will

By the same author

will

will self

Grove Press
New York

The publisher is grateful for permission to reproduce the quote from *Diary of a Drug Fiend* by Aleister Crowley, which appears here by kind permission of Ordo Templi Orientis

This book is substantially a work of non-fiction based on the life, experiences and recollections of the author. In some cases names of people, places, dates, sequences or the detail of events have been changed to protect the privacy of others.

First published in Great Britain in 2019 by Penguin Random House UK

Published simultaneously in Canada
Printed in Canada

First Grove Atlantic hardcover edition: January 2020

Library of Congress Cataloging-in-Publication data available for this title.

ISBN 978-0-8021-2846-1
eISBN 978-0-8021-4642-7

Grove Press
an imprint of Grove Atlantic
154 West 14th Street
New York, NY 10011

Distributed by Publishers Group West

groveatlantic.com

19 20 21 22 23 10 9 8 7 6 5 4 3 2 1

Pour NK, avec mes plus profonds remerciements

I've often thought that there isn't any 'I' at all;
that we are simply the means of expression of
something else; that when we think we are ourselves,
we are simply the victims of a delusion.

– Diary of a Drug Fiend, Aleister Crowley

I

May 1986

Standing in the Clapham Road on a sunny Tuesday morning, Will thinks: *You're standing in the Clapham Road on a May morning in the mid-1980s . . . Is this . . . it?* The space above him is no *only sky* but an ice-cream-head-aching void, its pale-blue depths tinged lemony by the early-summer sun.

'Is this is who you are?' he queries aloud – then runs on in a moaning undertone: 'A frightened young man of twenty-four . . . fraying – no! Fuck it – *falling* apart.' Will fumbles in his sad little grab-bag of received wisdom and comes up with: *When addicts are getting plenty of junk, they look anonymous – but when they start to withdraw, their image sharpens, then disintegrates . . .*

Still standing in the Clapham Road on a bright weekday morning, with the traffic grumbling along beside him, Will feels his sweat-stiffened socks beginning to . . . *melt*. Soon, he thinks, I'll be immobilised: a sick junky, petrified by withdrawal, and sunk deep in silent, solipsistic agony . . . *a suffering of the cells alone*. Yes, he'll be immobilised right here, on the wide pavement beside the shitty little shopping parade.

There's a bookie's, a chip shop, and a plastic shop like the one in Burnt Oak Will worked in on Saturdays when he was a teenager. His first real job – if by that is meant a manila wages packet, with inside a well-worn tenner, a fiver, some coin . . . *riches*. Crawling around on the dirty chequer-board of linoleum with a sticker gun – pricing up Atrixo hand cream, while lumpy and careworn legs, thickly hosed, shuffled about him: *Issat the hand cream, love? Gissa tube, willya?*

Yes! Gissa tube – a tube magically metamorphosed into a giant morphine syrette, the sort Brother Bill served his apprenticeship shooting up.

There's also a chemist's on the corner of this shabby parade – a small one. No doubt the pharmacist got his qualifications in Kampala, and never imagined he'd end up here, among . . . *stores selling artificial limbs, wig-makers . . . a point where dubious enterprise touches skid row*. Soon enough, Will thinks, the locals will come . . . *stumbling . . . drooling . . . squealing* for their methadone: little green bottles labelled POISON that are, in point of fact, their poison. *Mm-mm*.

True, there's nothing remotely euphoric about methadone: it just makes you feel as if you're buried up to your waist. Buried up to your waist – and possibly by that fact alone . . . *enjoying a happy day*. But Will doesn't have a methadone script – doesn't have twenty mils of green gloop to pour on the wateriness of his own dissolution.

Why? Because, if he did, he'd be *a fucking no-hoper loser*

junky. Really. The sort of idiot who goes out kiting, scores, cooks up, finds a vein, flushes the works then squirts wide arcs of claret across the dingy wallpaper — Or the kind who jemmies call boxes for smash, like Pete and Mike did before they got nicked, and Mike's parents sent him to rehab' . . . *the fucking featherweight.*

No – Will doesn't have a script. He does have fifty-seven pence, though – enough to buy a banana, which he could wrap in a sock. *Doing a chemist's* – it has a certain ring to it, such that in the addict world, the men and women who do indeed do them are highly esteemed: brave bandits, stealing from the plutocratic drug companies so they might give to their own poor . . . *habits.*

Diconal and Ritalin in pill form – wet and dry amps of dia-morphine, Tuinal capsules, Mogadons and other benzos – Tenuate Dospan spansules, *uppers, downers, twisters and screamers* . . . God knows what delights might be locked away behind the counter piled high with sponges and Strepsils – certainly the necessary medication for what ails Will: the infected sores he's fretted into being on his face and body – and the *hot wire* in the crook of his arm that he speared *ten . . . twenty?* maybe as many as thirty times during the short, sodium-stained night.

Will feels them – the sores and the needle-punctures feels them clotting up and scabbing over, as the pus . . . *gleet . . . ichor* congeals. How d'you call an infected cat?

3

Here, pus-pus-pus! And the cat comes, lolloping across London in its dirty-white Volkswagen Fastback, which purrs noisily as it smarms between the off-white stucco terraces running from the Cromwell Road down to the river, then, hearkening to the rising hysteria of the drivetime DJ, bounds up Queenstown Road and pounces on the fraying end of Silverthorne Road.

Yes – Silverthorne Road, where Will remembers attending a party five or six years ago. Mikey Dread the reggae musician had been there – and Hugh, together with his sister, Genie. Genie had been flush from the smuggling run in those days – and she gave Will a wrap of gear, before passing around a spliff spiked with some more. Later, out in the street, slithering along the icy pavements – it'd been winter – he'd almost fallen in front of a bus, so intent had he been on extracting every last toke. And why not?

The hoary old homily – deployed by his mother so many thousands of times throughout his childhood, Will thinks of it as *her line* – would've repeated on him then, just as it does now: *Waste not, want not . . .*

Yes, waste not, want not – waste not so much as the tiniest smidgen of gear, lest you find yourself here, on the Clapham Road, shifting from one clammy foot to the other, and deafened by the ultrasonic screaming of your wanting flesh.

And waste not, either, the opportunity when you come fast out of the first bend, and see traffic tailing back from the junction with the Wandsworth Road, to slam your foot on the accelerator. Yes, Will can still hear the fluttery roar of the 1600cc air-cooled engine as he'd swung the car into the opposite lane and the revs picked up.

How long has he been scoring through John? Genie made the introduction early last summer. It was a hot day and they'd been skint apart from their score money, so trudged all the way up the Kennington Road, then the Clapham one, until they reached the squats: a long, low block of flats, vestigially mock-Tudor, with pitched roofs and bits of decorative half-timbering. Up on the central gable there was a plaque with '1916' inscribed on it – a bad omen, Will thought at the time.

In front there was a strip of bare earth, a row of sooty-trunked trees, some fucked-up old caravans up on bricks – broken-down trucks and cars the same. When winter came and rain fell, this area became a soggy morass – churned up by the feet of the traveller kids who lived and played there. *Somme hope.*

That first time they'd scored off Rosie, a plump-for-a-junky, light-skinned black woman Genie knew. Will remembers shooting up in Rosie's kids' bedroom, while sitting awkwardly on the lower bunk – and then shifting to a leaking sagbag, from the hollow of which he'd first retrieved a dog-eared copy of Crowley's Diary of a Drug Fiend.

5

He remembers flipping through its pages, while Genie and Rosie talked animatedly in the adjoining kitchen – recalls marvelling at the immemorial quality of the drug culture he was swagged in, its ossified moth-eaten mores and tatty mythology. Will knew perfectly well that until very recently there'd been scarcely any junkies in London, yet now here they all were: thousands of the wheedling, whining fuckers – and all claiming direct descent from the likes of Crowley and Brother Bill, as if they'd been some sort of smack-head Pilgrim Fathers, set sail on a golden-brown sea.

But the Beast had slouched away – most probably to Bedlam – leaving behind only its moulted fur, caught by the hem of a velveteen drape, then draggled back and forth by some warm and oniony draught.

Later on Genie and Will had visited other portions of the labyrinthine squat – and in one of them they'd met John, who had a pencil moustache and said he'd served with the Paras in Ulster. But then you hear a lot of that sort of martial bullshit from junkies.

Still standing . . . *yeah, yeah, yeah* in the Clapham Road, with the sky's chilly-blue weight bearing down on him, and the glazed buns in the bakery window evilly gleaming, Will thinks of churned-up Derry mud sucking at the teenagers' platform soles, getting their kicks chucking bottles and bricks – while opposite them, grimly determined to do their duty, is a squad of Johns.

Johns twitching in their khaki battledress while they hold their rifles out to one side, so simultaneously aiming, and making the characteristic, soliciting gesture of junkies the world over. *Ye-es*, John had served the Queen in Ulster – *now he's serving up smack in Stockwell.*

He and Denise and little Amber squat a two-bedroom flat on the lower-ground floor of 1916 – which is how Will thinks of the old block. There's 1916, and rising up behind its low bulk are two gaunt towers, that preposterously, have been named after Absurdist playwrights. Twenty-two storeys high, Beckett and Pinter loom over the surrounding streets of Victorian terraces – Will's never been inside either, although he knows that Helen, an old housemate from Oxford, is living in a flat on the tenth floor of Pinter. Living with her boyfriend, Freddy, who Will remembers as Struwwelpeterish, with a huge red hooter, lopsided grin and stiff straw hair.

But he's a user, isn't he . . . a useful fact Will files away as he at last makes a move towards the bakery, while groping in his pocket for the two twenty-pence pieces, a ten and some coppers. *Fucking riches . . .*

. . . *so waste not, want not.* It'd been around five – at any rate, after dawn – when Will realised work wouldn't be possible without a proper hit rather than these ersatz ones:

Christ! How that fucking citric stings! Appalled by the Tottenham cakes, their lurid pink icing *infested* with desiccated coconut, Will rubs the crook of his elbow. Stinging didn't really capture this – no: it's more of *an agonising bite* – as if some miniature piranha had swum inside Will's mainline, and, as he writhed in agony, chomped its way towards his heart . . . *a fantastic journey indeed.*

No – don't dwell on that: go to work. He should be in Chiswick by now – should be parking the Veedub on the short stretch of road that cuts across Turnham Green, the one with no yellow lines. Stupid cars – they're not really auto*mobiles* at all, but for the most part empty metal sheds you've to pay ground rent for. Will hasn't got a parking permit for Kensington, where he's living. There'd been one on the Scirocco – but the sports coupé is long gone in a puff of . . . *coke*, and he hasn't got his shit together to apply for another one.

Most mornings – well, a slim majority of them – Will's up and off to work before the wardens are about. Before he had the job in Chiswick, he'd get up early enough to move the car a few streets away, to where the parking isn't zoned. Or not. The penalty-charge notices, which are encased in bright yellow-and-black-plastic sachets stuck to the Veedub's windscreen, are well-nigh impossible to ignore – yet he finds it easy enough: simply tearing them off then shoving them with the others into the glove compartment . . . *waste not, want not.*

Will's mother says her fondness for this expression originates in her hardscrabble childhood, during the depths of the Great American Depression . . . *You kids can have no conception of what it was like* – but he thinks this is yet more of her histrionic bull-crap.

Yes, Will should be in Chiswick, parking up his shed full of parking tickets, paper bags gummy with icing, dirty polystyrene cups and fag butts. He should be heading for a different branch of Greggs – the one on the High Road, where, on dutiful days, he buys an apple Danish, a healthy banana and a silvery sachet of Capri-Sun orange juice (from concentrate).

. . . *Concentrate – yes* . . . Will checks his watch, which tells him he's due to clock in in less than ten minutes. Still, the important thing is *I'm not late yet* . . . moreover, so far this morning his timing has been superb: the Veedub picking up speed as it shot up the incline towards the Wandsworth Road. And more speed – such that its air-cooled engine sounded like . . . *a church organ about to blast off for heaven.*

Yes! Waste not, want not – waste not the intensity of life, lest you end up as just another dull little bourgeois, queuing with all the others, content to eke out your days *waiting for the cheapest lightshow in town!*

However, there'd been no rising sound to accompany Will's ecstatic death, instead, the car's radio crackled with the tinny beats conjured by soon-to-be-cashiered experimentalists banging an iron bar in a studio: *Ting-ting-ting-TING!* While a bint with a posh accent cried that she – in common with Will – wanted money. Strongly suggesting that she – like him – had been wasting it.

Ting-ting-ting-TING! Ting-ting-ting-TING! Will's scabby hands had gripped the vibrating steering wheel as the Veedub raced up the wrong lane: if a car had turned left from the Wandsworth Road, or the lights had changed before Will reached them, he'd've been wiped out. As it was . . . *magically* . . . *mystically* . . . his arrival at the lights coincided exactly with amber flicking to green. Will expertly dabbed the brakes, wrenched the steering wheel — The car skidded as it cut across the blunt snout of the Transit at the head of the queue, then bounced jauntily away east, to the accompaniment of outraged horns: *Mad, mad, maaaad fuck-errrr!*

But then the best things in life are free – while the worst retail at a tenner a bag.

A minuscule little envelope, folded out of a scrap of paper torn from a glossy magazine – a dinky heap of beige powder, which, when shot up or snorted or smoked, would sweetly burn away all his pains. But Will doesn't have a tenner – he has fifty-seven pence. Not quite enough for a couple of apple Danishes. Already, Will sees himself: standing in the cool, stone-smelling vestibule in front of John and Denise's locked-and-barred front door – already he hears himself cooing, lovelorn, through their letterbox: *John* . . . *Denise* . . . *I've brought you some* . . . *breakfast*, which will surely do the necessary sesame, and open their cave of delights.

This, despite its having been only five minutes since John swore blind through this self-same letterbox he'd only his get-up hit – but he was lying, right? He's a junky – and junkies lie: that is their nature. They don't really speak, as such, they just open their mouths to utter *what is not* . . . so would be consummate ironists, if they weren't so intent on being taken . . . *so fucking seriously*.

Seriously, Will thinks: You're seriously going to buy two apple Danishes then take them back across the road? You're seriously going to offer them to John through the letterbox, then, if he holds out, plead with him, willing him to *say what is not* . . . Namely: *Only kidding, mate – I picked up last night* . . . *Lemme jus' do the bolts an' I'll serve yer* . . .

Greasily, the coins slither between Will's fingers: I'm sweating, he thinks, and soon enough I'll be immobilised. He checks his watch again, cursing himself for a *fucking, cunting* moron: 'It's always the multiple profanities with you . . .' He continues this admonition aloud – then lapses into another memory of his mother: standing at the stove at Number 43 in her pale-blue Terylene dressing gown, cooking and cursing: *fuck, shit, piss, damn* . . . she's always been

so impressively florid. And that, he thinks, is her legacy –
along with anxiety, depression, multiple neuroses . . . *I'm
feeling neuro*, she'd say, having invented her own collective
noun to encapsulate the vast swarm of her obsessions and
compulsions. Yes. And insomnia too – something she's also
bequeathed him.

So much so that last night –. Well, what night? A bilious
one – a jaundiced one: a night sullied by the streetlamps outside the big sash windows of the beautifully appointed flat.
Yes, a pale-yellow night – its urinous tang *catching in the back
of my throat* . . . Heroin and cocaine – you smell them as they
enter your veins, proof positive – as if any were needed – that
the secondary qualities of things exist not in the phenomena
themselves, but only in the mind which perceives them.

Yeah . . . shooting up the shit coke he'd bought at retail
prices from fat old Michael up in Kentish Town. Sixty-
fucking-quid a gramme! Cut to fuck – and on tick as well.
Cut to fuck the way Will taught the poor old innocent to do
it when he sold Michael the connection for a oner.

'Lissen, mate,' he'd said, 'waste not, want not, and all
that jazz – this charlie Chess sells, it's better than fifty per
cent pure, so you can step on it at least seven Gs in the
ounce – if not fourteen, if you're outing it to dumb yuppies.'
Will even told Michael about mannitol – such a better cut
than icing sugar – which was why he'd ended up with so
much of the baby laxative . . . *in my fucking bloodstream.*

Still, it is a better cut – 'cause it fluffs up the coke: fluffs it up puffy as the cumulo-nimbus clouds clumping up in the cold-blue heavens over the Hampstead Garden Suburb. A sky little Willy looks up at from where he sits: a paved embayment, tucked under the hedge bordering the front garden, where he plays with his toy Dinky and Corgi cars.

Dumb fucking little Willy! You infantile shit! Shooting up crap coke that's been cut *to your own bloody specifications!* Now you regret it, don't you, you crybaby. Yes, crying 'cause you're sick – standing there with an old handbag of Mummy's full of your toy cars, 'cause you've run away . . . run away on your own birthday. And now, instead of finding yourself at the beginning of a great adventure, you're just lost.

Standing in the Clapham Road on a sunny weekday morning in late spring, Will begins to slap his own face – open-handed clouts that will, of course . . . *ruin my make-up.* A passing mother tut-tuts, pulling her children closer to her. They're going to school – whereas little Willy's no longer on his walk to Grandmama's house, oh no – he's going straight to hell. A hell that's neither Stygian, nor ruddy with eternal fire – on the contrary, a hell that's a flickery-white void . . . *like last night.* Which was no night at all – since there'd been *no repose . . .*

After the smack ran out, he'd been fixing up coke every quarter-hour to begin with – then every *ten minutes . . .*

five . . . *three* . . . until he was wandering the rooms of the flat – *no!* Not wandering – following a precise figure-of-eight route: one circuit of the big, glass-topped coffee table, scattered with all his paraphernalia, and beneath the hooded eyes of his great-great-grandfather, Nathaniel Woodard, a constipated-looking Victorian eminence . . . *no baby laxative for him!* whose four-foot-square daguerreotype is propped up on the marble mantelpiece.

Then a second circuit – this time of the bedroom, revolving the double bed, tightly tucked into its powder-puce coverlet, and passing beneath the equally reproving gaze of Dennis Bovell. There's a large poster of the reggae singer stuck up on the bedroom wall, portraying him with a mortar board crushed down on his dreadlocks, and captioned BRAIN DAMAGE. In an antic mood, some years ago, before things got so very . . . heavy, Will tore it off the wall of the Town and Country in Kentish Town.

Yes, round and around, again and again he'd gone – for addiction is just that: a ceaseless and Sisyphean go-round. The drugs go into the system – and the system metabolises them out again. The addict goes out to score – and comes back in to use: round and around. Until every so often, he goes round and around at such a velocity that he ends up, as now, oscillating furiously on the spot, and condemned to remember all his previous paralyses.

Waiting, aged just three, at the bus stop on the North Circular – and a lady in a tweed jacket asking him, *Where are you going to, little boy?* And Willy already resenting that 'little', while forthrightly replying, *I'm running away from home.* Whereupon the suburban lady . . . *the fucking grass,* whispered something to her male companion, who went to the phone box a short way along the road, and made a call.

Yes – oscillating furiously on the spot, havering between the judgement of Nathaniel and that of Dennis, all the while the plastic leech of the syringe resting in the crook of his arm. Oscillating furiously, and, as he'd pressed the plunger home *a touch more . . . and more,* he'd heard it: *Waaaste nooot, waaant nooot!* her hokey homily whooshing into and out of his inner ears, while the blackness welled up at the periphery of his vision, and his bebop heart began to play arrhythmic drum fills and hit rim-shots on his resonating ribcage.

He'd waited, paralysed, listening to Brother Ray's rising chorus of grunts: *Uh-ooh! Uh-ooh! Uh! Ooh! Uh! Ooh! Baby, one more time! Just one more time! Baby feels so good! Waaa!!!* Acutely conscious that, were he simply to press his thumb right home, it'd be a cartoonish death: *That's all folks!* as the aperture screwed shut forever.

Instead, he'd completed the figure-eight circuit again and again – his vision darkening *again annagain . . .* until at last the aperture screwed fully open on the reflection of his own troubling face, on which, as he'd regained consciousness, he was applying Max Factor foundation in a thick layer, hoping to mask the wounds he'd worried into existence.

For it's always the same: no matter how many times Will admonishes himself – *It's just the cocaine* telling him this infinitesimal whitehead is the tip of a massive iceberg of pus – he still believes, so picks viciously at rubbery flesh numbed by the drugs. Besides, isn't the night-time the right time for *making . . . hate?* For hating his *miserable fucking cheating ugly pathetic failure's face? His pretentious mummy's boy's pussy-whipped mush?* And therefore isn't the morning the right time to cover it up? Because, although in its cool light the spots, sores and other blemishes appear monstrously disfiguring, it only takes a dab of the foundation, and then a few *dabs* more, to show it's *no big yabba-dabba-deal at all.*

So, standing in the Clapham Road, outside a branch of Greggs, on a bright and zesty morning, Will looks just . . . *fine.* No junky he – he can't possibly have a drug problem. Why? Well, because he drives a car, and he has a job, *and he brings home the bacon . . .* Moreover: he has a degree from a distinguished university – albeit not a very distinguished one. Yes, Will looks just fine: short back-and-sides, suit jacket in a light-blue check, navy-blue serge trousers with an ironed crease, an open-necked lighter-blue shirt, and black leather lace-ups to complete the conservative camouflage.

Yes: Will looks just fine – and he looked just fine, aged

just three, as a precocious Huck Finn, lighting out for the territory with an old handbag of his mummy's slung around his neck, and his white-blond fringe tickling his squinting eyes – eyes that nonetheless saw the police Rover pull up at the bus stop, and his mother scramble from the back seat to run and comfort him, *the lost boy* . . .

Yes, Will looks just fine: a twenty-four-year-old tele-marketer for IBM based in their Chiswick offices – at least, that's what he is according to the laminated script card he reads from when on the job: *Good morning, I'm calling from IBM in London, may I speak to Mr Frean? He's no longer with the company? Well, in that case, can you put me through to who-ever is currently responsible for your purchasing?*

The problem is that yesterday – and the day before, as well – somewhere between this request, and the voice of the next corporate drone buzzing in his ear, Will's chin dropped down to rest on his chest, while his eyelids unrolled, so hiding his pin-prick pupils. A better punter than he is a salesman, last Friday in the Assembly House, in Kentish Town, Will'd wheedled away at Dick until he was given five twenty-quid bags on tick.

Over a lost weekend, then, for the next two days, Will wheedled away at himself until the gear was all gone — Which was why, instead of identifying prospects for IBM's salesmen, he'd pitched, head-first *againannagain*, into that plush inner-space of . . . *mothball-scented fur coats*. There he'd floated, free from all cares and woes, until an irate voice yanked him back into the real world of chicken-salad on seeded baps and vending-machine tea.

Because the telemarketers wear headsets that tether them to their phones, so they remain communicado even if unconscious. Yes: yanked back into the world by this beige umbilicus, 'Boing!', Will's eyes would snap open, and he'd see the concerned face of Carole, the thirtyish and mumsy manager of the Telemarketing Department – then hear the frustrated yodel of another equally bored phoney in Stockport, Solihull or Southampton: *Hello? Hello? Is there anyone there? Hello? Are you still there?*

Good questions. One and all. Because Will isn't altogether sure he's still in Chiswick – his absenteeism being, well . . . *chronic*. Why wouldn't it be? If he was entirely diligent, the take-home from the IBM job – even combined with the money he makes from his two weekly cartoon commissions – would be nowhere near sufficient to cover his costs. He may ignore the penalty-charge notices and chance his arm taking smack on tick, but Will's perfectly aware of this widening gulf – one only temporarily bridged by the various 'loans' he contracts for – mostly from Chloë, his long-suffering girlfriend, and, of course, his Depression-era mother.

Standing in the Clapham Road, staring down between his feet, Will sees the fossilised outlines of last autumn's leaves, together with crumpled-up IOUs and utility bills, stern letters from bank officials – all the irritating *pepperworks*, generated by creditors who aren't quite as understanding as the women in his life.

'Apple Danish's, what? Thirty pee, is it? Aww, c'mon, love – I've fifty-seven here.' Will jiggles the change on his outstretched palm. 'Giss two, willya?'

Charm, Cocteau observes, is that quality which enables its possessor to solicit the answer yes, *before he's even posed the question.* Clearly, Will isn't that charming – but he must have something, because the girl in the white nylon-netting snood, her face as livid as his own, wordlessly tongs a second apple Danish from the tray, drops it in a paper bag she deftly twirls into a parcel, then passes it across the counter.

Will hefts it, and wonders whether this little bag of sugary insubstantiality will really be enough to . . . *get me a bag of smack?*

He's back on the far side of the Clapham Road, stepping over a low wall and making his way between the dimpled flanks of some old caravans. No one's stirring in the travellers' encampment – it's too early for totting, or for pretending to sharpen knives, or for murdering, for that matter. A body was found here a couple of weeks back – a runaway from the North, with a paring knife in his heart, wrapped up in plastic sheeting on the back of a flat-bed truck.

Or so John claims – although, Will concedes, the paring knife is a convincing detail. So convincing it might be enough simply to utter the words 'paring knife', and a corpse would be cultured around them . . . *white* . . . *pearlescent rather than putrefying* . . .

Will's been thinking magically for a long time now – so long, it seems merely an extension of childhood fantasising: no reality – let alone a Reality Principle – having been interposed. He'd have more respect for *my savage mind* if it'd only come up with lyrical incantations, sophisticated spells and elegant rituals. Instead, Will simply tries hard to visualise the obvious counterfactuals to his desires: the dealer won't be in – or he/she won't be holding. Or, if they are holding – and Will's skint – he/she won't give him tick.

Will tries to render these scenes with as much detail as possible – mentally limning the dirt beneath the dealer's fingernails, or the half-eaten banana rotting on her battered kitchen unit – convinced that if he takes on this diabolic role, God will . . . *do the right thing.*

It's only been a quarter of an hour since he was last standing, wheedling, in front of the multi-density fibreboard door – while John wheedled back at him: 'No, mate – fucking no. I ain't got nothin' – only me fuckin' get-up an' that. No way I'm going to pick up before this afternoon, either – he ain't up till then anyway. Now go away, willya, please . . .'

His grim little speech winding down the curtain on Will's fantasy: aerial shots of a mellow Will at the wheel of the Veedub, racing back across Chelsea Bridge, the window rolled down, his arm resting on the sill, and sportive breezes tousling his happy healthy heroin-maintained hair, as he makes his way joyously to work, on time, for a righteous day full of conversion calls.

You ARE interested in purchasing new computer equipment? You ARE the person in your company responsible for purchasing? You WILL make an appointment for one of our salesmen to call on you? No. None of that. Because magic isn't real – only rip-offs.

Standing there in the dank vestibule, John's words buzzing about him ... *flies in my eyes*, the air, the blood – the very piss and shit had been drained out of him, such that Will'd sagged, knock-kneed, against the jamb.

No gear – no hit. He'd soon be immobilised – *clamped*. And this immobilisation would be worse than any previous one, because there are too many bills, fines and creditors for him to ignore, too many unreturned phone calls and ripped-up letters: he'd had one from his father last week, and with it was a Polaroid of the *old faker* ... he'd put it in the fridge's freezer compartment – Will shivers – it's still in there, his father's plump, ruddy face now coated in rime, and when he opens the door it glistens in the light of a five-watt bulb.

No, it's no longer an option for Will to take to his bed for two or three days and *sweat it out* . . . He's already done this at least three times this year – four or five last. It's dismaying: lying there in a foetid sopor, imagining the streets outside, their gutters running black with liquid misery – and when, after seventy-two hours, you feel some quickening, some rise in spirits, it turns out only to be the puppet master, yanking your strings so that you stand, wobbling and sweaty – but ready to go *once more unto the breach!* and score.

Yes . . . Will had wheedled – begged quite shamelessly: 'Please, John – please. For the love of God – please . . . Surely there's someone who's holding – someone you can ask? If I can't score, I can't go to work . . . Please, John – I'm on my fucking knees out here.' And he had been – on his fucking knees on the cold stone floor, his peeled lips pressed painfully against the letterbox . . . *SWALK*.

But John had been implacable: 'Nah, fuck off, willya, Will – jus' fuck off. We've gotta 'ppointment anyway – somefing t'do wiv Amber, so be a good chap and make yourself scarce . . .'

But Will isn't a good chap – not this morning: this morning he's a *protoplasmic blob* . . . barely held together by the junk remaining in his system. Heroin slooows everythiiing dooown: the intestines' peristalsis becomes glacial, saliva evaporates, *the cock stops*, while mucus hardens . . . *cellophane crinkling up in the nose.*

Sometimes, in the small hours, on a run, heart pounding, head lost in heroin's greenish shadows, Will will find himself standing in the bathroom of the Kensington flat – which is tucked up in a sort of little turret, accessed by a curlicue of stairway – addressing his shrivelled penis thus: 'Rapunzel, Rapunzel, let down your hair, so that I might climb your golden stair . . .' then laughing hysterically. 'Cause it's gotta be funny, right – it's got to be a laugh, this wanton misuse of your own young body – if it ain't funny then nothing's funny, and if nothing's funny then it's *GAME OVER*, as the last *lumpa-lumpa invaders* chomp their way *through your necrotic flesh.*

Staring up at the 1916 roundel, Will, who's well sub-cultured, thinks not of unimaginable pains or incredible slaughters, but the Defence of the Realm Act, the first British measure to outlaw the sale of heroin and cocaine. He tries another magical tack: I've brought them some breakfast – so they'll have to offer me some gear in return, right? Mere manners would dictate such a course: the gear being a sort of condiment, or possibly *confiture . . .*

Will tries this off-the-peg vision on for size: the three addicts – John, Denise and Will – sitting on some *terrasse* up above the Côte d'Azur, their pasty skins warmed by the sun's rays, as they pass the breakfast things between them. The crockery and napery is snow-blindingly-bright – the cutlery coruscates. Denise asks for the butter – John passes it. Then Will, in turn, solicits him for the heroin, a small silver bowl of which rests beside the coffee pot. *No trouble, chappy* . . . he says, passing it across, *no trouble at all* . . .

The May morning sunlight detonates against 1916's façade, and its diamond-shaped windowpanes . . . *explode.* Will senses the build-up of commuter traffic behind him, as the cars, trucks and vans hump along the Clapham Road towards the city centre: a steely testudo, ever forming, dispersing and re-forming. Will thinks of the desperate manoeuvre he pulled off on the way from Kensington: 'You coulda fucking killed yourself . . . No, really, you could've . . .'

Sometimes – although not very often – Will revisits those frozen moments when another driver's face looms at him out of a vortex of deathly possibilities – only for it to be swept centrifugally away. Then he advances the contrary proposition: the driver's face thrust towards his own in a spray of shattered windscreen glass . . . *a death-borne Aphrodite.*

But he pushes this image away – just as he pushes away the one of his mortal form, lying limp on bare boards, its costume soaked, its face and neck pummelled repeatedly by Genie, who sits astride him, trying to save Will from the soft yet inexorable impact of an overdose. While beside him lies the plastic leech, ruddy and bloated, having *drunk its fill* –

*

One of John and Denise's windows is wide open. Bizarre enough – given their quite reasonable obsession with security. Yet more bizarrely, as Will looks on, a middle-aged and middle-class woman emerges through this window, wearing a trench coat, below the hem of which flickers the hem of a floral-patterned dress.

Will would very much like to intervene: this nice woman is clearly way out of her depth – way down the rabbit hole. She needs to hear received pronunciation, not John's impenitent whine: 'Yeah . . . yeah, we'll be sure to do that, Mrs Winters – I promise . . .'

Will drops back behind a caravan, from where he watches the social worker clamber awkwardly up out of the trench in front of the window. She stands, pats herself down, checks her open briefcase to see if any of her buff case files have fallen out, then makes her way off along the muddy path towards Stockwell tube.

Will leaves it for a minute – then breaks cover: with the crazy, half-formed idea of storming the window, confronting John, and so being able to plead his case face to face. For even now, seven years – more or less to the day – since he first took smack, Will still can't quite get used to the lawlessness of this jungle: can't altogether accept that reason, politeness, a *certain basic human decency* . . . simply isn't called for. The window's been rasped shut.

*

Cold stone and the fossilised esters of old urine. A few wires curl loose from where someone's thieved the copper tubing. Will pauses, fist raised to resume his *knock-knock-knocking* on this hellish door. For a moment his watch's face is picked out perfectly by the morning searchlight – it's less than a half-hour since John told him to fuck-right-off, yet Will still tries his juju: visualising himself, once again, en route to work, happy and whole.

Then: 'clonk!' and 'clonk!' again.

Silence for a while, before he hears something human – or possibly excremental – stir, deep in the bowels of the flat.

I'm late for work now, Will thinks. He hasn't taken the morning train – he won't be working from nine to five *and then* . . . No. Moreover, there'll be no bubbly young woman to welcome him home to the high-ceilinged rooms of the Kensington flat – only a spoon, which, rather than fleeing with some dirty-minded dish, will be where he left it, resting on the marble mantelpiece, beneath the hooded eyes of Nathaniel Woodard.

While in it will still be several little lumps of dirtied cellulose: bits of cigarette filter, through which syringe-after-syringe full of scuzzy water – in which first heroin, then cocaine, and latterly just citric acid was dissolved then drawn off . . . *if air bubbles could kill you, there wouldn't be a junky alive.*

Will folds his skinny form down to the ground . . . *down to the ground.* And, *oh, the feeling!* of the rusty knee and hip bolts, 'cause he's a badly designed robot, is Will – one that runs on smack, so soon will be – *I might've mentioned this already* – immobilised.

He lifts the metal flap to project through the slot: 'John! John! I know you're in there, mate . . . John!' But there's no reply, or any further stir – only the brightly incomprehensible chatter of a radio in some other flat. Will tries again: 'John! John! It's me, mate – Will. Lissen, I know you said to leave it a couple of hours, but I'm desperate, mate – fucking desperate . . . Lissen, I can go over the odds – considerably over the odds . . .'

Even as these weasel words leave his mouth to wiggle through the letterbox, Will's overwhelmed by the absurdity of his position, which is at once cosmic – and utterly commonplace: a snivelling, shitting-his-whack junky, with no money – and, worse, no front, no willingness to kite, lift, do a chemist or otherwise contribute to the commonwealth. *Yes*, Will's *a fucking amateur*, who kneels on the floor outside the barred door of another junky who isn't even a dealer himself, only someone who scores for others so he can nick a bit of their gear.

One gloomy lunchtime late last year, with the rain cascading down outside, Will and Genie had sat waiting with Denise, little Amber, and one or two other punters *silent and immobile in separate misery* . . . while John went to score.

Then, suddenly, Genie'd shot upright in the broken-backed old sofa: 'Oh, fuck!' she'd cried. 'He's been gone too fucking long!' She ran to the door, unbolted it – and bolted. Will followed her splashing through the muddy puddles to the Clapham Road, then full-tilt down it to the pub on the corner of Lingham Street.

He'd caught up with Genie in the gents', where the ambience had been pretty much the same as the flat they'd just left: cold, with trickling water and the stench of defecation mixed with disinfectant. Standing there in his habitual donkey jacket, pale eyes wide and pinned, was John, who'd been blatantly chopping out tiny piles of smack on the sink's scuzzy surround.

Will got what the *fucking tea leaf* was up to immediately – what amazed him had been Genie's telepathy. If that's what it was.

Telepathy . . . yes, and prescience as well. Two years before, Will had witnessed another instance, in central Australia, on the long stretch from Adelaide up to the Alice. The coach was almost empty, with only a few sweaty travellers suckered to the sticky seats, and sunk in their own silent torpor. It had left the dusty opal mining town of Coober Pedy, and, after a few clicks on the metalled surface, begun hammering the interminable corrugations of the dirt road.

Right at the back slumped two Aboriginal men, who, after

hailing then boarding the coach in the middle of nowhere, had fallen straight to sleep. Tatty nylon curtains pulled across the windows sipped at the soup-hot zephyrs. Will had tried to concentrate on his book: an account of the white explorers who'd penetrated this region in the 1850s and '60s, in search of phantasmal inland seas, and well-watered pastures, only to be driven back by thirst, thorny scrub and the sheer tyranny of the distances.

Then, without any warning, the Aboriginal men simultaneously awoke: one went to the front of the coach and said something to the driver, who slewed the vehicle over to the side of the track. They then clambered down, and, without any farewell, or so much as a glance behind them, wandered straight off into the desert waste.

As the coach accelerated away, Will had looked back: the Aboriginal men, who weren't even carrying a canteen of water, were headed into an absolute void: a desiccated scrubland of regularly spaced and skeletal bushes set down on the sandy gravel. Craning, Will had watched as the great heat warped and stretched the men, so that their hats touched the sky, while their fifty-yard-long legs lagged across a salt pan.

And a few months after that strangeness, Will had been in Darwin, in the Territory, sitting on an afternoon veranda with Brian from the Lands Department and some of his Groote Eylandt mates: they'd been drinking beer, the bottles in little polystyrene stubby-holders . . . *squeaky*, and talking of nothing much, when all at once the Aboriginal folk became deeply agitated and switched languages.

Next, with no further ado, the entire mob – several hefty middle-aged women, two spindle-shanked young men, a bunch of kids – had decamped. It wasn't until he'd gone into work the following morning that Will found out what'd happened: according to Brian, they'd had news of a light-aircraft crash back in their country – three people dead.

'What d'you mean, news?' Will had queried, and Brian – that most prosaic and least magical-seeming of men, who'd driven round the world from Croydon to Darwin on a Honda-bloody-C90 – winked significantly, then said in an undertone – *as if anyone gave a monkey's* – 'They have ways of learning about things instantaneously – songlines can act like telephone ones . . .'

Will had been disposed to believe this anyway – but what'd made it more credible was Brian, whose colleagues slurred him as an Abo-lover, and who could've been any dull crat, in any guvvie bureau.

God is great . . . Gear is great . . . Therefore: gear is God . . . Still standing in the chilly vestibule, his head full of *false fucking syllogisms* . . . Will sees John in the pub bog: they'd stood over him, hawk-eyed, while he scraped the gear up and repackaged it. The shit – the snivelling little punk: Will and Genie had already given him a fiver just to score on their behalf. The whole sorry incident had been worthy of one of Genie's Cockney clichés – after all, what's the point of having a mum who lives off the Roman Road if you can't say things like *that's a diabolical-fucking-liberty, mate – you should be ashamed* . . .

Yes, the three of them had remained there while John scraped the gear back into its bindles . . . *a dull crat in his watery bureau.* They must've made an odd trio – but they were conspicuously ignored by the men who came in, pissed and left. But then that's the sort of pub the Royal Oak is: full of ancient, bull-necked Irishmen and murderous gyppos – all of 'em lashed into their donkey jackets with lengths of nylon-fucking-tow-rope. The healthiest-looking things in the entire mouldering gaff are the *fruit in the fucking machines* . . .

Later on, emollient following his hit, Will'd asked Genie about her telepathy, and she said: 'It was just a hunch – he'd been gone too long.' And what about the pub gents', what had made her seek him there? 'Logic – there's nowhere else he could've done it.' Yes, logic – not some third eye, implanted in Genie's spotty forehead and peering out between her greasy curls.

Besides, Will's ceased to lend credence to such mystic hoodoo – nowadays, he likes to quote Turgenev on the subject of enlightenment: *What's the difference between a white void and a black one?* What indeed. Because that's what heroin's done to Will: knelt on his chest and smacked him *again annagain*, great open-handed clouts, such that his brain vibrates in its bony pan: *Is it a white void or a black one? White or black? White/black . . . black/white?* Surely, it hardly matters once you're properly stunned – it all just . . . *fades to grey.*

Rooted in the dank lobby, Will's head rings with a jaunty hornpipe *Blue-fucking-Peter . . .* which he recalls vividly – not for John Noakes standing atop a Welsh mountain bleating, *It's really hairy up here!* Or for Valerie Singleton, fetching up from below the counter one she claimed to've *made earlier.* No, it was the programme's set that made the biggest impression on little Willy: freestanding shelving units, piled high with this and that – stuff made for, or used in, previous features – stood about in an unbounded space – a whitish and local void, out of which emerged these jolly presenters in their woollies, together with frisky Shep and faithful Petra.

It'd been the same with the Magic Roundabout: poseable Florence, swishing Dougal and dozy Dylan – the puppets sprang from the nothingness to sport between two-dimensional shrubberies, before Zebedee boinged into being, to tell everyone it was *time for bed.* Top of the Pops too – once Will had been old enough to appreciate it – seemed to be being broadcast live from a boundless – if more cluttered – space.

By then – their parents having had a bien-pensant fit, and

got rid of their own set – he and his brother had had to go next door to watch this vital cultural bulletin.

The Hamburgers – who ran a dry-goods shop in the Kentish Town Road – had no such anxieties when it came to their adoptive daughter, Ruth. So the three children sat in a solemn little row on Mrs Hamburger's plastic-encapsulated sofa, watching the large and lurid television.

Jimmy Savile, that *goggle-eyed loon*, hysterically yodelled the introduction – then the children wheeled away with the camera, to take in grown men, pretending to play star-shaped electric guitars, as they stomped about on silvery platform heels . . . *Fooox ooon the run!* The camera nosed in to focus on the studio audience: teenage girls and a few boys who gurned and fidgeted along to the music.

But it didn't matter how far the camera shoved between acrylic shoulders, or probed goose-pimpled thighs – there was never any end to this mad realm: only another spaniel-coiffed chanteuse, tinkling the ivories while she urged the pre-pubescent – yet already priapic – Will to *Baby, ba-aby, sugar me!* Whatever that meant.

The Top of the Pops studio was a multicoloured void – and, with the benefit of hindsight, Will understands not only that there's no distinction between this and a white void, but that all these televisual spaces were, in effect, representations of childhood itself: a vapid state of being, in which all sorts of phenomena – trees, buildings, people, cars, laws, customs, morals – loomed up out of an indistinct middle-distance, only to assume the conventional dress called . . . *reality*.

This reality: one in which he's fucked *in earnest*, and quite unable to *arise from his semi-recumbent position*, because *everybody hu-urts*, don't they, when their anaesthetic runs out? And still he hasn't learned his lesson, *dumb little Willy* – and still he tries it on: 'John! John! Lissen – I know you're in there . . .' Yes, in there – lurking in that sepia-streaked interior like some human turd that emerges unflushed from the watery maelstrom of the moment: 'John! John!' Will hefts the Greggs bag – as if by this act alone to magically communicate its sweet yumminess – hefts it, and calls through the letterbox: 'I've brought you and Denise some breakfast, John . . . Thought you might fancy it . . .'

Fancy it? Where do such frumpy locutions come from? Ach! Will knows where – somewhere neither they nor he wishes to go, because none of them wants a Danish pastry from Greggs, any more than they want the teapot warmed and the toast racked — No! They *fancy* great piles of pharmaceutical-grade diamorphine, pure and white as the driven-fucking-snow – snow driven by this: the relentless pulsion of their hunger for junk.

Will's sandbag head slumps, his legs quiver – he feels the grit beneath his eyelids. He experiences no lucidity – only the pitiless clarity that accompanies mounting hysteria. He tries again: 'Breakfast! I've got you breakfast!' And hears his words dropping to the floor – *'cause there's no mat.*

Junkies' gaffs are always like this: devoid of the most basic fixtures and fittings, because lampshades and towel rails, draught excluders and door mats, all deteriorate eventually – and when they do they aren't replaced, since there's no money for anything but the true essentials. At the opulent Kensington flat lent to him rent free by his wealthy friend Caius, Will is down to a single light bulb (saving the five-watt one in the fridge).

Last night, as he danced his figure-of-eight – from the pocket-sized kitchen, through the main room to the bedroom, and up the curlicue stairs to the bathroom, he unscrewed it – his hand gloved by a tea towel – and took it with.

It's a dismal state of affairs – though not as dismal as the one endured by little Amber: often, there's not even the money to buy her nappies . . . *Mmm, smell that rich substance!* Yes, and all the richer and more substantial for its sudden appearance in that dingy setting, with its sweating anaglypta wallpaper and scabrous linoleum floors.

A coprophiliac might well hang out here with the junkies, camouflaging his habit in theirs, and waiting to score for this: bandy-legged little Amber, who, with her mop of brown curls and sharp, delving chin, so resembles her captious mother:

Am-berr! Am-berr! Geddoutta'ere, willya . . . Yes, little Amber, toddling round the broken-down couch where the junkies sit, waiting for her father to bring joy back into their lives.

Little Amber, going *Choo-choo! I'm a train* . . . as she pushes a toy carpet-cleaner – though there isn't an off-cut in the entire gaff – then stopping abruptly, her legs getting bandier . . . and bandier, till one . . . two . . . three hard turds plop out, together with a half-cup of piss, in which they lie, gently rocking.

Ye-es, it's all part of the same eternally shitty present, Will thinks, as, his knees aching, something stirs deep in the recesses of his own bunged-up bowels. As he recalls, little Amber looked down with pride – *Yes! Pride!* – and Will had thought how appropriate the poor child's given name is, given she's stuck fast in her parents' addiction – imprisoned here, just as a fly might be caught in mid-wing-beat during the Cretaceous, so remaining that way *for millions of years* . . .

Animals, things – people, basically, they're made of the same stuff. His mother had euphemised bowel movements as 'BMs' *before the shitty seventies* – and both BMs and babies emerge from mummies . . . *so much stuffing*.

While Will had looked on, Denise bent down, her hand gloved in toilet paper, and picked up first one, then the second and third hard little turds. Lost, as now, in the chilly fastness of mounting withdrawals, Will had thought: If they can afford toilet paper, why don't they buy the child a fucking nappy!

'Look.' John's voice is posted back through the letterbox, directly into Will's waiting ear: 'Mate, I told you, right – push off, yeah? Jus' push off willya? It's too early for . . . anyfing.'

'But I've brought you and Denise breakfast, John – don't you want it?'

Will had anticipated building up to this clincher gradually, and that once the B-word was uttered, the chain would come off, the bolts shot, and within minutes Will would be hunched up in their dank bathroom . . . *dowsing for a vein*. Instead.

'No' – John's voice is utterly toneless – 'no, I don't fucking want it – now push off, there's a good chappy. Don't want you out there 'tracting 'tention . . .'

Traho, trahere . . . to drag, comes to Will from some black-jacketed primer – and dragging behind it comes Marzie – Mr Marsden – who taught him Latin throughout prep school, and was his form master in his final year. Marzie, in his Batman gown, the nicotined fringe of his white hair falling across an imperious brow.

Because of his own antinomianism, Will had sensed a kindred spirit in Marzie's simmering contempt for his lily-livered charges. Marzie would break off from dinning *traho, trahis, trahit . . . trahimus . . .* into them, to tell anecdotes of his wartime service in the Royal Marines, the message of which was always the unrivalled capacity of the human animal for a *colossal balls-up*. The new recruit checks to see if his rifle's clean by placing his eye against its muzzle – then pulls the trigger.

If you dozed in Marzie's class, your repose would be interrupted when he aimed the blackboard rubber with unerring accuracy, and your head . . . *exploded*.

'. . . so fuck off!'

'But breakfast, John – Danish pastries . . . from Greggs . . .' Will re-delivers his feeble entreaty – together with a faint, but distinct, sob.

'Danish-fucking – pastries? Aw, fuck OFF, willya . . . please.'

Will tries another tack: 'Can't you at least open up, John, so I can give 'em to you?' After all, Will's mother carps in his inner ear, *Waste not, want not* . . .

'Can't be arsed to find the keys, mate – 'sides, I don't want no fuckin' pastry.'

Bare feet squelch away – Will's losing him: desperate, he cries, 'You could let me in the window – I saw a woman climbing out of it just now!'

'Yeah,' John calls back, 'that was our fucking social worker, come to check on Amber.' And he retreats to the bedroom, slamming the door behind him. The letterbox flaps a puff of disinfected air in Will's face.

*

Why doesn't John *get it*? Why he can't feel Will's *warm face*, and the *closeness* of his *lips*? Why can't John sense the *invasion* of Will's *scent* — the scent of his fucking fear?

In Will's measureless inscape, the schoolgirl choir – clad in acrylic, chiffon, and all things bright and artificial – wafts this way and that. A bearded man with a hook nose strikes an attitude: the crotch of his jeans bulging, his electric guitar's bulbous machine-head raised to ejaculate a solo.

Will's ears howl with middle-class maledictions: You better let me in, John – or else! I have friends and relatives – I've an Oxford-bloody-degree! Granted, it's only a third – but still . . . it means I'm like your social worker: you've GOT to let me in. Even my shitty little telephone marketing gig is more legit than anything you've done in years – you're a fucking thief and a parasite, man, whereas I'm a bona fide taxpayer! So, you've gotta let me in, and give me your get-up so I can drive to Chiswick, call Quality Die Casting in Bromsgrove, and find out if they want to *upgrade their fucking computer system!*

Will's words echo away. The girls' choir fidgets silently with the beaded tassels of its collective maxi-skirt – the bearded man slumps, his guitar dribbling spunk. Abandon hope, Will preaches, all ye who enter this fucking shitty stupid life – abandon hope, and *waste not, want not . . .*

He should've squeezed the syringe tight, so injecting death deep into his black heart — Should've done it while there was still enough cocaine left in the scuzzy solution to give him a heart attack or a stroke. Yes, in the anaemic pre-dawn, under the accusatory eyes of Dennis Bovell, he should've allowed it in: the darkness that wells at the periphery of his vision . . . *my life*.

No. No hope now – no more *painting silver shadows on a rose-coloured land . . . all hope gone.*

Will's elsewhere too. A sudden transition. Because it's like this: either you stay, forever havering on doorstep or corner, waiting for the man – or you go. Will re-discovers himself on the corner of Grantham Road, standing beside the dirty-white hummock of the Veedub . . . *Styrofoam cup crushed into leaf mould . . . cracked cassette oozing silvery tape-trail . . .* The paper bag's contents are as useless to him now as Denmark itself – so he lets it fall from his numb fingers . . . *down to the ground – down to the ground.*

He looks up – and the two tower blocks rear up from behind 1916, their dirty-grey façades threatening the gentle May morning with . . . *grievous-bodily-harm.*

Will remembers a trip to the Isle of Dogs with Hughie, to look at a prospective council flat. It was a few years ago, in winter, and they'd been squatting together in Brixton. It'd taken ages to get there, and the flat turned out to be on the top floor of a block identical to these two.

The view silenced them all. Will, Hughie and the bloke from the council had stood, staring down first at Millwall with its defunct docks – then lifting their eyes to take in the great grey immensity of the city. In the far distance, a break in the clouds illuminated the gnat-like planes circling over Heathrow. The tower block had swayed a little in the wind, and Hughie pretended, goofily, to stagger.

Poor Hughie, Will thinks, with his plinkety-plunking on his acoustic guitar: *My girl don't stand no cheatin', my girl . . .* And his chopping out of tiny little lines of amphetamine sulphate, while saying, *Little and often, Will – that's the way to do drugs: little and often . . .*

Another vision: this time of Hughie in saggy underpants, his puckish face madly grinning, and hopping from one foot to the other, powerless to do anything, as the bottles of home brew he'd lined up in the vestibule of Number 43 exploded, one after another, sending creamy spouts a yard high.

Hughie and his girlfriend Carol had stayed with Will and Chloë at the broken family home for a month in the long vac', while Will's mother had been away in the States. The house was on the market and half cleared already. Hughie had been working in Soho at the Club – Carol, Will and Chloë were all office temping.

The stench of yeast – and the sight of *chopping Hughie . . . plinking and plunking Hughie . . . ever-grinning Hughie . . .* Will thinks Hughie was probably the most vivid person he's ever known: a joker, grinning up from a card forced upon Will by life itself – a card that's now been discarded . . . *into the white void.*

Cursing and farting, the traffic rolls over uneasily in the road-bed, waiting for the lights to change. Will shakes his hurting head – there's got to be a Plan B. *Gotta be some way I can score – Helen.* The name pops back into his head: *Helen and Freddy.* Freddy's a smack-head – or at least a user, and Will has her address in the little leather-bound book he extracts from his inside pocket. There, in among the notes he's made in his cramped cuneiform, he finds it. Yes! Preposterously, the two of them are perhaps *inside Pinter* at this very moment . . .

It might be possible, Will hypothesises, if one knew the city exhaustively – indeed, had the entire A–Z imprinted on one's cerebellum – to examine intently a single rush-hour London street, such as the Clapham Road, and, using this data – speed, density, weather conditions, traffic lights' phasing and roadworks – to extrapolate the vectors of every other vehicle in the city.

With such a head-borne and continuously updated map, someone could avoid all tailbacks and jams. Will could perform his Silverthorne Road manoeuvre in complete safety, again and again, so reaching IBM's Chiswick offices before ten. He wouldn't even be docked *an hour's wages* . . .

*

Scabbed with paint, kicked and dented, the lift doors part and Will limps along the tenth-floor corridor to the door labelled '67' – another inscrutable slab of multi-density fibreboard that *flays* his raw knuckles as he knocks . . . *has no one heard of bells or buzzers?*

It opens immediately – and here's Helen, clearly on her way to work: her pretty face – freckled and vulpine – appears in the gap, chin-strapped by the chain. 'Oh,' she says, 'it's you, Will.'

She doesn't seem at all surprised to see him – and, better still, Freddy's loitering behind her, his Marty Feldman eyes popping.

'Right, mate,' Will says, and Freddy grins: 'Saw an ad' in the paper, she did.'

'Sorry?'

'Helen saw this ad' in the paper: Have You Considered Making Your Will? So she reckons it was a sign – or somethin' like that.'

Yes, Will thinks, it was a harbinger of my arrival – I've ascended to this: a mystical plane about as elevated as a *fucking futon* . . . He asks Helen: 'Can I come in?' as he exults: Yes! I'm expected – albeit in a mad, hippyish way.

On the basis of this welcome Will instantly recalibrates his entire near-future: minutes hence, he'll be snorting up a thick line of smack through a cored biro – then, a few more after that, he'll be back in the Veedub, bombinating up the Earls Court Road.

'Yeah . . . 'course . . .' Helen undoes the chain and swings the door open, 'it's just that Freddy's in a spot of bother with this bloke –'

'This fucking nutter!' Freddy jerks about, his skinny frame *a gesticulating hand* . . . that, together with his ooh-arr accent, makes him both endearing – and asexual. He's more of a misshapen cuddly toy than a man – like Laura, the clown dolly Will's mother knitted for him when he was little.

Although Laura soon haunted him: grown monstrously large, she'd stand outside the house, her white woolly face blooming in the dark windowpanes, when he went upstairs to the lavatory to pee on winter evenings. Perhaps this is why Will feels no particular guilt about having *cuckolded* Freddy – and the Shakespearean term seems particularly apposite, given he and Helen have been a couple *since the Elizabethan-fucking-age* . . .

Will remembers Freddy's face manifesting in the frigid stairwell of the house he'd shared with Helen and four other young women in his final year at Oxford. Will was staggering from his ground-floor room, peaking on acid, when he encountered Freddy – who'd been instantly and entirely sympathetic, saying something like, *Whoa! I know where you're at, man, take it easy* . . .

Will was quite unable to follow these instructions – since they issued from the sewn-on mouth of a *fucking clown dolly-of-a-man* . . . Besides, did Will genuinely perform a sexual act with Freddy's girlfriend, or had they only nuzzled frantically, to keep warm?

Not in north Oxford – but a year or so later, around the time Will'd gone to check out the flat with Hughie. Helen and Freddy been squatting in Brixton as well, in a flat on Josephine Avenue once owned by the racing driver Stirling Moss, who'd spraunced the gaff up, adding a breakfast bar and a control panel equipped with switches meant to raise the shutters and dim the lights – but which had long since blown its fuses. When Will went round, they'd all lain there on the ratty old fitted carpet, stoned, and peered out at the defunct present through the broken futuristic blinds.

But yes . . . Helen came by Arlingford Road a couple of times when Freddy was away in the sticks. Came by when it was so cold the piss in the milk bottles under Will's creaky old bedstead had frozen. He'd been hunched up on top of it in a grubby sleeping bag: a stalled locomotive, puffing out condensation – and, without preamble, she'd pulled off her jeans and wormed inside with him.

Now, Helen wears black leggings and her hair's dyed black – while she and Freddy both sport loose-knit black pullovers, hers with a Betty Boop appliquéd to the front, his with a skull-and-crossbones. Looking at her freckled face, framed by many little Artex *pricks* . . . Will re-feels the wiriness of her multi-bleached hair, the grinding of her pubic bone against his and the granularity of her sweaty breasts.

Will sags, so his cheek rests against the broken entry phone – he can imagine well enough what *a spot of bother* with *a fucking nutter* means, so there was no point in dragging up here.

'You okay?' Helen touches his elbow, and Will snorts, coughs, chokes down a cold oyster of phlegm – then brings up: 'I'm utterly fucking skint, I've got a raging habit – an' I'm clucking. Other than that, I'm kushty.'

They all laugh – and Freddy says, 'If I can just pay a fiver off my tab, he'll give credit.'

'The fucking nutter?'

'Yeah.' Freddy grins. 'He knows I'm good for it . . . eventually.'

'Good?' Helen scoffs. 'What's good got to do with it? He said if you didn't give him your whole giro this week, he'd kick your fucking head in.'

It's Freddy's turn to sag – as if a giant thumb's been pressed into his fundament, his elasticated limbs crumple up so.

'You've fuck-all, then?' he asks Will, who cackles back: 'I jus' told you – only dosh I had was fifty-seven pee. Managed to blag these pastries off the girl in Greggs – was hoping my largesse would persuade this bloke I score off in the squats to serve me.'

'You've got some brass neck.' Freddy goggles at Will, his big eyes welling.

'I was hoping,' Will says, shrugging, 'to charm him.'

'Look,' Helen intervenes, 'I've gotta go to work – what're you gonna do, Will, hang out here?'

He gazes past her shoulder – the lemony light of the earlier morning is turning orange. He sees himself slumped in yet another sagbag: the one right there in their front room. True, if he stays with Freddy something might happen to change their fortunes – but if it doesn't? If he's going to be sick, Will would rather be so beneath Dennis Bovell's accusatory eyes than Freddy's watery ones.

'Me? I've got to go to work too – d'you wanna a lift?'

'Got a spare fag?' Freddy asks – and, feeling that since the apocalypse is indeed now, he may as well nuke his supplies, Will gets out his pack and slides it open.

'Woodbines, eh,' says Freddy, 'old man fags.'

Will takes one as well, leaving a single slim white missile. *Yes . . . old man fags – the fags smoked by entropy itself . . . then crushed into a flying-saucer-shaped-ashtray heading for a black-fucking-hole . . .* They light up: Bryant & May's dinky baton conjuring . . . *sulphur and woodsmoke.* He inhales, experiencing the acrid hit as a weird reagent coating his ulcerated gullet and wire-brushed lungs – turning them instructional colours . . . *purples . . . magentas.*

*

47

In the lift Will wonders if it's worth crying. He follows Helen past the piled-up black plastic bags acting as Pinter's gate piers, then beneath the filmy eyes of its front windows – puffing the while, his eyes smarting . . . *pricking.*

He certainly could cry if he made the effort – and who knows, it might work. Will's aware he's possessed of that quality his mother calls 'built-in orphan power': he could hit on Helen for a tenner – or at least a fiver. True, she'll've been fending off Freddy ever since their crusted eyes opened on the *nothing new* . . . but a final feeble twist might yet open that . . . *piggy bank.*

Will knows she'll have some cash – just as he knows that beneath Helen's unisex leggings and baggy black jumper, her body is voluptuous, with wide hips, and a quiff of ginger pubic hair. *She has long, pale-pink nipples – expanding aureoles . . .*

But as they come up to where the Veedub's parked, Will abandons the idea. Why? Because the recent past *repeats on me* – as unwelcome as a kipperish burp: he and Chloë, standing exactly here, a few weeks ago, and arguing about money . . . *and smack.*

Standing beside her parents' brand-new Mini Metro – the daguerreotype of Will's great-great-grandfather had been laid flat in its boot, so his hooded eyes stared up through its hatch. They'd been transporting it from his mother's flat to the Kensington one . . . *for decorative purposes*, but went via Hendon first, where her parents were having some sort of party.

Will remembers polite faces, canapés . . . *cubes of cheese.* Nothing surpasses the nausea of cheesiness . . . *puddling in your gullet.* He'd considered shoving the toothpicks into his own eyes, as they chatted chummily away. Then they'd driven south in the Metro, his threnody so persistent – he had nothing, was sick to death, was going nowhere in a worthless world – that Chloë hadn't noticed where they were heading, until they were bickering in this precise spot.

Chloë had been wearing her missionary grandmother's mauve silk and gold-embroidered cheongsam, brought back from her time in the Heavenly Kingdom. Her hair was up – with a chopstick thrust through it and twisted, so her pretty features seemed *stretched tight.* Or it could've been disgust – because no one likes it when their lover begs and pleads with them, which is what Will had been doing: *Just a tenner . . . that's all – all I need's a measly tenner . . . Just so's I can get straight, sort my shit out – then I'll get clean . . .*

On and on, his entreaties increasingly humiliating to them both, until finally she gave in.

He isn't indulging in a pathetic scene like that now – not with Helen: 'I'm heading back over Chelsea Bridge,' Will says. 'Any good to you?'

49

Helen says, 'Nah, not really – I'm temping in the Borough, I'll get the tube.'

They flutter into each other for a peck, and she squeezes his upper arm, undertoning, 'Look, I hope you sort yourself out, Will.'

Her face is diamond-shaped, with pretty facets – while her spiky hair is dyed a sort of aubergine colour this month. *Sort myself out* . . . He sees his body parts scattered, and his ghost-self arranging these into *fleshy, bloody piles* . . .

'I'll be all right,' Will says. 'They don't call me the Feminax Junky for nothing.'

'Oh, yeah,' she laughs, 'you used to take loads of them at Juxon Street – you did that thing with kaolin and morphine too.'

Yes: the Feminax Junky – who'd visited the chemist's on Observatory Street daily, and bought enough to ease a thousand menstrual go-rounds – and sufficient of the diarrhoea preparation to stopper a thousand arseholes.

Will'd gobbled the pills up, heedless of the paracetamol and caffeine they also contained. As for the bottles of kaolin and morphine, these he lined up in his room: silent ranks of little brown soldiers, standing to attention while their soporific brown heads slowly detached from their chalky-white bodies.

Then he'd siphoned off the morphine suspension, either

drank it right away – or else poured it into a tray and baked it in the oven until the gloop turned into a weird dun substance, cracked like the surface of a desert salt pan. This, he'd scraped up with a spatula and smoked in his homemade water pipe – the big one made from an old litre catering jar, and in which he'd immersed a platoon of toy plastic US Marines, *together with their landing craft.*

When Will applied the lighter to the morphine crud, it glowed evilly, and thick white smoke boiled down into the vessel, such that the tiny amphibious troops roiled in these miniature elements. But did this DIY junk really do anything? It was on a continuum, he felt, extending from over-the-counter pills with a soupçon of codeine in them, to the very Prince of Narcotics. Will needed painkillers, though, in his last year at Oxford, when his sinusitis grew acute – a metal vice, ever tightening behind his face: the result, some *malicious fucking quack* had informed him, of cocaine getting into his sinuses then becoming infected. Christ! That hurt – hurt enough to get him to stop shoving stuff up his nose . . . *and begin fixing it up in earnest.*

He'd craved smack – of course – but it'd been a rare bird in Oxford . . . *hardly ever breaking cover.*

Helen's gone — yet Will still havers on the corner of the Clapham Road. Feminax. Fuck that. He could chuck 'em back like Smarties and they wouldn't stop this inexorable . . . *rot.*

He can't go to work. His eyes slither about on the pavement, from this *turd of irrelevance*, to that *inadmissible shit* . . .

. . . *Seconds to go*, now: eyes squeaking in their sockets, all fleshy surfaces hooking into each other, ghastly hypersensitivity – his very skin stretching out in *a clammy layer that coats the city* . . . Throughout the long night of shooting cocaine, Will has punctured his arms *one hunnred an' aytee!* times: mostly hitting the bull's-eye in the crook of his left arm.

It was a Lilliputian contest: the scores of darts embedded in his flesh trailing fine cables — Now, the *trahens* will commence, as his corpse is hauled back across the river then cast into the plague pit of his bed. There he'll writhe in agony, longing for a silken skin to enfold his squamous one – then he'll come, his involuntary orgasm being only one of the grotesqueries exposed by the long fetch of opiate withdrawal.

Helen has gone – and Will doubts if she was ever present. Isolation grips him – he boils in the bag of his own corrupted skin as he digs out his car keys and unlocks the Veedub. That hurts. He pours himself into the vinyl bucket of the driver's seat – and that hurts too.

A year ago Will was driving the Scirocco Caius had given him. The turbo-charged red wedge could do around a hundred and thirty on the flat. He'd been working at the adventure playground in Richmond last summer, and when, come lunchtime, his resolve invariably crumbled, he had the necessary wild horses to drag him all the way back to Kensington, where he'd have a hit, before they dragged him back again.

One delirious evening he and Caius had horned up a great mound of coke and driven from London to Oxford in twenty-six minutes . . . *Gee, it must be great riding with him.*

But the red wedge is long gone – converted into an ounce of cocaine, which in turn is gone: *waste not, want not . . .* Will stares about him at the utilitarian interior of the car – gaining a little succour from its cream-painted metal fascia, the chrome-lidded instrument-binnacles, solid, rubberised switches and knurled knobs. In a Heraclitean world the Veedub, more than ever, represents some sort of certainty . . . *there are certain things.*

Will bought the car from a social worker who lived on the Broadwater Farm Estate. It'd only been a few weeks after the riots, and the red-brick walk-ups, and the glass-strewn grass patches between them, dripped *with a silent horror of blood . . .* The social worker . . . *Terry? Bobby?* had had enough – he was getting out. A black guy, with delicate features fraught with worry, he told Will he knew many of the mob personally, but they'd been almost unrecognisable to him as they surrounded Blakelock, so distorted were their faces by . . . *evil, I'd have to say evil.*

Will'd paid five hundred for the car – which was an

unlovely thing: scuzzy-white, with the same engine as a Beetle, but *a crushed one* . . . Now it scuttles across the junction and heads through leafy, sun-drenched streets. Not that Will appreciates what *noontide fucking wakes anew* – for him all is epidermal corruption: perished and scabby mortar, peeling paint and tarmac lumpy with fungus, London's skin and Will's own having entirely engrafted, such that they share the same *wanting* . . .

And there can be no pleasure at all in the life of the ever-desiring – only temporary gratification, on this Eastern mystics and Western philosophers agree. But Will knows that now even transient pleasure is denied him – why, if every chemist in the city were to be done, and all the pills and potions mixed together into a mighty salve, then rubbed into their rubble-strewn hide, neither he, nor the omnivorous city surrounding him, would feel any better.

As the Veedub blats back along the Wandsworth Road, its rear-mounted engine gives Will *lots of little shoves* in the back. The car handles stiffly and holds the road firmly – although in wet conditions the rear-wheel drive means it's susceptible to skids. The step-through clutch can also be awkward – sometimes Will catches his foot under the rubber matting as he's changing up or down rapidly, and thinks *I really must do something about that* . . .

Thrumming under the railway bridge by Wandsworth Road

Station, man and vehicle leave the thoroughfare and plunge off along a branch line, one that leads . . . *deep into the zone.* There's no control possible over the car – besides, it isn't a car any more, but a single-carriage train, and up ahead, all the points *have been welded* . . .

It's a familiar sensation – although usually experienced heading towards, rather than away from, the dealers. When Will, after hours of fretting and pacing, succumbs. On his way to score he'll realise the truth yet again: the Stoics were right, and free will is merely the feeling we have when our desires coincide with what has been determined for us.

Which is this . . . Some days ago, back at the Kensington flat, he spilled a can of ratatouille, and the sauce splurged across the glass-topped table in the little kitchenette, seeping beneath its wickerwork surround. To Will, now facing Fortuna herself, naked and unarmed, this image is inconceivably vile . . . *a slimy blot*, still viler than the open sores on his thighs and buttocks, ones he'd covered up with flesh-coloured Band-Aids. He remembers sitting on the unleavened bed in the lakeside hotel at Pokhara and piercing these pseudo-skins with a safety pin then squeezing out the infective . . . *sauce.*

It'd been there that his dream of following in Vance's nomadic footsteps had died – so he'd snuffled up another line of smack, then lain back as his imagination mounted, up and up, through valleys choked with rhododendrons, to the eyries of animistic isolates. *Yeah, yeah – poor fucking Vance*: he'd pitched up in London late last summer, when Will was picking up weekly. It was only a convenient Number 52 bus ride from the Kensington flat to Chess's gaff – then the same back again, with lips and tongue numbed to non-existence: *all heart*, it was drumming so against the ounce of coke tucked casually in his breast pocket *'cause he's a dedicated follower of fashion!*

The afternoon Vance arrived, Will sat him down on the powder-blue sofa, in front of the glass-topped coffee table. The tall sash windows had been half open, and, as they'd sat, snorting, sniffing and beer-swilling, the cries of playing children rose up from the gardens in the middle of the square. Contemplating Vance's dirty-tan skin, which appeared paler . . . *more sickly* in the northern light, Will'd thought, *Now the boot's on the other foot . . .*

Throughout the autumn, as they'd sopped up gramme-after-gramme of Kensal Rise Kokaine, Vance's skin grew yet paler.

Will had introduced him to Caius and Jasper. The former was amused by his hearty appetite for drugs, while the latter, sharing his love of cricket, took Vance to a late-season game played on the hallowed turf. For a while Vance had been in some sort of arcadia, in a London full of clichés: mole-faced members in their enclosure, stoned on gin, while, outside the MCC ground, tit-helmeted coppers waved down Cockney cabbies for tinkly voiced tiara-wearers — But by the time winter came, he was in a bad way – not even restorative congee at Wong Kei in Chinatown could bring him back from this ashen brink: a negatived version of his Aboriginal other self – a *burnt-out shell of a man* . . . bent over the tin foil, then wandering a black-and-white beach as he hit *an all-time low* . . .

He'd slumped for days in his sleeping bag on the powder-blue sofa. Both grew dirty – while Vance grew seedier. Then Will got a job, courtesy of Jasper – who, being a fully paid-up member of the suited and executive class, had such things in his gift. Will's mission was to tour the country interviewing data-processing managers about their, um, data processing – which seemed pretty *fucking reductive* . . . He took Vance along, to keep him awake at the wheel after long cocaine nights: Thompson-and-fucking-Acosta, barrelling down the M4 to Filton *with pterodactyls swooping around the car* – then Will, in a come-down ague, ground out toothy shorthand, while the British Aerospace data-processing manager droned on, and the paper softly slapped as it concertinaed from the printer.

Meanwhile, outside in the car park, Vance chopped out lines on the open hatch of the Veedub's glove compartment.

Honest lumber-jacking, really – compared to the cosmic-fucking-joke of his own labours. Will, still *st-st-stammering* along the Wandsworth Road, and fixated by the clods of dried earth falling from the back axle of the lorry in front, scans his curriculum vitae. He's had wildly inappropriate jobs, such as driver–labourer for Thomas de Vere & Sons, a general builder in Stoke Newington, or wacky ones, such as running the kids' project for the council. There'd also been a satiric interlude, when he'd been contracted by the Lands Department of the Northern Territory Government of Australia to assess the demand for building land in the Territory, an area six times the area of the entire United Kingdom, with a population of around a hundred thousand.

In between there'd been dynasties of day-dreaming, cramped eternities of clock-watching as he'd shuffled paper temping for this or that faceless corporation . . . *the Sudanese Bank of Carmarathon*. Really, he should've stuck it out at De Vere's, there'd been an honesty in the toil, if not the Tolstoyan absorption into 'the people' he'd sought. When ancient and horny-handed sons of the sod bellowed *Shift dem fuckin' bricks* . . . or putlocks, or acrow props, or scaffolding poles, Will had felt nothing but pride. Proud – and grateful to've been given a valuable education in the basic physics of toil: everything has its tipping point. *Under western* . . . Cork eyes, he'd driven the little dumpster up the planks, pulled the lever, and the rubble cascaded down into the skip.

That'd taken some balls – especially when sweating out the previous evening's gear. Because that'd been another reason for taking the job – a health kick, like Brother Bill kicking with laps of the pool at the New York Athletic Club.

The De Veres had been good bosses. On Will's second day, piloting the flat-bed truck along the Queens Avenue, one eye on the patrolling brasses, the other on the wheels of the parked cars, he thought he'd seen something, and braked hard. Because that was another of his mother's neurotic foibles: *Always keep an eye on the tyres of the parked cars, if there're kids about to cross the road without looking you'll see them . . .* The truck slewed, sideswiping a Jag.

A fucking Jag!

Will's boss, Richard de Vere, always had a troubled expression on his pear-shaped face. He'd been cross – yet hadn't even docked Will's wages.

Some six months later, Will was rearranging roofing tiles and chimney pots up on the roof of the warehouse, when Richard's narrow temples rose into view, followed by his broad jaw. It had been summer, and behind him Clissold Park was looking particularly . . . *frothy ma-an.* Richard had asked Will what he wanted a word about, and Will said he was giving in his notice, and Richard said, What? – genuinely astonished – and Will said it again, I'm leaving . . . Richard shook his head. What you want to do that for? To which Will, *the fucking snot,* had replied, It's just *I think I can do better for myself with an Oxford degree . . .* Of course, he couldn't, and Richard de Vere's response still resounds, years later, *I think you're making a big mistake – I was about to give you a raise . . .*

Horns blast Will from this reverie: career driver–labourers are waiting behind him to take the right into Silverthorne Road – a sweeping one, that'll dash lumps of aggregate down on to the road. There's a gritty feel to this area, Will thinks: the southern littoral of the Thames, which was *pasted* in the war, and is now *smeared* with detritus. Yes, and the businesses that process it: car-breakers, scrap-metal dealers, and the council tip at Cringle Dock.

The Veedub jitters over potholes as the four chimneys of Battersea Power Station thrust up from the mid-distance. Will steers the car through the chicane under the shitted-and-feathered railway bridges, and emerges into a scattering of raindrops.

Yes . . . Will thinks, that's it, there will be no more sunny May mornings – none at all. There are only rainy Tuesday afternoons, and debts, and persistent skin infections. Silent, somnolent, still afternoons in deepest suburbia, with no one to phone, and the acute understanding that whatever else may happen *you'll never leave here . . .*

At the junction with Battersea Park Road Will has a small fit: 'I'm fucked! I'm fucking fucked!' Screams that're accompanied by a frenzied tom-tomming on the steering wheel.

Yes, there's already no one to call – his mother will be at work, Chloë too. Besides, Will's forgotten where he is in his cycle of deception-and-confession – can he convincingly represent himself as the victim of his addiction, or will this come across as *yet more fucking lies* . . . They're both attending Families Anonymous meetings now – although not together – and the dreadful jargon *enabling, complete abstinence, letting-bloody-go* . . . comes to their lips . . . *un-fucking-bidden.*

Exiting the Queenstown Road roundabout, Will fixates momentarily on the drizzle-dampened expanse of Battersea Park. When he'd been working for the GLC, he'd meet the others here, in the keepers' yard, where they'd kept the panel vans. Then they'd head off into the wilds of London, from Thamesmead in the far south-east, to Ally-Pally in the north, Will spread out on the mounds of warm plastic in the back.

True, at the time he'd been *bored out of my fucking mind* . . . by the interminable afternoons, patrolling the parched defiles between the inflatables – huge structures, cemented together out of plastic tubes, and kept so taut by industrial blowers that they squeakily resonated as scores of screaming kids jumped up . . . *and dropped down.*

He'd been bored – but not that sick. He was only doing bits and pieces of gear – and he'd been frightened, feeling himself rapidly sinking in the *quicksmack* . . . mixed together out of water and powder. It'd taken Will three long years to get a proper habit – but then he had. Oh, yes – a serious habit, with serious consequences.

Driving back from Filton, with Vance slumped in the passenger seat, Will had struggled to stay awake. As soon as he got back to the car he de-cored the biro he'd been note-taking with and truffled up another thick line. It was no good, though – he was beyond stimulus, the needle on his toxicology meter well inside *the red zone* . . . where things got weird.

Poor Vance! He'd come to London in search of wonder, but then tumbled down Will's rabbit hole, snorting lines from the shelves lining it as he fell.

A dangerous road, the A303 – especially when swept by heavy showers. An arterial road that drivers treated *like a motorway* . . . Will remembers jockeying to pass cars cloaked in primal chaos, the Veedub's wipers carving brief swathes of realism out of his coked-up impressions of *spray, speed and sunlight*.

They'd splashed past the object of their detour – Stonehenge, its mighty sarsens huddled up in the rain – then, shortly before merging with the real motorway, came this bizarre interlude: in the middle of the carriageway, a Citroën 2CV, balled up like a sheet of waste paper and burning merrily. The traffic slowed and parted to either side – the accident must've happened only moments before. Gripping the steering wheel, grinding his teeth, Will had cruised by. *There must be people still inside!* The combusting consequences that, by rights, should've been the sequel to his and Vance's stuporous condition.

He'd been aware of this – and conscious, also, that, in common with Turner's conjurings of rain, steam and speed, this one of *rain, smoke and flame* . . . while glimpsed only for seconds, would remain with him . . . *for centuries.*

Drugs can do this, Will believes: they memorialise chance and fleeting occurrences, fixing them forever in fantastical varnish . . . *My head aches,* he sees himself spread-eagled on the bare boards of Mumsie's gaff off the Roman Road, Genie sitting on his chest and punching him in the face. The Will-dummy splutters as she pours a cup of cold water over it. It'd been his second heroin overdose – his first had been with Genie as well, back when she was still squatting in West Hampstead, in regal pomp, in the tall and isolated house at the end of Hemstal Road.

Yes . . . Genie sitting on Will's chest and punching him in the face – an eternal recurrence, ever resurrecting him to this grisly go-round. To this – and to her anger: Christ! She'd been fucking furious – *it masked her fear.* Genie knew how to use her fists – and she'd used them on Will: regular blows that made her brown curls bounce. As he regained consciousness, it'd been first of that, then of this: the blatant fucking injustice of surviving an overdose. Why? Because as you pushed the plunger in, you'd been simultaneously aware of these three things: you'd taken *too much*, you were *going to die*, but it was all right because *you felt no pain* . . .

Resurrected, a cold and wet Lazarus, you suffer a less than miraculous headache, because all that analgesia has been wasted, contra your mother's homily.

Now, as the Veedub splashes past Marco Polo House, Will recalls going to pitch his cartoons to the Art Editor on the Observer, which has its offices in this bizarre ziggurat of white-and-grey marble . . . *with its ornamental balls*. She was a sympathetic-seeming woman, who, while not exactly bowled over by his wit and artistry, was at least . . . *civil*.

They sat at her desk while she flapped the plastic leaves of his portfolio. Around them the open-plan office hummed and clattered. So as not to witness her indifference, Will turned to the wide expanse of tinted windows: 'The glass isn't shatter-proof,' she'd said – or words to that effect: 'Almost every day a passing lorry or car shoots up a stone from the roadway and it breaks a window – they've had to clear all the desks at the front of the building.'

She'd told him, kindly, he was welcome to try again, then Will had made his way back between the desks of the straight-goers, towards the traffic's fusillade.

Christ! Pitching cartoons to the newspapers is a depressing – no, soul-destroying – business, one that makes the entire world seem deeply unfunny. Even when he does have a commission, Will feels drawing cartoons is *a dumb-fucking-occupation for a grown man* – especially one who can't draw properly.

And remembering he's a strip to deliver tomorrow, Will groans out loud, seeing himself at the kitchenette table with a 2H pencil and a Rotring pen, his blank A4 page neatly aligned with *the fucking ratatouille stain* . . . Although maybe it's this that's the real subject of Will's drawings: not the cartoons of people and things, but the white void surrounding them.

Now, fleetingly, as the Veedub charges towards Chelsea Bridge, he sees his younger selves as a series of pen-strokes on the blankness of his past – a void in which his brother's creepy teachers also lurk, beckoning that tubby and compliant child to join them in their cars . . . *for a spin*. A void into which Will, soon enough, disappeared as well – a zone at once unlimited and sequestrated, in which he'd been free to smoke, drink, and eventually . . . *score*.

After the OD at Vallance Road, he'd left, soggy and groggy, then forced the Scirocco through the heavy lunchtime traffic, aeons late for work at the adventure playground in Richmond. He'd then had to stop for petrol. Standing on the forecourt, festooned in oblivion, he'd managed to splash it all over his hands and trouser legs. Driving away, reeking of the stuff, he'd fumbled out a cigarette, stuck it in his numb mouth, fumbled out his lighter and rasped the wheel.

'Woomph!' Audibly so.

Then a few stunned seconds while the message got through from his legs to his brain: *We're on fire! We're on fucking fire!*

After which everything had *sloooowed riiiight doooown.*

It'd taken decades for Will to decide to stop the car – then centuries to find a place to do so, and millennia for him to bump it up on the kerb.

Next he'd been standing on the pavement, in the dead-centre of his daymare – and he'd been on fire: his jeans merrily combusting, blue-yellow tongues of flame licking towards his groin. He'd had time to think – as he took in the peculiar odour of human fat frying – how to an observer he must closely resemble the cover of the Pink Floyd album *Wish You Were Here* . . .

Or there – but not exactly where Will is now, staring bleakly up from under the flesh-coloured lids of the Veedub's vinyl sunshades at the crane's davit, angling out over the river from beside the southern approach to Chelsea Bridge. It's too early in the day for such dizzy delights – but at other times he's seen them: daredevils who've paid for the privilege, bungee jumping from the crane. *A surrealistic sight* . . .

As is the cloud momentarily blocking the May morning

sun. Can this be the same lazy little puff that sauntered in Will's wake, as, strung taut as its cabling, he drove across the bridge an hour or so ago? *Does it matter?*

Anyway, if it is, in the intervening time it's grown into a bigger, and *yet more pathetic-fucking-fallacy.* Will's realisation coincides with raindrops spattering the Veedub's roof. Although, given the road ahead is already sheened, rain must've been falling for a while — *Sheened . . . ?* No: *awash,* with the thin coating of water that lies unabsorbed on tarmac after a cloudburst, providing the perfect surface for a car to aquaplane.

But that's okay, because, although the coach ahead is slowing, preparatory to making a right-hand turn across the oncoming traffic and into the coach park by the bridge, there happens to be a nearside lane.

It'll be just like the Silverthorne Road manoeuvre, Will thinks, eyes flicking to the wing mirror: *so long as my luck holds . . .*

It doesn't: there's a car coming up fast in the nearside lane. *There's a fucking car COMING UP FAST IN THE NEAR-SIDE LANE!*

So fast, if he were to yank the Veedub's steering wheel to the left – given their relative velocities, trajectories, and the Fates, who have, with each pierce and pull of their needles, stitched together his several stupidities – they'll collide.

Will's eyes flick back to the road ahead — And it's at this

crucial juncture, when speed is, for once, truly of the essence, that Will's thoughts . . . *congeal* into this sticky epiphany: despite the police, the thieves and the paranoia, there's nothing remotely exciting about heroin addiction. All the drug imparts is the golden-brown repose Will longs for, a state of gilded gradation, in which the distance between the Veedub and the arse-end of the coach ahead – which judders, and farts out wisps of blackish exhaust – would halve, and halve again, forever forestalling the inevitable impact.

While leaving him with plenty of time in which to contemplate his surroundings: the delicate tracery of the crane's struts and the bridge's cables silhouetted against the bright May sunshine, which explodes once more from behind the pathetic cloud. Will thinks of lolly sticks and feathers stuck together with duck shit, slowly revolving on the oily surface of Battersea Park's boating lake.

He thinks of pedalos – then of childhood. He remembers another May morning, seven years ago, when, sitting in the passenger seat of Pete's mum's Triumph Dolomite, he'd wound down the window, leaned out and vomited.

He'd felt properly heroic then, certainly: for where there'd been discord, she, with her *texture like silk* . . . had indeed brought . . . *harmony*.

*

The coach's rear end looms larger in the Veedub's windscreen. If this were a two-dimensional world, the worst he'd have to fear would be absorption into its scuzzy whiteness — But it isn't: his eyes flick once more to the offside wing mirror – and no: *the situation remains ongoing . . .* the car's drawn level in the inside lane, and the Veedub's completely boxed in.

At once, Will's right foot slides from the accelerator to the brake, while his left depresses the heavy clutch. His intention is to just dab the pedal, and brake lightly.

The moral worth of an action is not, however, to be judged by the intentions of he who performs it – Will knows this, despite his hurting head and indifferent philosophy degree. No: it's to be judged on the basis of its consequences – and, while his intention may've been to dab the pedal, since saying goodbye to Helen back in Stockwell, every action he's performed has been peremptory: wrenching at the Veedub's steering wheel, ramming it into gear and jabbing at the radio's buttons to summon this disc then that jockey.

So, Will doesn't dab the brake pedal – he stamps on it, and the brakes lock.

Immediately, he feels the car's tyres part company with the road. His dependable mobile shed, which had forged its way happily through the spray past the burning Citroën, is *running amok!*

At last, there's a break in the oncoming traffic and the

coach ahead swings to the right – the carriageway is clear, and for the first time in his life, Will fervently wishes to . . . *go to Chelsea.*

It's too late, though, because mounted on its millimetres-thick cushion of water, the Veedub starts on its own deviant trajectory: a long, looping skid that'll take it past the right-hand turn, and – if it misses the cars that've slowed momentarily for the coach – to an impact with the parapet of the bridge, within the next few deliciously elongated seconds.

For here at last, in the skid itself, is the repose Will's been seeking not simply this morning but for months – years, even. As the Veedub lazily pirouettes, he's ample time to reflect on his own colossal folly. 'Ample' – a fatherly word, this – one it's impossible to pronounce without sounding orotund. So, for a few moments, Will's father joins him in his death-ship, sitting implacably in the passenger seat, a great dolmen of a man who gently remonstrates, *Really, Will, old chap – I don't know why you've got to be so very excessive . . . I mean to say, I myself have always enjoyed a drink and a smoke – these are some of the pleasures life has to offer – but always in moderation . . . Everything's better enjoyed in moderation, don't you know . . .*

Yes, Will's got plenty of time to reflect on his folly – a great waste of it, full to bursting with his yet greater wanting.

He's time to regret the drugs and the debts and the betrayals – the weeping, the wailing and the rotting of his teeth. He'd wanted to be a writer – *to lounge about in a silk suit, smoking opium* . . . but, clearly, that's not going to happen now.

He's guilty, he knows, of hubris – of daring to differentiate himself from the great mass of individual wills simply striving to exist. Only the day before yesterday, in the shambolic aftermath of another smacked-out night, he'd taken the Polaroid his father had sent from Australia – a photograph which showed the old faker in full verbal flood – and applied the flame of a lighter to it. Waiting – then waiting some more – until the plasticised flesh bubbled then melted.

Next, he'd applied the lighter's flame to his own forearm – which seemed as distant and objective as Australia – and waited until the flesh bubbled then melted. Then waited some more . . . *smelling bacon fat.*

The steering wheel whips uselessly through his numb hands, as, anticipating the collision, the car begins to self-disassemble: its hub-cabs popping off, its tyres peeling away from the wheels – and those wheels twirling off their axles.

The Veedub's bonnet, together with the boot's hatch, fly up and away – while the seats eject themselves. The car's transforming into an orthogonal diagram of itself – the sort Will's seen in workshop manuals he's idly leafed through. Crumpled-up fag packets and scraps of tin foil smutty with smack-ash float up from the floor – while the ashtray springs from the dashboard, the butts crumpled into it uncoiling. The glove compartment falls open, and the penalty-charge notices stuffed inside fly out, as all the rest of the rubbish – the sandwich wrappers, tin cans, silvery juice sachets and paper bags that once held Danish pastries – *rises up into entropy*...

Yes – all of it: all of these disparate things – together with Will's own hopes, dreams, fears and memories – are flying away from each other into the white void of this wonderful May morning.

2

May 1979

Don't care was made to care . . . Don't care was made to care . . . Don't care was . . . MADE TO CARE! Will shouts out his mother's hackneyed homily in the pressurised confusion of his own mind. He will indeed be made to regret his lack of *empathy* – another of Mum's fave words, and one that's never far from her sad, saturnine lips. Because she wants it, and needs his sympathy as well – requiring him to sit beside her where she slumps, sobbing on the stairs, the phone's handset lying in her lap.

Yes, don't care will be made to care – but, for now, *there's plenty more unfeeling to be done . . .* Will rises unsteadily, so he's standing upright on his bed, which he's positioned immediately next to his bedroom window. Why? Well, the better to see the world, of course – the world? *Bollocks.* Suburbia is all he can see: the overgrown back garden of Number 43, with its tousled hedges, shaggy trees and back-combed lawn. To the left is Mrs Cohen's garden, to the right the Hamburgers' – by contrast, both rectangular plots have been fanatically clipped, cut, weeded and pesticided.

Will remains poised, arms and legs akimbo, as he listens to the needle he's just placed on the single hiss and pop its way around the dusty groove. During this pause, he holds fast to this talismanic memory of earliest childhood: on a trip to Chicago with his mother – for his grandfather's funeral, he's been told, although he's no recollection of this – he was laid sleeping in the loft bedroom of his much older cousin, and woke to find *Zeus descending in a shower of gold* . . . a thick beam of light lancing through the dormer window, in which swirled myriad motes.

If he squinted, the beam withdrew – if he dilated, it advanced. This was the true innocence, he thinks: a time when world and Will were one and the same –

'Gettup in de mornin' . . .' Now, it's words and guitar chord that're one and the same – a closed loop of lyrics and music, flung from the turntable to lasso his scrawny neck. Will undulates as the singer slowly bemoans his struggle for subsistence – then, as the guitar chugs up the scale, dragging bass and drums behind it, so Will begins to skank: his skinny arms pump in the slack sleeves of his olive-green US Army T-shirt, while his skinny legs bicycle in the baggy legs of his pale-tan combat trousers.

It isn't exactly dancing, Will thinks, he's *embodying the music* – a good expression, one which captures the way certain guitar riffs, when combined with specific words, cannot be resisted – they push buttons deep inside, which in turn release great gushes of adrenalin, 'Poor me, Israelites!'

*

Will's finding it hard to gettup in de mornin' nowadays – with only a few weeks to go before the exams there're no classes any more, and, with his place at Oxford conditional on his scraping only a couple of passes, he scarcely needs to revise.

Days seem to float on the surface of reality, filmy and insubstantial, with nothing to fill them but the crude black doodles of Will's desires: he's found himself, wheezing in the empty, airless house, longing for a bomb with which to blow it all to smithereens – he sees tatty paperbacks and broken crockery strewn across the road, his father's voluminous flannel underpants draped over a rose bush in Mrs Cohen's front garden.

As for slavin' for bread – emphatically not. Whatever his mother says about wasting and wanting – and however much his father sheepily bleats about *things being a bit tight* . . . all Will can see around him is the fusty upholstering of the middle-class lifestyle: cushions, curtains and carpets, all furred with dust.

True, a couple of afternoons a week he works in the post room at the small publishers where his mother's the production editor – there are fines to be paid off: for driving with undue care and attention, and taking a vehicle without its owner's consent. The vehicle in question being the puke-yellow Austin Maxi parked on the drive outside – a little unimaginative, that, stealing your own parents' car, although, on the plus side, there's a certain precocity involved in reaching the age at which you're legally entitled to drive having already been banned from doing so.

Will doesn't like to think of how lost and ineffectual his father appeared, standing in the witness box at Highgate Magistrates' Court. In point of fact: thinking about his father at all is a torment to Will, as a hot hive of embarrassment spreads beneath his skin.

At seventeen, Will's old enough to sense the shape of his father's insecurities – which are social quite as much as financial. He returns again *annagain* to this shocking scene, which had occurred a couple of years earlier, when they were staying at the opulent country house belonging to a wealthy colleague of Dad's.

Father and son had been walking in the West Country, and Dad – *as was his wont* – had invited himself to stay. After dinner – which had seemed convivial enough – conversation slid from the general and the philosophic to the personal and the political. Will hadn't quite been able to peel away all the onion-skin layers of irony from their host's table talk, nonetheless he got this: he was systematically and snidely humiliating Will's father – implying he was a bore, an intellectual makeweight and – the proof being in his and his son's very presence – a sponger.

Dad's face is red to begin with – redder when he's been drinking – and reddest of all when he's both tipsy and embarrassed. He'd *burned* – while Will burned with him, fuelled as much by contempt as pity.

As for poor Israelites, Will doesn't know any – unless you include Darren Silvers, who lives with his single mother in small flat full of knick-knacks and net curtains near Henlys Corner. Will's own mother is an Israelite of sorts – but her Jewishness seems quite different to that of the English Jews who live around them.

It's difficult to imagine any of them coming out with one of her outrageous one-liners: *She thinks she shits chocolate ice cream . . .* said of some demure young miss or other that Will fancies, and so in that instant stinking out all his perfumed dreams. There'll be no escape from the Mother planet – Will realises this intuitively: even if he does blast off for new worlds, he'll touch down only to find her footprints already in the dust. There'll be no giant leaps for this specimen of mankind, only *baby steps . . .*

There're four marijuana plants growing in pots downstairs on the kitchen windowsill – Mum's been cultivating them assiduously, as she does the geraniums growing on what she grandly calls 'my terrace'. The plants would be a lot healthier, were it not that every time they recover, Will goes down and prunes them again.

Mum says *pot's a bore* – and that she smoked reefer with Timmy Leary in the fifties, and that he too was a bore. She grows the plants only out of a desire to connect with her adolescent son – which is also why, when she last went to the States, Mum brought him back a copy of Cocaine: A Drug and Its Social Evolution by Lester Grinspoon.

Will finds the book's title considerably more stimulating than its content, which is academic to the point of tranquillising. The title implies that cocaine is going somewhere, while Grinspoon (an obvious nom de plume: the 'grin' of the cokehead when he's plied his 'spoon') is the man to take it there. Will has shelved 'Cocaine' with his other drug books: there's a second by Grinspoon, the title of which – Psychedelic Drugs Reconsidered – he also finds hilarious. Beside it are Burroughs's Junky and Naked Lunch (the latter Will received for the Lower Sixth Form English Prize, and has his school's book-plate glued to its inside cover), Thompson's Fear and Loathing in Las Vegas, De Quincey's Confessions of an English Opium Eater, together with one or two other dog-eared accounts of narcotised debauchery.

Hobby doesn't seem quite the right term to describe this, Will's consuming interest. If drugs were a hobby, he thinks, then the books would be uniformly jacketed, like I-Spy booklets, or Shell Guides. Neither are drugs a genre *like science fiction . . .*

Still skanking on his bed, Will feels the reggae guitar's chopped rhythms stir his sluggardly heart – or is it the two amphetamine blues he swallowed twenty minutes ago already doing their work? His eyes zag to the oak tree looming outside his window, and he sees in its gnarled basketry a crystalline planet, where jewels grow instead of flowers, and wheeled anthropoids drive their bodies between steely trees . . . *which would be cool* – although drugs have really taken the place of science fiction in his life, offering him direct experience of alternative worlds, rather than the effort required to imagine them.

Will thinks of last year's trip to Bath, with Mike, to see Tom and blow his parochial mind with their multicoloured collection of *uppers, downers, twisters and screamers . . .* namely: ten blotters of acid, a half-ounce of Pakki black, four black bombers, twenty-odd amphetamine blues, a couple of Mogadons Mike'd nicked from his mum and a bottle of amyl nitrate. 'Course, there's no way the two of them could've got through all of that in a couple of days – but then, there was their host and his brother to consider. Besides, *once you get locked into a serious drug collection . . . the tendency is to push it as far as you can . . .*

Either to the point where pterodactyls swoop about the sky – or a bright red balloon, which had slowly floated into the steep and wooded combe where Tom's house was, just as they were all peaking on the acid. Will had indeed *pushed it further . . .* encouraging their host to search out the carefully concealed key, open his father's gun compartment and loose off a couple of rounds, not at the balloon – but in its general direction.

There were some girls about, but they hadn't dropped any acid. The following week one of them grassed Tom up to his parents, with predictably dire consequences. Will wonders if it was the honey-blonde whom he'd seen, lying across Tom's brother's bed in the early-morning sunlight, wearing only jeans with a Snoopy patch on the knee.

He can still see the vulnerable bumps of her spine – he'd so wanted to go to her, wrap his own shaky frame around her . . . *and cry.* But then Will often experiences such wild excesses of emotion – the possibility of an ephemeral engagement with a passer-by releasing him from the interminable torment of watching his older brother . . . *eat cereal.*

Tom had done some of the acid, though — Whereupon he freaked out, despite Will's best efforts to babysit him, by plunging his head inside a miniature garden inside a goldfish-bowl. Crazy! After all, what could've been more beguiling than those bonsai trees and mini-mosses bejewelled with infinitesimal dewdrops?

Tom had flung the rifle away, even as its report flatly cracked across the combe. Will fished it out from beneath one of the cars cluttering up the driveway – which was when he'd seen the trial bike. Shortly after that – and thanks to a stroll in the miniature garden – he'd *broken on through* to another dimension, one where there were no petty distinctions between interiors and exteriors, so confidently wheedled the key from its owner, and drove the bike inside the house . . . *and halfway up the Möbius stairs.*

He'd been scrambling towards Tom's brother's bedroom – probably to impress the blonde girl. Will doesn't believe there was much damage – only a scuffed skirting board . . . *or two.* Besides, what did Tom expect? Still, a very angry and upset letter arrived the following week: Tom and his brother were grounded for the whole summer – and reparations would have to be paid. Neighbours had also reported stuff to the police.

Will wonders if he'll ever see Tom again – which would be a shame. But, then again: *Death to all moderators!*

Yes, indeedy — The following morning, pie-eyed and knock-kneed, Will and Mike had sneaked away into the parched summer day *dandelion spore stuck to softening tarmac . . .* They couldn't afford a return coach ticket, so hitched, and ended up in the baking afternoon somewhere near Blackbush in Surrey: a landscape of sandy heath and fly-blown bracken that, whichever way they wandered, faded into a *hot . . . white . . . void.*

An ancillary portion of Will's brain registers this: ringing and knocking that isn't in time with Desmond – whose wife and kids have packed up and left him. Well, that's Israelites for you, always on the move – or at least they should be. The Israelites who live in the Hampstead Garden Suburb seem pretty firmly entrenched to Will.

His mother, while at pains to make it clear he was an anti-Semite, is nonetheless fond of quoting G. K. Chesterton: *The Jews are like everyone else, but more so . . .* and extrapolating from this that the English Jews must, therefore, be like the English *but more so . . .* And how crap is that?

Lying behind her sallow-olive skin and comedic mole is a vaudevillian realm, full of snappy characters wearing loud check suits and smoking ten-cent cigars – guys like Will's grandfather, of whom all he knows is that Jack Rosenbloom kept a card-index of one-liners, and that instead of a billfold he carried a mother-of-pearl-inlaid money-clip, stuffed with dollar bills, so's to give himself the lustre of being moneyed, while having little of the substance.

By contrast, there are the Smith-Simonses, two doors down, with their absurd and recently acquired hyphen – imagining they can somehow pole-vault their way into the upper-middle classes with this little typographic stick.

Gravel and earth spatter against Will's bedroom window. At once, the Israelites scatter beyond the Jordan – *an effect*, Will thinks, *that should've preceded its cause.* He suffers badly enough from déjà vu, forever arriving in new places by ripping through well-known scenery, and equates this feeling with precognition: a hard tackle when he played rugby, a fist randomly smashed in his face, the bonnet of the family Austin Maxi buckling on impact with a tree – they too had been sucker-punches: the world feints, Will looks the wrong way, then *Wham!* it hits him in the *fucking face* . . .

Shaky-legged, he steps down from the bed, lifts the plastic hood, then the needle.

Returning to the window, he opens it and calls down, 'Wotcher.'

The pink, earnest face upturned below offers a 'Wotcher' of its own, followed by 'I was beginning to think no one was in, I've been ringing for ages.'

Yes! Ages . . . dynasties of god-kings with extravagantly curled and richly perfumed beards, drinking sherbet and goosing houris dripping with gold — Playing kiss chase with them, up and down the Babylonian terraces *bright with sinuous rills* . . .

'I'll meet you out front,' Will says, rasping shut the metal-framed window. He picks up his jacket – a tan gaberdine one that dates from the early sixties. Checking the pockets, he feels a Marlboro box, a match one and his stash box: a flat tin, dating from the still trendier fifties, that once contained Dilly Duckling Cough Pastilles.

Will reveres this satiric object – its lid bears a cartoon of a bright yellow mummy-duck, wings-on-hips, admonishing a couple of ducklings who're catching their *death of cold* in a cartoon pond. To him, the lid captures in its narrow, painted dimensions the cultural antinomies he sees around him: between high and low, or decades as marketable commodities and . . . *time as a flow.*

Then there's this delicious irony to suck on: *Specially Made for Children – indeedy!* Nestled in the tin are a lump of Red Leb' wrapped in clingfilm, another little filmy bundle of blues, together with a couple of a Mogadons and a wrap of coarse, amphetamine sulphate.

Pete says things like 'Don't be daft.' He's what Will's mother calls 'a gentle soul', by which she means to say, ineffectual, and of no great significance. Her savage dismissals counterpoint, Will thinks, her wild inclusiveness: the *waifs and strays* picked up in tea shops, on buses and in the deserted aisles of remote provincial libraries, when she's off on one of her *little trips* . . .

Pete has a mole too – but his is larger, lighter and just off-centre on his dimpled chin. His family have a semi a bit like Number 43, three-up, three-down – yet somehow a little meaner in every respect: the brickwork paler, the front and back gardens smaller, and bounded by creosoted fences rather than privet hedges.

There're no books to speak of – at least, Will's seen none on the rare occasions he's visited. Instead, there's a large colour television, always on, and several broken fruit machines clutter up the hall and the living room, where, when he isn't on his rounds, Pete's white-haired father sits in a big black vinyl armchair, sucking on an Embassy filter, drinking a can of Double Diamond and watching the racing.

He owns scores of the machines, which are sited in pubs and cafés throughout North London. To Will, Pete's family have an odd glamour – the effect, he's aware, of seeing them through his mother's estranged and estranging eyes. They seem very pink, very white . . . *and very petit bourgeois.* Pete even refers to his grandmother as 'nan' – a sure sign of yet more déclassé origins.

Nan . . . is a term Will's mother would damn as . . . *non-U*: a refined judge of social distinctions, she's schooled Will and his brother in them since infancy, when she instructed them to call shit 'BM' and shitting 'doing a BM' – the Mitford-mandated abbreviation now, to Will's ear, sounds . . . preposterous, as if old children's books were being retro-actively bedizened: the Indian uncle arrives at the Bastables' house by the Common, bearing all manner of exotic gifts – the most unusual of all being a large and glistening BM in *an ornately carved sandalwood box.*

Will stands on the hushed landing, beside a reproduction of Matisse's 'Still Life with Oysters' he's stared at while falling asleep thousands of times. There's cold metallic pill-sludge at the back of his throat, and dust tickling his nostrils – Pete's house smells companionably of lager and fags, but Number 43 is gently putrefying now its *parental authority figures* are mostly absent.

Bananas rot in the fruit bowl, while the dog's intestinal parasites . . . *burrow deeper*. The entire semi, Will senses, dangles from cables, as it's swung out over the dark roadway: a bathysphere, about to be lowered, yet again, into the deep, dull suburb.

Will wonders if he's possessed of that quality most prized by his mother, for which she's coined the term 'built-in orphan power'. Yes, built-in orphan power – which suggests a mummy's boy raised to the status of a super-hero, one capable of sympathising with *the entire-fucking-world* . . . If it wasn't for the fact that *don't care was . . . made to care*: first by Wilkinson's sword, withdrawn from its plastic scabbard then held tight between thumb and forefinger. *One, two, three, four* . . . gills through which his sharkish arm breathed . . . *blood*.

It didn't matter anyway – he'd hated wearing T-shirts. His arms looked so fat in them – and horribly white.

It'd been typical of his mother, who couldn't resist an opportunity for drama, to make her announcement on his birthday. The party for his ninth one had been the best he can remember – or is that simply pathetic nostalgia? Life before the Fall, with Mummy and Daddy and Little Willy and Johnny?

Bullshit. Arrant bullshit. Still, nostalgia or not – amphetamine p-p-pump p-p-priming the flames of recollection *or not*, she'd made hamburgers and French fries, and Will could tell his schoolfriends were impressed.

There'd been, he thinks, *some of the usual paper-ripping games . . . kazoos . . . Smarties . . .* But at the very end, when it was dark outside, they'd pulled the curtains, doused the lights, and *the wild rumpus began . . .* Once cushions were pulled from sofas and chairs the warm darkness grew arms and legs, as the boys touched, grabbed, grappled. Had it been wrestling, cuddling, or both?

It hardly mattered – the sensations were thrilling: an abandonment at once savage and tender. When his mother switched the lights back on, the boys looked at one another, at once further alienated – and far more complicit.

Mothers had arrived to collect their sons – Will handed out the going-home presents . . . *more bourgeois barter.* Then, he'd gone with his mother as she drove the last few guests home. Finally, on the way back, when he was altogether replete and happy, she'd told him: *Your father has left us, and gone to Rome to be with an Italian woman . . .*

Night after night, ivoried by forty-odd watts, the Matisse reproduction had hung before his eyes: the knife and mug crudely depicted – the oysters illegible blobs. No wonder he couldn't see the world for what it was, when he'd been subjected *night after night* ... to this post-impressionistic lullaby. *But then you gotta be cultured, yeah? You gotta know yer Monet from yer Manet*... Will hates the skin that forms on porridge – and suspects culture may be a skin that forms on society, tacky and colloidal. It couldn't be anyone's ambition – except a *complete fucking pseud* – to simply make more of this stuff, could it?

Gettup in de mornin'? Get up in the night is more like it — 'cause he had, and tottered on foal legs to the laundry basket in the airing cupboard ... *a nest, right*, where he'd recline, *each in his narrow cell forever laid*... his nostrils full of competing aromas: musty and soiled versus laundered and clean, until one or other of them would scoop him up and return him to his penitential *and precocious* art criticism.

Pete's waiting out in the car – but Will's *figuring and figuring* the carpet with each beat of his revved-up heart.

You little cunts wired, or what? The man was bearded, fat and wearing only a leather waistcoat and jeans, his face splashed with brightly coloured splodges. Sunlight streams in through the decals of tattoo designs stuck to the dingy windows of Mick's Tattoo Parlour, while lorry traffic hammers along the Pentonville Road outside.

'I said, you little cunts wired, or what?' Their guru glowers up at them, and Will and Pete shift uneasily from one foot to the other: doubly naughty schoolboys, given they're not only wired, but have also bunked off to come up to King's Cross and get a tattoo done.

Haltingly – yet convinced by reason of upbringing that honesty remains the best policy – they'd both admitted that they w-w-were indeed w-w-wired. *Cop a load of this!* Mick snarled, reaching below the scuffed tabletop covered with little ink pots and electric needles, to come up with a huge zip-fastened plastic bag full of amphetamine blues. *I can get hold of more of these than anyone can fuckin' use – hundred for a tenner, or seventy quid for a thousand – interested?*

Interested? Will and Pete had been terrified. It was enough speed to send them first skyward, then, when they'd achieved escape velocity, *deep into criminal space . . .* They'd only just begun buying four-for-a-quid off of Steve, who played pool in the Station Café at Finchley Central. Anyway, they'd come to get tattoos, for which they'd only seven quid between them – not enough, it transpired, for both to get proper coloured ones. Will's puma head cost a fiver, while Pete ended up with a poxy little star inscribed on his shoulder – just the outline.

They'd had to get the tattoos, though – there and then: otherwise they'd be shown up for the poseurs Will knew, in his heart of hearts, they were – rather than the wild anarchists he wished they were. Pete has a gold stud in his left earlobe – Will has two silver hoops. But it doesn't matter how many times you squirt your ear with butane and shove a needle through it – it can still heal back up. But a tattoo is forever, right? And no one they know has one of these marks-of-the-common-Cain.

Will thinks of his puma as a sort of anti-pass, which will never expire, so ever preventing him from crawling back into the warm and enfolding arms of the hated bourgeoisie.

No sailing back in a little boat through a night and a day to where someone loves him best of all – let alone his supper *still being warm* . . .

His mother still cooks occasionally – mostly dull pasta dishes. She no longer practises the feverish domesticity Will remembers from his early teens, when she baked bread or cookies most days, as if to fashion a warm – albeit ephemeral – heart for their increasingly detached home.

Will remembers this – and also the shameless hysteria, for her admissions are part of it: *I'm a woman, and I'm hysterical!* Then she'd threaten to *hand in my motherhood badge* . . . that invisible symbol of all the caring, feeding and wiping of boys she's been obliged to perform in her life, acts of love, which – she makes no effort to hide this – have come to disgust her.

BM looks like chopped liver – which, in turn, resembles shit. As Will and his brother grew older *the mask slipped* . . . and she ceased bothering to hide. At supper, she'd spontaneously push out the bottom plate of her dentures, gifting her a tribal lip plug. But she'd say nothing about this – and her children had had to deduce her toothlessness from Steradent tubes and semi-concealed glasses of water.

Her language – unlike that of the colourless English Jews – was vivid: *Your father's a fucking shit . . .* she'd casually remark, while *fuck, shit, damn . . .* would just drop from her lips. Is it any wonder her *Benjamin – her baby boy . . .* finds it impossible to think of her as an ordinary mortal: she's immense, a vast and ever-mutating presence, with Olympian – let alone built-in orphan – powers.

Stoned, or feeling otherwise surrealistic, Will sees her huge beige face, accentuated by the large frames of her glasses, leering from the clouds — Clouds that mount up ahead in the mid-distance, as he walks in one direction, to East Finchley tube, or in the other, to the Market Place, where he catches the bus to Golders Green.

She's unavoidable. He doesn't need to tell her what he's doing this evening, or where he'll be staying tonight – she already knows. At least, she does in a general sense – there's a paradox: her omniscience is combined with self-confessed impotence: *How the fuck can I help you if you won't DO WHAT I FUCKING TELL YOU TO DO!*

It's begun to sully her divinity – turning her into some . . . *demiurge*, who sits waiting for Will, at the end of a warped corridor, in a brown-Windsor-soup-smelling guest house, in a sleepy market town. Sits waiting for him, in her flesh-coloured girdle, waiting to press him to what she calls . . . *my bosom*, and cuddle out his tearful social anxieties: the he-said, she-snogged of the denim milieu he rubs along in.

When she wants to be attentive – and what she calls *utterly charming* – she'll sit you down at the kitchen table, and it'll be as if an invisible vent has opened in her forehead, from which, SMERSH-like, emerges poisonous misinformation: baking aromas, mixed with the moist sandalwood odour of her bountiful flesh.

Not that she has ways of making him talk about everything. She knows nothing of the white nights he suffered for months after her *pity party.* Nothing, either, of how he learned to wield Wilkinson's sword – or of the delicate soldering that replaced this practice once he began smoking: between drags, he'd apply their red-hot tips to the *wanting* flesh on the inside of his forearms and wouldn't stop until he *brought home the bacon smell* . . .

As for dissolving coarse amphetamine sulphate with tap water then drawing the mixture up into the barrel of a hypodermic syringe through a viciously barbed needle, no, he's never vouchsafed this to Mum. She may want to share in his enthusiasm for drugs – but only so long as she believes it to be academic.

Will has injecting equipment *my works . . . stashed* in a pair of hiking socks that have been chucked at the bottom of the cluttered walk-in closet in his bedroom . . . *the artlessness that conceals artfulness.* It's true that the only peers pressuring him are literary ones, while the instructions he follows are on paper – but follow them he does. Too scared to attempt a vein-shot, he sits on the edge of his childhood bed, his hand shaking, the metal mosquito's proboscis probing his little apron of belly-flesh.

Carefully and crazily, he sows this puckered-up field with hard little seeds, such as he's seen beading the cicatrised foreheads of African tribespeople, photographed by the National Geographic.

There's nothing older than a pile of old magazines – *even if they're still glossy.*

There's a thigh-high pile of National Geographics rotting away in the corner of Will's bedroom. *World upon world . . .* alternate realities, counter-factuals and forked paths, leading into and out of one another: the possibilities are ending faster than any likelihoods are emerging, and Will feels this cosmic foreclosure acutely.

Which is why *you crank it up!* You crank up the arm and you crank up the leg: you crank-skank up the system so much that it oscillates wildly in the wave tank of the world. You crank it – Elvis pumps it, while Poly screams, Thrash me, crash me, beat me till I fall . . . You crank it up 'cause you've stuck your finger in the mains for a dare, and your legs and arms spasm uncontrollably . . . *let's do this thing!* Until you no longer feel the speed burning beneath your skin – and you no longer hear the soundlessness of the suburb. Throughout it all, Pete remains sitting in his mum's Triumph Dolomite, parked up at the end of the drive – *closer to the Golden Dawn*, and wrapped in an ironic uniform of red Harrington jacket, jeans and Converse sneakers.

At last . . . *by way of the* Beast, Will arrives at his father: that large and obdurate man – who's nonetheless a flickering presence: a belated Edwardian, caught by Kodachrome, so that a black-and-white world shows through his wide and ruddy face.

He's here, in the bathysphere, coming up with his anachronisms – *Here's a fiver to go and buy yourself some dancing pumps* – then he's gone. Here – then gone. *Here – gone.* The Italian woman had phoned Will's mother and asked her – or so she gleefully reported – to tell *my husband to stop bothering her* . . . Could there be any greater humiliation than an errant father – yes, there could, a father who couldn't even *err fucking properly* . . .

When he'd first left, it was too bizarre an occurrence to be thought about – let alone related. When, three years later, he'd gone again there was a boy with separated parents in Will's class at school – and the humiliation of being in any way associated with this *wet*, who'd put his head down on his desk *and cried* . . . was *in-fucking-supportable*. They'd ended up as friends – of course. Still were – sort of. Although Orlando doesn't have Will's appetite for drugs – or indeed any at all. *Dumb-fucking-straight.*

The winter his father abandoned their family, Orlando, his mother and two younger sisters remained in their large, vulgar mansion on the Bishops Avenue. According to Orlando, his father – a wealthy businessman – then refused child support, so his mother – who's given to her own histrionics – had to sell the fittings and fixtures from under them. The reduced company of four trod these bare boards bemoaning their fate.

Will, who was attending drama classes at the Highgate Institution on Tuesday evenings and considering a theatrical career, had been impressed. They were pretty, Orlando's sisters – both pretty, and also had Shakespearean names. His mother was sexy too: what, in short, did he have to complain about, enfolded as he was in this chiffony chorus of femininity, all of them *softly whispering they loved him?*

Besides, their paterfamilias's departure underlined their dramatic unity: he really had exited – he didn't keep tottering back onstage. Whereas, after a long winter of power cuts and candle-lit suppers, during which Will's mother had assured them again *annagain* they were on the brink of starvation, due to their father's miserliness, he'd returned – and was immediately reinstalled at the kneehole desk in the corner of their bedroom.

Seated there, with great stolidity, long shanks canted to

one side, because there's *no fucking kneehole big enough to contain them* . . . and covering sheet-after-sheet of the feint-ruled foolscap he favours, with his beautifully regular but scarcely legible handwriting. *Pissing it out* . . . a long, blue-biro line of description and enquiry that adds up to . . . *what?* Will's tried reading some of his father's stuff, but finds it *unbearably stodgy.* The prose equivalent, Will thinks, of the meals served in his grandparents' Brighton home, before his grandfather died and their cook was retired.

Doris, who'd had a red and permanently dripping tip to her nose, served up sausages embalmed in their own fat, petrified potatoes, and volcanic steak-and-kidney pies venting steam through craters in their thick pastry crusts. It wasn't so much cuisine – Will's mother was fond of remarking – as a form of internal mortification: just another example of the English upper middle class's perverse masochism.

Doris's chocolate cake had been her most celebrated dish: heavy, and with a granular texture, it appeared on a stand, bare of icing. Will and his brother used to joke that if you failed – as their grandfather adjured them – to masticate each mouthful forty times before swallowing, then the sharp end of the slice would be visible, poking against your stomach wall. How they laughed – at their mother's behest – at the stodgy English absurdity of all their father and his family did and said. *Don't care was made to care* – and, so far as she was concerned, making this selfish, self-absorbed man care had been just one of her daily and soul-deadening errands.

When he was present, she'd a funny way of going about it, though – snapping, sniping and occasionally screaming. Sometimes hurling things at this big bolster of a husband, who, while possessed of dull certainty in his professional life, deployed a thrillingly negative capability in his personal one: 'Calm down, Bunchy,' he'd say mildly, as cups, plates . . . knives, whistled past his ruddy cheeks. Or else he'd just ignore her.

Standing on the landing, his heart audibly thudding in his ears, Will feels this great parental pushmi-pullyu still curvetting in the empty house. His father yet sits at his kneehole desk – his mother still stands below, in the hall, beside an old framed map of *Suffex*, a dripping spoon in her shaking hand, as she half hisses, half shouts up the stairs: *The dinner is on the table! The dinner is on the table!* Fury to which he responds – as he has, does and probably always will, this once-and-future (but seldom present) father – with a phrase seemingly calculated to infuriate her even more: *Just coming . . .*

That there's a sexual undertow to their storminess is something Will's always been ickily aware of: this unstoppable American force, hurling herself against this immovable English object – *dinner's ready/just coming . . . dinner's ready/just coming . . .* It was a duet that went up and up the scale, but never reached any crescendo, only relapsed into the slow handclaps she'd encouraged her young sons to give their father, when he did at long last appear.

Yes. And if he wasn't writing one of his interminably boring books on town planning or public administration, Will's father might well be found wedged in the narrow defile of the upstairs lavatory, a linen-backed Ordinance Survey map rugging his knobbly knees, his distempered flannel underpants down round his lumpy varicose ankles, and his reading glasses tipped forward on his long nose, as he imaginatively promenaded and complacently shat.

There were never any locks on the lavatories or the bathroom at Number 43 – which meant that from time to time Will would walk in on him, either shitting – or bathing, the cloud of his pubic hair wavering *waterweed* . . . Lacking any sense of physical shame or embarrassment, the old man would simply look up . . . *and smile.* This insouciance Will grudgingly admires.

Moreover, his semi-public toilet was complemented, throughout Will's childhood, by his performance – in the same yellowing flannel underwear – of his daily exercises: physical bends and jerks codified for Canadian Airforce personnel, which he'd completed at the most leisurely imaginable pace, as if engaged in some balletic Chinese martial art.

*

Half submerged in the glacial tarmac river of Brim Hill . . . *the pressure – the dreadful pressure* is rising inside Number 43, despite there being no one in the house besides Will and Brownie – who his father jocularly dubs *the stipendiary dog* . . . because he's required to pay for her maintenance. His parents' pushing and pulling has compressed the stale atmosphere in the gloomy little rooms, with their palpable air of neglect: hanks of dog hair twined in tufty upholstery covers, toothpaste blobs spattering the bathroom mirror . . . *rotting leaves wadded in guttering* . . .

The crushing weight bearing down on every square inch of his body explains, Will thinks, why he remains cemented here, staring at the deformed oysters, the knife, the fork . . . *a bottle anna cork, thass the way you spell New York* . . .

Simon sometimes has cocaine – Tom Hogan too. But Will hasn't taken enough himself to make a meaningful judgement as to the drug's *social evolution* . . . He's read another book besides Grinspoon's – one about the high times of a Californian playboy, who flew light aircraft full of the stratospherically expensive powder into the States over the Mexican border. The author made it all sound like a jolly, Billy-Bunterish sort of jape: snorting lines at the controls, as they brought the Cessna dallying down to land.

Cocaine has a pretty good image – it isn't like speed. Speed thuds, drums, juddders . . . *shudders*. Speed's a drug that throws a party *without telling the neighbours* . . . Speed charges the dying cul-de-sacs and sleepy crescents of the Suburb with an exhilarating and useless energy.

The first time Will took it was at a party in Gospel Oak — one he'd arrived at alone, on a tip-off, to discover the front door thrillingly kicked in, broken glass and popcorn all over the carpets. Someone's parents were going to *fucking crucify them* . . . But that hadn't mattered at the time, because out of the convolutions of music and bodies emerged a geezer sporting an SS officer's peaked leather cap, complete with death's-head badge, who'd had a bag of blues in the pocket of his leather jacket, two of which he'd sold to Will for the princely sum of fifty pence.

Best fifty pee I ever spent . . . Will remembers the *giant steps* he'd taken home in the early hours of the following morning. Had they been across Hampstead Heath, or *on the moon?* His sweat-soaked clothes cooling, the trees gesticulating, and his mind teeming with ideas, gags, comic routines and surreal juxtapositions, such as *orient/orientate* . . . which bothers him still: his mother favouring the former – but surely it's possible *to orientate yourself towards the orient?*

Back at Number 43, Will had obsessively arranged and re-arranged the objects on his bedside table: a flick knife, a little soapstone stash box, an old harmonica . . . Fiddled, as he'd riddled with himself: a happy, bantering sort of self-consciousness, and the first time he'd ever felt . . . *truly contented.*

And when you're intimate with someone, like that . . . *Well, you riddle . . . and you fiddle . . .* rub-a-dub-dubbing his rubbery little nubbin of a penis, Will hadn't experienced a sexual thrill – the amphetamine took him beyond the erotic, to a realm of the purest excitation, and the most complete invulnerability – a place where he could never experience rejection by those mocking, and silkily seductive, sylphs, who softly whispered *I love you* . . . from the dark wings of his imagination.

Yes, invulnerable he'd been: at the controls of a Panzer rumbling through the Hampstead Garden Suburb, the dawn flashing from his silver Totenkopf, as the pasty-faced frummers fled inside their mock-Tudor houses and hid between their humming fridges, awaiting the passing of the Angel of Death – which is what some of the kids at school call Will to his cadaverous face.

In the morning, not having slept a wink, Will walked beneath lowering, maternal skies to the bus stop, rode to Golders Green, took another bus down the Finchley Road, then walked to the playing fields behind the Blue Star Garage.

He'd stood on the touch line, still *totally wired* – still rubbing his wizened penis through his jeans. One of his old teachers had come up to talk to him, and Will remembers how beautifully indifferent he'd felt towards this man, and whatever judgement he would've made . . . *if only he'd known.*

Will's friend Mark had been not exactly underwhelmed –
but certainly nowhere near as excited as Will by this loss of
drug virginity. Will remembers gabbling at him as Mark
limped, mud-spattered and exhausted, towards the changing rooms: just two little pills – and you were transformed
into . . . *an Übermensch!* Mark certainly claimed to love drugs –
I love drugs! – as anyone else might an enthusiasm for the
cinema, or rock music. He usually had a lump of hash – and
he drove his Mini Clubman *with a certain dash*.

Once they began doing speed, Mark drove it to the sleepy
streets off Southend Green, parked up, then he and Will
would mount to the top of Parliament Hill. Sitting there,
passing the final spliff of the night between them, they'd
watch as the rising sun silvered the myriad glossy rocks of the
oceanic city – watching, and philosophising: surely there
was more to it all than this? Than black plastic bags, and
broken social contracts, and nuclear piles melting down into
the living earth?

Pivoting away from the pains of his adolescence –
Wilkinson's sword, and the spit of fag-roasted flesh – Will
wanted to be free. Add amphetamine to this heady mix,
what did you get? Will, doubled over on the bench, leaning
in to Mark's precociously moustached face, desperate to tear
the half-formed syllables from his mouth: *For fuck's sake,
man, spit it out – I NEED TO KNOW!* Yes . . . Will loves
speed – loves too the all-nighters that are its inevitable

sequel. But Mark, having failed to win his place at Oxford, has to get good exam results – so is no longer what Will would call . . . *serious.*

Will has an ideal of intimacy – one formed by the reading suppers he enjoyed throughout his childhood with his obsessively doting mother: her with her Penguin Classic, him with his yellow-jacketed Gollancz, either side of plates and cups, wordlessly bonded in absorption of words, their only exchanges infantile ones – and, even now, they still lapse into the *diddums, noo-noos and boo-boos* . . . that should be reserved for babies – or pets.

The dog needs to be let out to piss before Will leaves – he senses her presence in the house. Christ! Will cannot bear the sight of Brownie – whose name is an analogue of her nondescript appearance, rather than some cosy reference to maternal baking. He loathes her passivity – and despises her still more when 'Walkies!' summons her, squirming with self-abnegation. Brownie is, Will thinks, a sort of *personification* of the family. She – like them – is miserable, she – like them – is neurotic, she – like them – no longer belongs here, at Number 43.

Will wonders about the night ahead – what constellations of caring and not caring will revolve across the suburban heavens? He believes Mark and the others find him both funny – and outrageous: qualities he plays up to then hates himself *and them* for. Surely, now he's officially going out with Chloë, he should feel a little bit more secure? Through mustachioed Mark came the others: his brother, Philip, equally dark and hairy, with a braying, infectious laugh, who's already up at Oxford, and so unbelievably sophisticated.

Tom Hogan's a friend of Philip, and he has sisters: Sally and the impossibly Botticelli-beautiful Roisin. Mark and Philip are at the centre of a glittering group, mostly a year or two older than Will, who're either in their final year at one of the better North London fee-paying schools, or taking a year off before university. Oxbridge – or, at the very least, Bristol or Sussex.

Then there's Simon Church – even among Jewish kids with goy names, Church's seems especially inappropriate. Will's mother says Jews arriving at Ellis Island were forced by bullying immigration officials to change their unpronounceable East European ones – hence her ridiculously maidenly Rosenbloom. But Will rather doubts this – after all, the Churches have been nowhere near Ellis Island, so presumably they voluntarily transformed from outcasts of the Pale to conformists of the London suburbs.

Simon still lives with his parents in an especially comatose cul-de-sac off Middle Way, in what Will's mother calls the 'echt suburb'. Brim Hill is to the north of the North Circular, where, after a few streets of pseudo-rustic detached villas and Arts-and-Crafts-inflected semis, the Hampstead

Garden Suburb peters out. Technically the family home is in the Suburb – but the nearest tube station is East Finchley, and to Will's mother this verges on being shaming.

Simon's a mole of a young man, with a thick pile of brown hair and blinking myopic eyes. He's an epileptic, and wears a chunky silver bracelet engraved with the rather alarming instructions that need to be followed if he succumbs to a grand mal seizure. Will – by way of letting everyone know he's reading the Russians – calls Simon Rogozhin, and asks often if, in the run-up to his attacks, he experiences the same wild epiphanies as Dostoevsky's antihero.

Simon's parents are equally troglodytic in appearance, while their dark and softly humming home – with its brown carpets, green linoleum, and glass-fronted shelves lined with the gold-tooled spines of book-club tomes – feels subterranean. Simon's an only child, and is reading law at one of the London universities. He professes socialism – *but then we all do*. He also, while not being particularly camp, loudly trumpets his homosexuality – and this is surely more genuinely counter-cultural. Will, generally speaking, approves of homosexuality – together with violent anarchism and drug addiction, it's part of a trinity of subversive activities he quite fancies.

Will doesn't think of what he got up to before puberty as homosexuality exactly – they were too young, there was no penetration ... *spunk clear as distilled water ... bitter as battery acid.* Then, when testosterone did arrive . . . *in force,* well, it'd been a great wave indeed, but one with a very feminine crest. In his mid-teens Will feared he might actually drown in his own lust.

Simon's the first openly gay friend he's had – and Will's enormously impressed. This last winter of discontent, while the coffins piled up in the council mortuaries, and Sid and Nancy danced their deathly pogo-de-deux before the eyes of the world's press, the gang had gathered most Friday and Saturday evenings at this or that parental home, before heading out in borrowed cars, on mopeds and motorbikes, to party after identical party . . . *I've done my time.*

At Number 43, Will had Sellotaped the newspaper clippings to his bedroom walls. Now that the family's peeling away, his mother doesn't give a damn about the wallpaper. The clippings detailed, over a couple of weeks, the killing, the arrest, the bail, the hounding and the overdose. Will got that the punk prince and his princess were playing out a tale old as Grimm – while this near-live-action tragedy was also a harbinger of . . . *a craven new world.*

Sometimes, Will imagines he was in the room at the Chelsea Hotel, when, strung out and crazy, Sid wielded the knife. Was – *or will be.*

Simon has a taste for schlocky Studio 54 disco – Sister Sledge his special favourite. The Sisters sing, 'All that rushin', gets you down . . .' and, since his favoured tipple is vodka, with Schweppes's just launched new mixer, all winter they'd sung along, 'All that Russchian, gets you down . . .' then laughed the special laughter that only comes when a joke's so in, it's a humour-bomb detonating in spiritous shockwaves.

Tonight, the gang's gathering at Simon's house, where he has an attic den – one with the same leatherette-and-mirrored furnishings as the others Will's hung out in throughout his childhood. Playing snooker and backgammon – pulling the arms of superannuated fruit machines. When the others had been getting barmitzvahed, he'd played Jewish as well, so attended shul a few times. The kippah he'd had to borrow would be gently wafted skywards by the thermals issuing from the under-floor heating system: a little circlet of black crêpe-paper returning – unlike Will – to Yhwh.

Ooh, 'allo! My name's Julian and this is my friend Sandy . . .

Oooh, 'allo, Mr Horn – lovely to vada your jolly old eeks . . . A few years earlier there'd been a different sort of impersonation: Will and his brother had revered Kenneth Williams and Hugh Paddick's sketches on Round the Horne.

They knew these exchanges pretty much by heart – knew also their campness was camouflage for dangerous desires and barely legitimate practices. But then that was the tenor of the times: everyone hiding in plain view – their parents included. Will's father's best friend, Victor-the-Vicar – and his mother's concert-going companion, Dion – both were pretty obviously Julians or Sandys. As they'd grown older, Will and his brother had taxed their father with this – but, despite his lazy liberality, any talk of deviant sexuality put him in another of his own anachronisms: *a pother*: 'I don't know why you boys're always going on about sex,' he'd say. 'Not everyone is a sexual being, y'know – I can't imagine for a moment that Cousin Wogs or Cousin Dreda ever so much as thought about it in their entire lives.'

Will thinks this probably was the case. They'd had to visit Cousin Wogs and Cousin Dreda, who lived in Hove, in an unbending terraced house not far from his grandparents' . . . *through empty post-nuclear streets . . . past St Ann's Well . . . God must've retired – senile now, he plays bowls all day . . . The world turns so slowly – all passion must've been spent, or be unspent – or was never accrued to begin with . . .* He remembers – or quite likely confabulates from period film and television dramas – white mob caps and black bombasine dresses.

Cousin Wogs had a nickname consonant with her mouthpiece – for she only ever spoke through her glove puppet, Sunny Jim. With his scarlet silk robe, lacquered yellow-and-black features and his sinister queue of real hair, Sunny Jim was a grotesque – although, in Hove terms, hardly an anachronism. When their father took the brothers to see these ancient maidens, Wogs got out Sunny Jim and squeaked inanities through him, while they bit into rock cakes.

Perhaps ventriloquism runs in the family? For Will and his

brother had also been mouthpieces, squeaking out innuendos for their parents, who for a while also hid the truth in plain view, which was that they hated each other *very much* . . .

. . . *I was like a seal* . . . His mother had sat sobbing on the bottom step of the stairs Will teeters at the top of: *I was like a seal, I tell you – like a seal* . . . He cannot purge these words from his mind: *I WAS LIKE A SEAL IN BED!*

Such a peculiar thing to say – no wonder her words still resound in the empty house. She was no Johnny Morris – yet, aged twelve, Will had heard in this proud howl a black sort of animal magic. As now, he'd been havering – while she, in nightie and dressing gown, sobbed into the Bakelite night, summoning other weepy seals to join her and the softly whispering chiffon girls. A choir then further augmented by big-breasted young women, uncupping themselves from the pages of *42-Inches Plus*, a priceless paperback over which Will and his brother had taken it in turns to masturbate . . . *for years*.

Will saw the seals, wailing, sway across the stage – saw the big-breasted young women thrust their nipples towards the cameras, while the chiffon girls swayed *the other way* . . . As for the bearded man, his bulbous machine head rose higher *as he played his licks and riffs* . . . And now, Will hears the seal women once again, their skins slick with their own sexual secretions, their Labrador eyes brimming as they sport in greenish sheets of sea: *Don't care was made to care! Don't care was made to care!*

Yes. Quite likely Will would be made to care – but the order's been placed, so . . . *things will take their course*. It might be tonight – or maybe tomorrow – but at some point in the next two or three days it was going to happen: a loss of innocence far more important than the ham-fisted fumbling that had taken place in his bedroom, with his then girlfriend, a little over a year ago. Fumbling that led to a frantic nuzzling, which in turn resulted in his penis just about entering her vagina. A first for both of them – he'd wondered then, wonders again now, whether she'd felt the same: that all the foreplay they'd undergone had been far sexier than this oofing incompetence.

As they'd tangled on the taut covers of his childhood bed, Will had been aware only of his mother, turning end-over-end in the same moist darkness, her helmet of brown curls alternating with her sensible Marks and Spencer's shoes, as she cried out to the cosmically aligned planets, *I was like a seeeeeaaaaal . . . !*

Abruptly, Will turns on his heel, enters the bathroom and stoops to peer in the mirrored cabinet above the sink. Are the white toothpaste stains on his face or the glass? If only he could put his spots there as well? He smooths his hair back – sneers his lip. Will feels the world's scrutiny as an excruciating hive all over his skin. How can it be repelled? This gaze pinioning him here, where he's picked and squeezed his way through adolescence – a gaze that once pinioned him to the corner of Judd Street, in King's Cross.

Because Will went back. Pete got the poxy star – and that's why he's waiting outside Number 43 at the wheel of his mother's Triumph Dolomite. But Will got the puma's head tattooed on his shoulder – in profile, its jaws open – and he savoured the needle's bite. Then he went back with a tenner and bought a hundred blues off of Mick, and retailed them at four-for-a-quid to trusted mates. Will's profits were sixty speckled blues for every forty he could shift — Soon enough, he was dropping a half during lunchtime break, *just to make the afternoon go with a bit of a zip*, the second half at tea time, then one before supper – and two before heading out to join the great herd of underage drinkers that watered in the Hampstead pubs, moving en masse from the Holly Bush's snug confines, to the noisy front bar of the Coach and Horses on Heath Street, to the Freemasons Arms by the Heath – with its big walled garden, which in summer would be trampled by the teenagers.

Will had picked up at the tattoo parlour several times – until Mick said the Old Bill were getting suspicious, so he was shifting the business to his mate Pablo's gaff. Pablo was a Spanish punk who wore white leather trousers and squatted in one of the walk-up council blocks behind Judd Street.

Dogs slinking through puddles they'd pissed themselves . . .
Anarchist slogans spray-painted on the tiled walls . . . From
behind fire-resistant tiling Poly Styrene sang of germ-free
adolescents — and, on the fourth or fifth time Will did the
run, when the door swung open, Pablo was holding a shiny
little gun – one Will readily identified as a chrome-plated
.32 Detective Special.

Standing there on the walkway, Will felt his mouth suddenly fill with puke. Pablo's girlfriend, who'd been wearing
a tartan miniskirt, fishnet stockings and a baby's bib, sneered
from behind him: 'Don't be freaked, man – it's just a fuckin'
replica.'

Was it, though? Pablo had aimed the revolver reverently –
so Will could look right into the dark nostril of its muzzle.
Then he said he didn't have the whizz yet – Will should
leave his tenner and come back in an hour. As he'd winkled
the note out then unfolded it, Will knew he was being
ripped off. He'd left the block, but only made it a couple of
hundred yards to the corner of Judd Street, where he became
glued to the pavement.

It had to've been a mistake – dropping his last two blues
before he knocked on Pablo's door: paralysed, his binary
mind click-clacked between the options: *give up/go back,
give up/go back – over and over, don't care/was made to care* . . .
don't care . . . He'd remained there all afternoon – perfectly
aware that this stalemate was for life — It didn't matter if

he strode back to the squat and boldly confronted Pablo – or he crept feebly away, because sooner or later the whole miserable situation would happen again *annagain.*

All speed did was spin the cylinder faster – it didn't make it any more or less likely there'd be a round in the chamber when you pressed the muzzle to your temples . . . *and pulled the trigger.*

Will was on the corner for hours – *totally wired*, his joints seized up, his jaw grinding. He was there so long, one of the bar staff in the pub opposite came to ask if there was anything the matter. It had been the great reflux of the rush hour that finally sucked in Will with it, back down into the tube. Safe, in the grey-veiled anonymity of the smoking carriage, he'd begun polishing the anecdote he'd tell his mates: *the didgy dealer . . . the gun . . . the sexy girlfriend hanging on the gun arm . . . Don't do it, Pablo!* And he'd anticipated their admiration: *Ma-an, you must've been shitting your whack—*

At last, the spell is broken: the speaker squawks as the needle lifts from the groove – the tone arm swings away, followed by the over arm, and the next platter flops on to the turntable. The tone arm swings back, the needle dips to inject the vinyl mainline with more chopped guitar chords and adenoidal desire – sounds that pulse bloodily in Will's inner ears: *Rox-anne! You'd don't have to put out the red light!* He sashays down the stairs, moving to the right, *strophe*, to the left, *antistrophe*, singing along to the white reggae in his pale head.

As Will reaches the step where his amphibious mother sat, the family's dog also appears, so suppliant she looks *knelt-upon.* Will's kicked Brownie in the past – kicked and also punched her in the muzzle, hard enough that her yellowing canines drew blood from his knuckles. In the cuddle-free years, Brownie's was the body he knew best: her six-titted and greying underbelly, her rubbery black lips and golden irises. The hassock-shaped mongrel absorbs the family's neurosis and misery – Will and his brother both understood this: knew it even as they bickered about who should drag her around the block, then stand watching her shiveringly shit on one of the wide and grassy verges.

'Wait . . . wait!' Will urges the frantic dog. 'Wait . . . wait!' He swings through the glass door to the vestibule, opens the front door and, leaving it ajar, scampers down the drive to where Pete is, indeed, waiting at the wheel of the Dolomite. 'Gotta let the dog out before we go,' Will pants through the open window – and Pete, looking, as ever, puppyishly eager to please, says, 'Cool.'

Will follows Brownie along the path between the garage and the hedge. Green garage door, *what's that secret you're keeping?* Not a fifties revival – they've never gone away: the damp old steamer trunks remain piled in there, their cardboard sides bursting, spewing out bundles of letters tied with string, and scallop-edged photographs: *Bobby in his football outfit, Ithaca, 1956* . . . These, together with the tea chests full of the stuff Will's mother and half-brother had shipped in from the States in '58 – fugitive spoonfuls of tea in their awkward corners. And, for a few months last winter, before the crash, Will kept a BSA Bantam he'd bought for thirty quid in the garage as well – a motorcycle he drove, unlicensed and untaxed, its pistons detonating, through the sleepy streets in a paranoiac lather.

Will knew it at the time – he was riding for a fall.

Acorns can be mashed up into a sort of flour – the kid in My Side of the Mountain did it when he ran away to live rough in the Catskills. Live rough, that is, until he'd skilfully hollowed out a giant tree and made it into the cosiest dwelling imaginable. Acorns pattered at the end of the summer from the oak behind the garage – just as the red berries pittered from the rowan on the far side of the garden. Aged eight, Will made a simple division to his kingdom. On the oak side of the garden he built – hammering planks into the poor oak's spread limbs, the nails smelling of the metallic blood they might engender. But on the rowan side he dug holes – deeper and deeper holes, down and down through the parched and sandy loam. The hole he'd dug in the summer of 1974 had been his last and his deepest – so deep it'd required props and boards to prevent its sides crumbling.

The family were impressed – Will's mother bought him a new garden fork, and his brother scattered a few bags of earth, Great-Escape-style, on the adjacent beds. The aim of it all had been what, exactly? Will claimed it was to hit the water table – but really he wanted to reach the centre of the Earth, or make his own getaway.

Dirt drifted down into the cooler depths, where Will lay on his back looking up at the coffin-shaped sky. He thought he might've had some joy – a little fun, a few seasons in the sun. The pathos of his early death had thrilled him deliciously — Now, one hand on the lawnmower's handle, Will considers the grassy dreadlocks twined in its rusting rotors: *Exodus: Movement of Jah people!* He remembers French cricket sessions with his competitive father, whose dummy deliveries provoked his son's involuntary erections: the bat raised so the ball struck little Willy's shins shamefully again . . . *annagain*.

Will considers his mother's much-vaunted terrace – not crazily laid, only a chequerboard of concrete slabs and oblong flowerbeds, in which she'd planted geraniums. Floating across this imaginary realm of sophistication in one of the voluminous muumuus she used to wear, a bottle of wine in one hand, a plate of cheesy canapés in the other. Her smile wide, her laugh merry – these were not the attributes of a seal . . . *a fucking seal.*

Brownie's performing a vile act of what might be either defecation or masturbation: her back legs parted, she presses her underparts into the long grass, and uses her stiff front legs to smear her rear forward. Will gets out his Marlboros, extracts one – why're the filters like this: dun coloured with lighter, *yellowish speckles?* – and lights it with a match he sniffs before dropping it into the snagged . . . *sulphurous* rotors.

He thinks of his father, dragging his yellowish underparts through the world with his stiff front legs. Will's father still hugs and kisses him – his rough skin sandpapering his son's tender cheek. Will remembers the excitement when the publishers' letter arrived saying he was to be featured in the forthcoming Crossman Diaries, and would Professor Self like to purchase a copy at a special discount?

In what for him – always so measured, so mild – constituted a lather of excitement, Will's father had done just that. They were sitting at the breakfast table when the much-anticipated volume was delivered and unwrapped post-haste. His glasses tipped forward on the ruddy end of his nose, Will's father searched through the index. He'd located the entry – but instead of reading it aloud, snapped the book shut, swilled the rest of his tea and quitted the kitchen.

It was left to Will's mother to find the entry again.

'Apparently,' she'd crowed, 'Crossman had dinner with your father, who – and I quote – "talked of all manner of things". As to the celebrated diarist's summation of this talk: "very boring".'

Then she'd laughed – a great shout of mockery, such as burst from her whenever she was given the opportunity to ridicule her husband – and, by extension, all vain and pompous men.

As for Will, sitting there in front of his blue-and-white-striped cereal bowl, fixated on a single soggy flake, he'd felt the familiar shame and embarrassment prickling beneath his skin *the pins and needles of outrageous fortune . . .*

Will shivers – it's been a long winter. On the dark mornings fog blanketed London's northern heights, and he'd walked to school kicking ragged holes in the near future. Early May now – but it was snowing in Scotland this morning. Enough, the radio said, to deter voters from the polls. Will takes another drag as Brownie at last sprinkles a few drops on the damp grass – *piss pearls*. 'Will I,' he thinks, 'remember them forever?' He exhales – savouring the Marlboro's acrid aroma – and looks up at the back bedroom.

For years now, he's been laboriously unscrewing the safety bars, then leaning out far enough for his smoke not to blow back inside. Now he's seventeen, his parents have given up censuring him – not that there was ever any actual policing to begin with. Will began nicking bone-dry Senior Service from his grandfather's silver cigarette box when he was twelve: he'd inhale deeply, then reel through the empty Hove streets, on the point of vomiting up *my very soul* . . . Yet it'd been worth it, *'cause fags're my friends* . . .

A James Dean lookalike with a Lucky Strike *smirking* in his kissable lips – or in the full-frocked fig of a Victorian dandy, with a cheroot matching his black mustachios: smoking is all about such impostures – performances as fleeting as the arabesques unspooling from the Marlboro's tip, he follows, Brownie at his heels, back down the passageway between the hedge and the garage.

The diarrhoea-coloured Austin Maxi squats, toad-like, on the drive's cracked paving. It's the last in the line of crap family cars: before the Maxi there was another Austin, a shit-brown 1800 – and before this a pale-blue Bedford. Will remembered going with his father to the showroom at Tally Ho Corner, and seeing the little car – really a small van, with windows hacked out of its rear panels – revolve on a dais.

Aged seven, he could tell it was a clunker.

Throughout Will's childhood his mother scorned his father for his unworldliness. She'd taught him to drive after they married, when he was already forty! *Late developer, or what* . . . She calls him *Monsieur Hulot, Pooter, the absent-minded Professor* – all nicknames Will thought affectionate when he was younger . . . *and perhaps they once were.*

Jittery now, eyes flicking from parquet, to doormat, to an

old golf tee of his father's, Will follows the dog as it skitters through the front door and into the *drawing room* – another of her classy coinages.

Brownie struggles up on to the sofa, which is covered in material the colour and texture of porridge. Memories are coming fast now, and, while Will sympathises with Pete's predicament – grown old in the cause of waiting, expired, then reached desiccated rigor, his . . . *Senior Service* skeleton broken over the Dolomite's steering wheel – still he havers, as his mother does on the bathysphere semi's threshold.

'Cause she's *claustro* as well as *aggro* – her pet names for her disabling phobias, which can leave her paralysed for hours, unable to face either the constrictions of the outside world or the barren expanse of her own domesticity: *There's your fucking-Sunday-fucking-lunch!* The roast beef and potatoes accompanied by unmown grass, since, despairing of Monsieur Hulot ever returning from the pub, she'd made the bold decision to serve them on the front lawn.

Yes . . . memories coming fast now — But then that's amphetamine for you: dividing moments by instants, until, arrow that you are, you find yourself . . . *suspended in mid-air.*

With two black-spot speckled blues resting lightly on the palm of your hand, options to which you give *weighty consideration . . . this one or that one? Don't care – or made to care? Boredom or nowhere . . . ?* Will took two copies of the Pistols' latest single with him to Canada last summer – thinking of it as carrying the punk gospel to the heathen.

When they'd arrived in Toronto, the customs official ignored the singles, with their garish sleeves depicting tourist coaches . . . *going nowhere*. But he gave Will's father a hard time about the two bottles of duty-free Johnnie Walker. In the car, Dad *bored on* to his old friend George about this, as they'd *bored through the boring Toronto suburbs* – complaining about how the Canadians were really Scots puritans, and how after the war, when he'd been travelling in the States, Dad had to come north to the border, in order to rendezvous with his Uncle Martin, halfway across the bridge at Niagara Falls.

You'll always find us, out to lu-unch! Uncle Martini – as he was referred to by the family – had been a remittance man, which always sounded incredibly glamorous to Little Willy. Silly old Martini was despatched to the former colony. When his ship had sailed up the St Lawrence and docked at Montreal, he looked out of his porthole, only to see a large sign reading CANADA DRY. Haver as he might between claustro and aggro . . . *there'd been no going back*. Which was why his nephew had rendezvoused with him, decades later, in the middle of the bridge, bringing two bottles of bonded liquor – because in the fifties you still had to have a permit in Ontario, while the allowance was only one bottle per month!

*

George lives, together with his large Catholic family, on the outskirts of Dundas – a dormitory town, slumbering under the outskirts of sleepy Toronto. *Boredom – or nowhere?* The professors drank the whisky and pontificated, while Will lay upstairs in a Spartan spare room, on an iron bedstead, smoking and reading about Sal Paradise and Old Bull Lee.

After a couple of days he took the bus into town and sold the Pistols' singles at a record shop in the Eaton Centre. Will marvelled at the aerial walkways, and high above these the slow-flapping mobile sculptures of geese, migrating beneath the barrel-vaulted roof.

He tried explaining punk to one of George's sons, who had shoulder-length hair, and knew nothing about either it, or the velvety underground into which Will wished, devoutly, to descend. *But you had to've been there* . . . in the Roundhouse the preceding November, where Will went for a gig billed as 'Three Generations of Punk'.

Will had seen the Pistols effing and blinding on the box – heard their anthemic anarchy too – but he didn't really know what to expect, despite familiarity with the venue: the old train shed's cavernous interior usually smelt of vegetarian curries, slowly stirred by old hippies in their *sad-fucking-drag*.

That night the atmosphere had been different: the smell the packed crowd gave off was chemical rather than organic. There were no dizzyingly long guitar solos to get the hairies nodding into their pint pots and muttering *tight . . . tight . . .*

The Troggs had encored their Wild Thing several times – and Will's heart had indeed sung. But the headline act – some Californian garage rockers – had been a no-show. It was announced over the PA that they'd come down with bad colds – but the whispers hissed round the house: they'd OD'd on a bad batch of . . . *sssmack!*

Will had scarcely heard this euphemism before – it slapped him hard. In the face. New words did that to him: *dialectic . . . philanthropic . . . copacetic . . . barf.* The last first having been heard on the bus back to Dundas. Will had bought a pack of twenty-five Players filter and a lighter with some of the twenty dollars. It was the first disposable one he'd ever owned, and, captivated, he'd lain on the iron bedstead, holding it in front of his eyes – tilting it first this way . . . *nowhere*, then that . . . *boredom*.

Lain supine, listening to the *snap, crackle and pop* . . . of the burning filter cigarette . . . *or filtre*, which is what it read on the obverse of the bilingual pack. Words certainly described realities – but were they in fact those realities?

Standing in the drawing room, blood kayaking through his inner ears, carrying *ideas . . . impressions . . . images . . .* Will stares uncomprehendingly at a painting his mother's retained from her previous life: a nineteenth-century New York scene of a man waist-deep in mud pushing a cart mounded with muck.

Will's been reading about Logical Positivists, and how they believe words are like little models of the things they mean, which implies reality may only be an endless story, ceaselessly being rewritten. Which in turn implies that to coin a new word – barf, say, or punk for that matter – was to . . . *let the barbarians in.*

That November night the few hairy heads in the Roundhouse were cowed rather than nodding, as a flying vee of youngsters charged their denim ranks. They'd worn shiny sharkskin suits and wraparound shades – their short hair was greased back, and some even sported SS-style full-length leather coats. Will wished he could be stripped right away, of his painfully passé army surplus battledress and saggy Wranglers. The young punks had arrived hot foot from the future – that much was clear – and their mission was to retrospectively alter history's very course, by making everything that had hitherto been positive . . . *negative. And vice versa . . .*

Rat Scabies's tom-tomming stirred the blood to froth in Will's ears – then Dave Vanian whipped the mic cord, and the punks began to *whinny and snort* . . . Yes, punk – this had very definitely been the reality compressed into that single syllable, and when the guitars stuttered out their chords, it'd exploded, sending its shockwave reverberating through Camden Town, and *all around the world . . .*

Yes! Will got a new rose all right – and *got it good.* After the gig he'd doddered back to the tube, high on its synthetic scent, and hobbled down the stairs to the platform. He'd sat on them, waiting for a train. A man came walking along the platform – a nondescript man, or, at any rate, one Will *hadn't bothered to describe.* As he mounted the stairs he'd casually swung a fist into Will's face. Hard. Stunned, Will remained motionless, dumbly bleeding as the man made his leisurely escape. Still, how punk was that? A random act of senseless violence – *guess I knew that I always would . . .*

And now . . . and now? Perching on the arm of the sofa, Will chucks back . . . *nowhere,* then returns *boredom . . .* to the Dilly Duckling tin. As he grinds the pill between his molars, he feels the very mortar between the bricks of Number 43 . . . *crumble*: the house is falling apart – as the gantry does when a Saturn 5 rocket lifts off from Cape Kennedy: bricks, tiles, wooden beams, paintings, cushions, paperbacks, willow-pattern plates – all of it collapsing in a great slew of uncaring neglect.

Yes! Will's *going up* to Oxford in the autumn – a punk rocket, with a coxcomb on its nose cone, blasting off from the present, destination: *the Renaissance.*

At last, he heaves his body upright – frog-marches it from the room, through the swing door, out the front one – which he slams behind him – and down the drive.

Wrenching the Dolomite's door open, he hurls himself into the passenger seat – slamming it shut, he immediately winds down the window. As Pete pulls away, Will's cigarette smoke staggers backwards in the slipstream — With it goes Will's father, unbuckling his thin leather belt from his voluminous grey flannel trousers, letting them fall away from his paunch, so he can rearrange his bunched-up yellow flannel underwear, and the tails of his Vyella shirt, before re-girding the entire assemblage.

With the smoke goes Will's amphibious mother as well, her curls encircled by the porthole of her bathysphere, her *weepin' anna wailin'* reduced to Pinky-and-Perky helium squeaks.

And Will's older brother – he too is jettisoned: see him, plummeting end-over-end, screaming and shouting . . . *livid as the acne erupting across his face.*

Pete lazily circles the steering wheel, and the Dolomite turns left on to Ossulton Way. The eight-track is playing, and sighings do indeed seem to swirl through the streets, as Will picks the crust of the sun from his smarting eye – then gets out the tin.

He takes two of the remaining blues and passes them to Pete: 'Plan's this, we get totally wired, stay up all night – then, tomorrow morning we should get our result.'

'You mean,' Pete says pedantically, 'the result.'

'No, numb-nuts,' Will laughs, 'our result – the result we've been waiting for for fucking weeks. He's gonna get it for us – the gear, the griff, the stuff, the business . . . the if-God-made-anything-better-he-kept-it-for-himself –'

Pete takes his paws off the wheel and pants puppyishly, 'You mean . . . the . . . smack?'

Will sees Brownie's greying muzzle – smells the canned meat on her breath.

'All right, mate – all right . . . stay cool – this book ain't for everyone, now is it.' Will says this – yet he's just as puppyishly enthusiastic, and salivating . . .*'cause we're both keen as . . . as keen as . . .*

Well, desperate to leave such clichés behind, together with the families they imagine they've outgrown. Will isn't old enough – but Pete's voted for the very first time today. Pointlessly, as his friend will soon cynically observe – because it's futile to resist: no mere cross can annul the vast Tory majority in the Finchley constituency, nor eliminate Mrs Thatcher, who, besides being Leader of the Opposition, is also their very own Member of Parliament.

Will feels an intimate revulsion – as one might to any family member. Aged thirteen, he'd been tasked with reading the lesson at the annual carol concert held in the church opposite the school: *A decree went out from Caesar Augustus that all the world should be taxed* . . . Afterwards, she'd shaken his hand – and held on to it, so he'd felt hers *rubbery . . . stiff – a laboratory clamp . . .*

A year later she'd paid a visit to the school, and by then

he'd read 'The Communist Manifesto', while she'd gradu-ated to become the bogeywoman of the left: an education minister who deprived poor kids of their free milk. Natur-ally, he'd chalked FUCK OFF, THATCHER on the wall beside the school's main entrance – and just as naturally he'd been *fucking grassed up* . . .

So the urinals had been *my Urals*, for he endured a smelly exile there for the following week: plying mop and bleach.

Last year she'd returned for an informal talk to the Lower Sixth in the library. Will had readied himself for heckling – but the Deputy Head took him to one side and made it perfectly clear that if he was in the least disruptive, his school career would be at an end.

Will has a certain smirking respect for the Deputy Head, who, during a fourth-year Social Responsibility class, told thirty-odd fourteen-year-old boys: 'I know the idea may seem preposterous, or revolting to you now, but in a few years' time you will hugely enjoy kissing women's genitals.' Standing there, in blue shirtsleeves, his fists buried in grey trousers . . . *he always looks me in the eye when he shoots.*

The school's a dump, though – too second rate to provoke any counterfactual revolt: a grammar aping a minor public one, what with its pathetically named houses, North, South, East and West – proof positive that it has no illustrious alumni whatsoever.

When the young economics master recently and shockingly died, the cheapskates screwed a small plaque to a shelf in the library with his name and dates on it: 'Not a cenotaph, not a gravestone – not even the whole fucking bookcase!' Will had crowed to his listeners. 'Just a shelf, that's all they felt he merited.'

Taking her seat below this, Thatcher had seemed brittle, her bouffant blonde hair spun-sugary, her accent a weird strangulation, as she tromboned between upper- and lower-class registers – yet she'd spoken clearly and with conviction, then been attentive and uncondescending to her teenage interrogators.

Will, the class anarchist, sat sullen and silent, his pistol holstered and on safety, his bombs stashed beneath his plastic stacking chair . . . *our day will come!*

The Dolomite rolls downhill towards the lights at the junction with the North Circular, and Will considers the falsity of all his horizons. In the mid-distance there's a wooded ridge, and for a moment he recaptures that *first fine fearless rapture* before its corruption by . . . *passé poetry.*

Will's read that these sorts of prospects – open, wooded and watered, gently rolling – are sought by humans so as to mirror the landscapes of their own evolutionary infancy. And it's true: this view had once seemed to him both magical and comforting – until, that is, he realised he'd been gazing rapturously at . . . *a fucking golf course.*

He'd also imagined he could drive his pram as a child – the big black Silver Cross one, his mother loaded with pillowcases full of laundry, which was pushed up to the laundrette at Prospect Ring in East Finchley. But that too had been an illusion.

The Dolomite's handbrake creaks . . . *old wooden stairs*, and the engine burbles as they sit staring at Henley's Garage.

'Fu-uck, man,' Pete splutters, 'that's bitter.'

'Shouldn't've taken them right away – shoulda waited till we got to Simon's.'

'Yeah? You're wired already.'

Pete's a calm and competent driver – as is Will's other wheel-man, Mike, who lives at the far end of Brim Hill, together with his family of *colourless English Jews* . . . A family whose calmness and security Will chews over covertly and . . . *bitterly*. Sometimes Pete drives Will in his mother's Triumph Dolomite – other times it's Mike in his mother's Triumph Toledo. *Round annaround* . . . North London they go, and sometimes further afield – but they never escape this privet prison.

As the car bounces across the intersection, and past the entrance to the park, Will remembers how Ruth Hamburger's lover appeared here one day: an old man in a sheepskin car coat and pork-pie hat, in among the children buying ice creams and lollies from the van parked at the kerb.

Will and his brother had *hoped to die* . . . rather than reveal Ruth's secret, but she hadn't been so circumspect. Waking in the middle of a summer night, Will heard the sodium-orange cries, until his mother came to soothe him back to sleep. The following morning she'd held out for *about three-bloody minutes* before telling them: Ruth had tried to climb out of her bedroom window, fallen and broken her leg.

The dark little Hamburgers had adopted Ruth as a baby, but she'd grown, cuckoo-like, in their nest of plastic sheeting and cut glass, until, lying on their shaven front lawn, her voluminous and cloudy nightie puffed up around her, there'd been no denying the truth: *she was a doughy-white shiksa!*

Poor Ruth! Trying to escape – trying to rendezvous with her married man-from-the-motor-trade. At fourteen she'd been too young to leave home, although much older than Will when he'd made his first attempt — On his third birthday he'd gone in search of his older brother, who, rather than join in the pleasures of Will opening his cards and presents at the breakfast table, was sulking up in their room.

'I'm gonna run away,' he'd said, deeply determined.

'Can I come, too?' Little Willy had pleaded . . . *and pleaded* – until his brother said he could.

Little Willy gathered up his new Corgi and Dinky cars, packed them in an old handbag of Mummy's and returned to the bedroom, announcing: 'I'm ready – let's go.'

'I've changed my mind,' his godlike elder brother said. 'I'm not going after all.'

Whereupon Little Willy had felt a surge of determination: 'I'm gonna go anyway!' he'd cried. 'I'm gonna go without you!'

And he had.

What remains of this incredible journey, undertaken without any companions – human or animal? He'd toddled along Brim Hill and turned down Ossulton Way – same route as they've just driven. Then he diverted along Hilltop, a more exposed, less leafy road, with meaner-featured semis.

Did he realise this then? He does now, and armed with a rudimentary understanding of the sacred drama, he thinks of suburbia in its entirety as ... *a dithyramb of the dull: strophe and antistrophe of semis dancing* along London's northern heights – but then? What can he summon up?

The Doppler wail of horns, and a frantic shout from the open window of the lorry that'd narrowly missed him. At the bus stop on the far side of the North Circular there'd been *a supporting cast of British character actors* ... a head-scarfed housewife with a wheeled wicker basket, a tardy City gent in pinstripe trousers with a tightly furled umbrella.

Yes! He'd escaped: a three-year-old bolter from the marriage of hysteria and solipsism, whom the concerned woman had asked, *Where're you going?*

'Fucking grassed up, I was – and not for the last time.'

'What?' Pete queries, yanking the handbrake again – for they've arrived in Simon's cul-de-sac full of entropy and pigeon-shit-blobbed Mercedeses. Will doesn't answer, only sits there, staring at the lid of his stash box: *Made Specially for Children* . . . an ironic gift, he thinks, that just . . . *keeps giving*.

'So.' Pete tries another tack: 'D'you know where you're gonna move to when your parents sell the house?'

'Oh, I don't fucking know,' *Little Willy* says, barging the car door open, 'just anywhere but fucking here.'

'The night is yet young, and we don't know what it may bring . . .' So says the BBC reporter at the Finchley declaration – which is being held in the Council Chamber. It's gone two thirty in the morning, but the party workers, volunteers and candidates all look wide awake in their sad-sack suits, slack-hemmed skirts . . . *and fucking anoraks!*

Will's father intones the phrase 'off-the-peg' with a sort of shocked reverence – as if the modernity of ready-to-wear clothing were simply too much to bear, being *on a par* with heart transplants and the space programme – *On a par* is one of Dad's as well, since life's course and the golf one often overlay each other in his rational – yet dreamy – mind.

Where once, every few years or so, the VOTE LABOUR sign was erected on the Iwo Jima of Number 43's front lawn, there now stands a FOR SALE one. Sunny Jim Callaghan,

Denis Healey – Ted Heath and Harold Wilson: these ruddy-faced men in made-to-measure suits have been fatherly presences in Will's childhood.

When he wasn't in office, Harold and Mary lived in the Suburb – as did other senior politicians from both parties. And since Dad is a political scientist, of sorts, the elevated realm of H. M. Government has always squidged together strangely in Will's head with Number 43's strained domesticity. *A permanent fucking crisis . . .* engendering revolutionary dreams.

'. . . Elizabeth Lloyd, Independent, eighty-six . . . William Stokes Verity, National Front, five hundred and thirty-four . . .' The Returning Officer – who also happens to be the Mayor – has taken his place in a high-backed and leathery chair.

The Council Chamber looks very much like the Magistrates' Court in which Will was recently deprived of his driving licence, after having taken the diarrhoea-coloured family car from the front drive and wrapped it around a lamp-post.

In Simon's attic den the night doesn't seem *yet young* at all: the heavy pub-style ashtrays are throwing up butts, the side tables are cluttered with empty cans, bottles and glasses – the atmosphere is stale and foetid, the lighting is flat . . . *and unconvincing.*

Vampirically, Will contemplates the dawn with . . . *fear.*

There's been a lot of coming and going throughout the night – and a fair amount of returning as well – but just now, Will and his host are the only ones present, fellow travellers on this long day's journey into *Tory benightedness . . .*

The ultra-cool Tom Hogan, together with his yet cooler girlfriend, Carys, breezed through before midnight, accompanied by the yet cooler Damian Price and his celebrated bong: a yard-length of bamboo, reinforced with black gaffer tape. Will took many and greedy hits off of this punitive device – he prides himself on his . . . *iron-fucking-lungs*, before they bore it away with them, to some other maximally trendy election party.

Mmm . . . Simon often mms . . . *I love drugs.* And he does seem to: lowering his squinting eyes to mirror or plate to snuffle up powders, or throwing his round head back so as to neck a handful of pills. That any given dose might trigger a seizure is, Will thinks, what makes Simon's drugginess quite so heroic: his life is a never-ending game of Russian – or possibly *Russchian* – roulette.

Sitting, a tumbler of his favourite tipple tucked between plump thighs, only Simon – a bona fide Party member – is paying attention any more: the exit polls have long since signalled defeat, so ushering in a Tupperware dictatorship, ruled over by the hated Milk-Snatcher, who's clad in a dark-blue dress with bows and pleats on its bodice, for this: *her ascension to power . . .*

Chloë, who took only half a blue, went to lie down in a spare bedroom a while ago – and for twenty minutes or so Will joined her, holding her slight, trembling body against his own: *You don't have to sell your body to the night* . . . He'd wondered whether he should try to make love to her – he ought to want to, but speed-sex only works if both parties are equally wired. In such entirely mechanical frenzy there indeed lies . . . *a certain ecstasy.*

'Anthony John Paterson, Liberal, five thousand, two hundred and thirty-four.' What does Will truly want? He hardly knows – if you'd asked him a couple of years ago he'd've said, *just lying skin-to-skin* . . . And romance, that too: romance of the kind Jackie readers dream of, their sharp little chins in their hands, a heart-shaped thinks bubble floating above their Silvikrin heads.

Will's mother had been away on one of her little trips when he'd invited Chloë for supper at Number 43 – not that she would've objected. On the contrary: Will feared her encouragement – for just as she's now abandoned any pretence of shame about matters bodily, since Will reached adolescence his mother's egged him on in his sexual adventures.

He'd bought candles and a bottle of Mateus Rosé. He cooked chicken breasts and new potatoes, and made a salad complete with grated carrot. He considers himself to be his mother's feminist son – which made him, he believed . . . *entitled*. A year older, and already having had a serious boyfriend, when they'd at last tipsily removed each other's clothes, Chloë knew her way round his body rather better than he did hers.

And for this – and so much else – he'd been thankful.

Waking at dawn in what had once been his parents' bedroom, Will lay watching the sun finger its way blindly across the rose-patterned wallpaper: ouch! Thorny. Chloë's small head – hazelnut round and brown – lay on the pillow beside him, and, overwhelmed by gratitude, he'd craned to kiss it . . . *dewily*.

What happened to that softly whispering gratitude – for he'd told her he loved her as well, and meant it. They'd wooed further during their interviews, when both had been staying at their respective prospective colleges: storeyed hulks within which were hidden third-rate provincial guest houses, complete with clammy lino, rusty bathtubs and the reek of overcooked vegetables.

The experience had nevertheless been properly, thinks-bubblingly romantic – the cycling girl students, their gowns flapping, and the drifts of yellowing autumn leaves *blowing down Turl Street* . . . He'd met up with Chloë in a café in the covered market and held her hand across the checkered cloth.

Yet only weeks later they'd been at a party in Hampstead – another parental home, daubed with dope smoke and decorated with beer cans – where Will found himself propped against a tiled worktop in the trendy open-plan kitchen, Chloë propped to one side, their hostess, Tilly, to the other.

Without quite knowing how it'd happened, Will realised he had one of the girls' buttocks cupped in either hand. He'd tentatively squeezed them – and they'd both leaned back, returning the pressure. Will's mother – who'd been walking around heavily inside his head – came to a halt, looking out through her son's lustful eyes.

Will hadn't really fancied Tilly – who has a face full of freckles, and poodle-ears of gingery-blonde hair – but there were all those miserable cuddle-free years to make up for, the ones during which he'd arrived at the conclusion that, were he to die without having had sexual intercourse, this would constitute *a greater human tragedy than the Holocaust.*

He didn't really fancy her – but quite clearly she fancied him, and so he took yet another of his mother's well-worn, homiletic routes: *the path of least resistance . . .* Oh, yes, Mum knows her way along that one – so joined them, early the following morning, after trusting Chloë had accepted a lift home, to thrash about in Tilly's parents' bed . . . *like seals.*

Ever since, Will's been bothered not so much by his conscience – but by the fear of getting caught: caught – or even *taken in adultery . . .* He's plagued by a recurring dream in which he's back behind the wheel of the family car, struggling to control the runaway vehicle, because he – in common with his cack-handed father – has only learned to drive *at a theoretical level* . . .

Anyway, they go together, right, relationships-and-adulterous relationships – like horses-and-carriages? That's the example his parents have set – was theirs, perhaps, an open marriage? A phrase deeply suggestive, Will thinks, of the sort of domestic arrangements the Man With No Name would have in a spaghetti western. Out there on the high sierra of their marriage his parents scream at one another with terrible complicity – and there are always noises *off*. . .

Will likes the theatre, although he already suspects the greatest performers are the audience, who – at the Hampstead Theatre Club as much as at the newly opened National – play the part of cultured middle-class liberals . . . *fucking perfectly*. Sitting close by them, he senses their imposture being transferred to his exposed flesh – then working its way beneath his clothing.

But how does he feel about this leap – or rather headlong plunge – into the wrong arms? 'Cause feelings're important, right? To feel too much, though – that's a psychological problem. That's neurotic – his parents' favourite term, to be applied as an adjective, *I do think you're being a little neurotic* . . . a verb, a noun – and repetitively, *neurotically* – as an adverb.

No. Will doesn't want to be like them: their egg-heads lopped open and their hands buried deep in each other's fucking psyches: rummaging around in there *to see if there's anything they can use* . . . He'd rather be a robot – the same robot who'd received the news of his father's flight with metallic indifference. And now that robot was *amphetamine-fuelled* . . .

Well, the other Duracell bunnies may've drummed away into the white void, then fallen by a featureless wayside – but this one just keeps on beating the retreat towards the dawn. That's why God invented speed: to stop you getting too pissed — 'Mm-mm,' Simon swirls the final ice flecks in his tumbler then takes a swig. His hand lifts off then lands . . . *expertly* high up on Will's thigh.

It would be churlish, Will thinks, not to reciprocate — so he does. Simon's thigh is incredibly taut and muscly: 'Naughty-naughty,' he giggles, rising from the leatherette sofa. 'Time enough for that in our brave new world – right now I need more of the Soviet stuff. Pils?'

'Yeah.' Will agrees to the suggestion — 'Cause that's how it is with booze, isn't it? You agree to the watered-down wine your father concocts at the Sunday lunch table – and despite a little cavilling your mother agrees to this as well, after your father comes out with: *The French do it* . . . Which, for a woman who often says *pas devant les enfants*, has to be a clincher. You agree to the watered-down wine, and, sub-sequently, agree with your brother to nick the occasional bottle from the pantry, glug it down, then vomit wildly and copiously.

Aged twelve, walking the Cornish coastal path with his father, they'd been soaked to the skin – and in a pub in Padstow, Dad rowed impressively with the publican, who'd eventually shouted out: 'You cannot buy your son a brandy, because he's clearly ONLY TWELVE YEARS OLD!'

It's to avoid disagreements like this that Uncle Rodney surreptitiously laces your lemonade with Barley Cup. But, anyway, beer flows down a sort of chute of least resistance, doesn't it? From Top Deck lager and limeade, to dusty bottles of Mackeson stout filched from your grandmother's pantry, to agreeing, aged fourteen – since you're tallest – to be the one who orders the pints.

You get away with this – and the feeling of enhanced maturity is so very, very agreeable, it's no wonder it soon becomes . . . *habitual*.

Poor Dad. After the row with the publican he took to his bed in a nearby bed-and-breakfast – and took a half-bottle of Bell's with him. Which was unusual – he was a merry drinker as a rule, one who – by his own lights, at least – did so 'in moderation'. He talked about this moderation a great deal – how desirable it was, how it shouldn't be abused – although, that being noted, to be more abstinent would, he thought, be equally pernicious.

Since he banged on so very much about moderation, Will toyed with the idea it was there his father wished the family could've resided: in Moderation, a yet duller and more anaesthetised suburb than the Hampstead Garden one. In Moderation, with his beloved Trollopian cleresy: *I should've been happy, I think, as a nineteenth-century clergyman, with a reasonable living, writing my sermons . . . shooting up fucking skag by the mulberries . . .*

Yes . . . Dad would be happy in some rural dead end – he is, after all, the sheep-faced scion of all those mutton-chopped ministers and divines, the ruminant faces of whom once stared down from oval gilt frames in the dim recesses of his parents' Hove house.

Little Willy found Moderation to be an elusive destination: alcohol-to-drunkenness seemed as short a cut as relationships-to-adulterous-relationships. He often missed out Moderation altogether – and one evening, shortly after he'd met Chloë and was trying hard to impress her, he found himself with his burning forehead pressed against the cold wing of a car, while he struggled to *paddle back up the chute . . .* so as not to vomit into the vortex that had opened up between his feet — a vent leading, surely, to an adolescent male hell, where, under the mocking eyes of every girl he'd ever fancied, he'd vomit again and again: *Sisyphean barfing.*

Looking up, he did indeed catch a moue deforming her pretty features – and that instant he resolved never to be caught out again: never to stagger or slur – let alone puke. There was no need for it, anyway: God had invented amphetamine so you could drink three, six, nine – however many gold-foil-topped bottles in which all the sugar had turned to alcohol.

Which is why there's another Pils wedged between Will's khaki thighs, and Simon's chortling, 'Look at yer foil knob!', while the insufficiently powered Pete and Chloë have flaked out somewhere deep in the chopped-liver-smelling – and chopped-liver-coloured – recesses of the hushed house.

'Labour . . .' the Mayor intones, 'Richard May, thirteen thousand and forty.' A scattering of applause, together with some strangulated appeals to Solidarity! Simon is rhythmically squeezing Will's thigh now – his heart suddenly hits a rim-shot: *Ooh-ooh, the Is-rae-lites!* Yes, this is what it's going to be like: Simon will be Julian – Will will be Sandy . . . *Oooh, lovely to vada your jolly-old eeks, Mr Horn . . .* Then things'll probably sour . . . Simon will stop calling Will 'Bunny' and instead hire an ex-airline pilot to shoot Brownie.

But can he really, um, face Simon's body? He's flattered by the attentions of an older man – and the others have noticed. Will's no fear of being called a woolly-woofter or worse – but sodomy, *shit-stirring, pillow-biting, fudge-packing . . .* Can anything with this many unpleasant euphemisms be pleasurable? Yet to be gay – or at any rate bi – that certainly appeals to Will. Doing drugs, getting your ear pierced and your arm tattooed, homosexuality – these are essential acts of rebellion: *fondue forks repurposed by Uri-fucking-Geller, then thrust deep into the cheesy heart of the British-fucking-bourgeoisie.*

The candidates are lined up in their polished wooden pew, below and to the left of the mayoral throne. An odd smile plays about those thin lips – a smile that appears, if such a thing is possible, elocuted. 'Margaret Hilda Thatcher . . . Conservative, twenty thousand, nine hundred and eighteen votes.'

There's a burst of applause and some yippees from the anoraks and suits lining the walls. Thatcher steps up to the microphone, her teeth bared — Simon grips Will's knee tight.

'The night is still young,' she flutes, 'and we don't know what it may hold . . .'

. . . immersed in Crowley's uniform, of im-a-gery . . . the Dolomite noses its way through the heavy rush-hour traffic on the North Circular, then slews off on to the Great North Road. The May morning is cold – unseasonably so, and all three of the car's occupants are shivering, despite the heating being cranked right up.

Will's ceded the front passenger seat to Chloë for this polar adventure – and she sits, Chi Chi-eyed, blearying through the windscreen, ragged with fatigue and head-bangingly hungover. Nevertheless, seen in the rear-view, the set of her small jaw tells Will she's determined – and she has to be, 'cause they're giving her a lift to her job at a small credit control agency in Edgware.

Will, who alternates between berating her for feeding the Moloch of capitalism and letting Chloë buy him drinks, tries Play-Dohing a witticism together in his own hurting head – something along the lines of *Well, we're all going to be paying for last night's excesses for the next four years!* But the words seem big and unwieldy – while his mental digits are small and weak.

Exhaust puttering against plate glass, the Dolomite trundles past shopping parades – but Will isn't thinking of the TORY LANDSLIDE, but of a more innocent era. He and his brother would wake at dawn, then, with commando-like efficiency, scoop the loose change from the top of their parents' chest of drawers, unscrew the safety bars on the windows of their bedroom, then climb down – first on to the leaded roof of the dining room's bay window, then, via the drainpipe, to the ground. Sure-footed, they'd been – unlike their next-door neighbour.

At the early-opening newsagent on the East End Road, they'd buy Black Jacks and fruit salads – four for an old penny – then walk back, their pockets and mouths stuffed with all this sweet chewiness, higher than the crap kites they sometimes bought, which inevitably snared in a tree or cable.

His older brother would climb back up, slip downstairs and admit Will to the house, so that he could sit at the breakfast table, worrying their mother with his lack of appetite. No! Will snorts, thinking he can only've been five or six at the time . . . *Little Willy was never one for moderation!*

'What's up?' Pete's a very tired puppy now – and when Will replies, 'Nothing – s'boring.' He doesn't push it – but instead pushes the buttons on the car stereo, so summoning the Prime Minister, accompanied by the swishy clatter of massed camera shutters: 'Where there is doubt, may we bring faith. And where there is despair, may we bring hope –'

'Oh, man! Shut the fucking cow up, willya?' Will groans.

'. . . and to all the British people, no matter how they voted, may I say this –'

'No, you fucking well may not.'

'Now the election is over, may we get together and strive to serve and strengthen the country of which we're so proud to be a part.'

'She thinks she's the fucking Queen!'

Slumped back, his gaze lancing up into the grey sky lowering above the grey streets, Will considers: can anything be worse than this? This place of dead roads and lost opportunities. God may well've invented amphetamine – but when the comedown begins . . . *the Devil drives.*

'. . . finally, one last thing: in the words of Airey Neave, whom we'd hoped to bring here with us, "There is now work to be done . . ."'

*

Will stands on the pavement outside Abbey Credit Solutions holding on to Chloë . . . *for dear-fucking-life.* Sliced into stripes by Venetian blinds, he sees green metal desks, typewriters, bilious IN and OUT trays, and a wipeable wall planner showing the debts chased, recovered or otherwise *solved.*

Licking out the inside of his mouth, Will tastes the crud judiciously . . . *as a connoisseur might, mmm, bitterest Nescafé* . . . The day ahead of Chloë is unimaginable: staring through achy eyes at a minute hand, poised *quivering* . . . He gets out the Dilly Duckling cough pastilles tin: 'Sure you don't want another one?'

When Will had first become aware of Chloë, towards the end of the previous summer, she'd been pleasingly plump – but she arrived back from India with her hips, shoulder blades, collarbone – all of it *poking out* . . .

Will's mother has been reading a book called Fat is a Feminist Issue, but he suspects it may be a masculinist one too, for he's been a witness since infancy to her struggles: the madwoman's daily confinement in the sinister and elasticated confines of a twenty-four-hour girdle.

Latterly, she's revolved from room to room of Number 43, wrapped in a bath towel, travelling from the bathroom scales to her bedroom, where she continues the doleful accounting, adding another 12st 9lbs to the list pencilled on the rose-patterned wallpaper.

'Fat-and-old, fat-and-old . . .' Will's mother chants in an undertone, 'fat and old.' Smelling the henna perfuming Chloë's hair, Will wonders if there may be some magical connection between the two of them, so that as the pounds melt away from her, they're moulded around his mother.

He w-w-w-would s-s-s-say s-s-s-something about this, he thinks, if h-h-h-he w-w-w-weren't t-t-t-totally w-w-w-wired.

Chloë folds her slim, cool hand around the frigid one holding the stash box and says, 'No, I'll survive – are you going home now?'

Will fluently dissembles, 'Yeah.'

'Don't take any more, will you,' she urges him – and he *pays into his account* by sincerely promising her: "Course I won't.'

He doesn't think of it as lying – more as a form of preparation: twisting the dimmer switch, putting on some mellow sounds, taking the phone off the hook so . . . *I won't be bothered* — In the dull white expanse of the day the set is rapidly and soundlessly rearranged.

'Where to now?' Pete asks – and it's only then that Will realises he's back in the Dolomite, cigarette smouldering between his Marigold fingers.

'We'll try Tom first – his gaff's in Notting Hill, off Westbourne Grove.'

Pete sets course for the south-west. Soon enough the car's toiling over the heroic concrete arc carrying the Edgware Road high over the North Circular and deep into the heart of London. 'Gissa snout,' he says, and Will gets out the Marlboro pack, retrieves the last lonely cigarette, lights it from the tip of his own and passes it across.

No. Chloë isn't in a need-to-know situation about their destination – any more than she is regarding his crafty activities in the back bedroom at Number 43: this is another area of the featureless studio altogether – one the camera zooms in on, discovering Will, dressed as Valerie Singleton, sitting behind a counter.

All you need is a toilet-roll holder, an old ballpoint pen with the cartridge removed and some sticky-backed plastic . . . Will/ Valerie reaches below the counter and brings out a crude oversized model of a hypodermic syringe . . . *This*, he/she intones, *is one I made earlier* . . .

On Ledbury Road a man in a cheesecloth shirt really is sanding the blades of a large propeller propped up beside a shopfront, across the plate-glass window of which has been elaborately inscribed – in plump multicoloured letters – the single word CURIOSITIES. Will watches the man as Pete expertly backs the Dolomite into a space. Simon's penis had been, he thinks, like his back: two turgid columns *knitting and pearling* together beneath sheathing skin – and it was this . . . this sense of raw, shuttling muscularity . . . that'd been not exactly repellent . . . *but not my cup of tea, old chap.*

*

'Make yourself a cup of tea, if you want one.' Tom Hogan says — He's so fucking cool, he's snuggled back up to the bare *foam shrimp* back of his girlfriend by the time Will's retrieved the key from the gutter and climbed up the three flights. *Doggy Pete* has been left out in the car.

'No . . . no . . . I'm all right.' Will looks around in the fleshy gloom of the bedroom, which smells of sex . . . *and something even more sexual.* He sees Tom's leather trilby lying on top of his piled clothing.

'Got any of that whizz left?'

'What the fuck, Tom?' Carys heaves herself up on to her elbows, her blonde curls *cascade*, and Will sees her breasts *whitely loom* . . .

He gets out his tin and chucks it on the mattress beside Tom, who immediately snatches it up, opens it, extracts a blue, cracks it in two and offers a half to Carys, who groans then *dives back down into the sex-salted sheets of the sea, like a seal* . . .

'Gotta go in this afternoon,' Tom offers by way of explanation, before tossing the two halves back. He reaches beneath the brass bedstead, comes up first with a dusty glass of water then with Damian's bong — Soon enough, Carys's sleepy breaths are joined by the lads' rhythmic sucking and spurting of the sweetly-weedy smoke. In the single beam of May morning sunlight insinuating itself between the velveteen curtains *a myriad motes roil and boil* . . .

'Have you got it, then?' Will asks after a suitably cool interval.

Tom coughs, 'N-No, 'fraid not. I gave your dosh to Damian – he's meant to be catching up with George around' – he gropes in one of the loafers under the bed and comes up with a watch – '. . . now. Look, if you're going over to his, take the bong with you, willya. Dunno how I ended up with it.'

Damian's mother's house is a tall brick corner-terrace on Savernake Road with *Gothic snot* on its weepy façade, and a long, overgrown garden that backs directly on to the Heath. Leaving, stoned, through a door in the back wall, Will's wandered up and down Parliament Hill, then on into more Narnian realms: by the railings of Kenwood, a single old iron lamp-post stands, its angular head wreathed, on cold winter evenings, in a misty nimbus.

His mother calls the park keepers – who wear fawn suits – *little brown men*, thereby poising them as painfully between whimsy and contempt as she is between claustro and aggro. If Will sees one of the little brown men trundling a wheelbarrow, or raking leaves, he thinks of Mr Tumnus – *and Turkish delight . . .*

Pete manoeuvres the Dolomite parallel to the kerb. The camber is alarmingly . . . *adverse* — For a while he and Will lean against one another, slumbering. Will's leery of bothering Damian this early in the morning anyway: this particular product should be packaged in darkness. To solicit for it on a sunny May morning would be, this mother's son thinks, *a terrible faux pas* . . . He already grasps not only the mores of the druggie hinterland but its occult practices as well, so concentrates, eyes screwed shut, teeth grinding on *what is not*: summoning Damian's dismissive face – *Sorry, man – nothing doing* . . .

Puppet that Will is, jerked this way and that by super-human desires, clearly only a supernatural solution can possibly work.

Throughout all of this the Dolomite's eight-track whines: it's Bryan, sitting in an empty café, and *complaining fulsomely* . . .

Will holds up the bong, sheathed in a Sainsbury's bag, and Damian says, 'Oh, all right – you can come in and wait, but keep shtum, I've gotta dreadful fucking hangover.'

'So,' says Will, 'have I.' He looks back at Pete's muzzle, flattened against the car window. If he wakes up he'll wait – he is, after all, *doggily faithful* . . .

Will follows Damian along the corridor to the kitchen, breath ragged, tongue licking peeling lips. There's a peeling poster advertising an off-Broadway production of Zoo Story, and a cork board covered with postcards and old shopping lists. On the windowsill a pot plant's tendrils are mixed up with the phone cable.

Will thinks, if you buy some Old Holborn at Savory's –

which is, after all, depicted on the tobacco's packet – you can then . . . *smoke Old Holborn in Holborn that's been bought . . . in Holborn.*

They sit and smoke. The tea Damian's made for Will tastes slimy – but he sips it dutifully, listening to his cold blood rattling through his ducts and pipes. *Yes!* the tomb has been opened, and there stands the new Prime Minister, a pith helmet rammed down on her nebulous hair: *There's work to be done!* she cries, and Will titters uneasily – what work can he possibly do with these hurting and nicotine-stained fingers, between which the roll-up smoulders.

Damian sits opposite, looking out at the world through his chilly blue eyes that seem to have no depth at all, and so welcome Will into their . . . *superficiality.* He's never wanked into a sock, squeezed a spot or vomited so copiously on a friend's mother's sofa that it had to be thrown away.

Is smack the cause of Damian's wry self-containment – or its consequence? He can raise one sandy-blond eyebrow – but knows not to overdo it. He and Tom Hogan both convey the same air of having prepared well for life's improvisations – right down to their costumes: three-quarter-length 'crombie overcoats in winter, Harrington jackets in summer, peg-top trousers or chinos, brogues or penny loafers.

Hungover or not, Damian wears a clean white crew-neck T-shirt, and looks to Will to be another of those emissaries, sent back from the future to the late 1970s, to witness fashion *being murdered* . . .

His pretty lip curls as he sneers out more anecdotes about Marvin, his eccentric – not to say schizophrenic – Rasta mate: Marvin took STP and spent forty-eight hours tripping up a tree on the Heath . . . Marvin has become fixated on Ivor Cutler, and goes each day to the Scots anecdotalist's gaff in Tufnell Park, where he kneels down in the hall and shouts through the letterbox . . . Marvin believes Cutler to be the reincarnation of Marcus Garvey, and that soon the White Starship Liner will land on the Holloway Road, and all the black people in North London will go on board and be flown away to a happy life *far, far from dis Babylon* . . .

Will wants to shout through Damian's letterbox: *What's it like?!!* And *Were you scared the first time?!!* And *Have you got a habit now? Do you think you can stop?*

The doorbell stutters then trills. Damian says, 'Giss that dosh, Will.'

Will stands to reach into his pocket – a movement that unglues his damp T-shirt from his ribs and sends shockwaves of revulsion shuddering through him: 'Didn't Tom give you my tenner?' he remembers, and Damian – who's already half out the door, grunts affirmatively.

George, who wears a US Army fatigue jacket and jeans, and has a bunch of black Hellenic curls, drifts, hands in pockets, into the kitchen . . . *stylized as a ballet.*

Damian says, 'Gissa sec, Will.' And, acknowledging the mysterious and omnipotent Man with a curt nod, Will rises and stiffly peg-legs it from the kitchen.

Will sits in Damian's darkened bedroom. It smells of cigarette smoke and aftershave. Another beam of sunlight probes between another pair of curtains, and Will thinks . . . *this is getting to be something of a motif.* It's a Tory beam of sunlight, of course, which jabs accusingly at the piles of magazines and the dollops of discarded clothing.

What's this *busy old rule-driven sun* trying to awaken Will to? The end of free collective bargaining and secondary picketing? They claim Britain isn't working – but Will is, albeit only a couple of hours a week at the publishers' in Camden Town, where his mother is employed as a production editor. Packing up copies of 'Greek Homosexuality' and 'After Virtue' in the post room – smoking in solidarity with Trev and Kev, the resident proletariat, while *joining in free collective complaining . . .*

Sitting cross-legged building a twig house, then destroying it with flung rowan berries . . . Clacking a slat of Formica detached from a tabletop . . . Blowing smoke into your own pubic hair and watching it . . . burn . . . Waiting for the man . . .

Will suspects his life won't have that much clock-punching in it anyway . . . *just kicking the fucking thing to pieces . . .*

Gold dust solidifies the sunbeam, Will straddles it, and it

carries him back to that Chicago attic. His mother told him he'd made everyone laugh at his grandfather's funeral – lecturing these old salesmen and shills about the difference between bulls and bears. Two years old and his stock had probably been *the highest it'll ever reach . . . and now?*

Don't care will be made to care . . . as he steps into the white void of adulthood, Will realises that not only is there no one there to admonish him, but there was no one throughout his childhood either. Moreover, nothing he made earlier will be of any assistance – while the softly whispering girls have been swept away in a cloud of shit-smelling chiffon.

Will's meagre flesh writhes in the savage slipstream as he plummets into the present: he's *tried and tried and tried-a-fucking-gain . . .* but no matter how many blues he drops, or lines of whizz he snorts, he's failed to reach escape velocity: junk, in common with gravity, now . . . *wins by default.*

The string of Indian bells looped around the doorknob tinkles as Damian sidles in. 'Here, mate.' Will turns and . . . *his hand swings out from the elbow, stiff-fingered, palm up.* A tiny paper envelope drops on to it. 'Enough for me an' Pete, issit?' Will asks – and Damian replies, 'Just about.'

In the Dolomite there's a bloom of heady condensation around Pete's mashed cheek. Will unlatches the passenger door with surgical precision, then lowers himself very slowly down into the seat. He pulls the door to with the catch held open, then releases it.

Pete hasn't stirred.

Will squirms about, pulling out a pound note. He retrieves his Dilly Duckling tin and balances it on his married knees. He opens the lid, removes the tiny envelope, shuts the tin, and very carefully detaches the folded triangular lip of the envelope so as to open it out, revealing a small quantity of pale-beige powder, which, moulded to the paper folds, resembles the mud finely networked with cracks left behind when a puddle has evaporated.

Will's conscious that his slightest movements have become painfully slow and precise, as he rolls the pound note carefully into a tight tube, the edge of which digs into his raw nasal membrane as he *bends to my fate* . . .

I should, Will thinks, be a more caring and sharing friend — Should've tapped the powder out on to the lid and neatly and equally divided it. He thinks this, because, with the merest sniff, two thirds of the light-beige powder simply *disappears!*

To be followed in short order by an exquisite aching in his nostril – a pain that rapidly fades into successively mounting waves of the purest . . . *pleasure!*

Pete stirs, twitches, shivers into consciousness – and sits up, rubbing his eyes with babyish fists. He takes in first the minuscule drug wrap, together with its tiny tan residuum – then his friend. Exhausted and strung-out Pete may well be – but it doesn't matter: he's no need to ask what's happened, because the transformation – while superficially undetectable – is nonetheless profound.

Will looks sympathetically back, understanding what they're witnessing: how, Caligula-like, by a piffling act of will, Will's transformed himself into a godlike figure – one who peers about him at the Dolomite's vinyl, leather and burled walnut interior from an Olympian height.

Pete says, 'Is that . . . it?' And when Will fails to respond: 'It doesn't look like much.'

With calm movements, Will refolds the envelope and returns it to the tin, which he replaces in his jacket pocket.

With divine grace he says to Pete, 'Sorry, mate, I think I may've had a little bit more than my share.'

'That's okay.' Pete stirs himself to turn the key in the ignition. 'I don't really care, to tell the truth.'

Will winds down the window. 'Don't care was made to care,' he says, then sticks his head right out into *lunch-time* . . . and vomits.

3
April 1982

Thrust onstage without any lines – him and me both. Him: crossing the far corner of the hummocky lawn, sliding from pock-to-pock in a mulch of winter leaves.

Him: slipping through a screen of sapling silver birches that whip-crack-awaay! at his leather car coat. He ducks down — why? Presumably, to avoid anyone who may be watching from the cottage windows – watching on the off-chance they'll see this: this large but otherwise rather ordinary man, with collar-length neutral-coloured hair, wearing leather and blue jeans, skulking around in the back garden at eight thirty in the morning.

Me: sitting here, keeping him under surveillance while smoking a whippet-thin joint made using dusty-dry rolling baccy and the last few crumbs of hash – Mm-mmm . . . tasty – the dense white smoke tumbling down on to a souvenir china toast rack from Betws-y-Coed.

Me: also in leather – although mine is hip- rather than three-quarter length, a critical distinction, I feel: I could conceivably pass for Brando in The Wild One – whereas he ain't foolin' anyone . . . My leather's made – or so the label in its quilted lining reads – from 'a quarter of a horse', and beneath this beastliness there's more: an old man's cardigan, a thick cable-knit pullover, a shirt and a T-shirt.

Why all the layers? 'Cause it's f-f-fucking c-c-cold up here in the Black Mountains — my teeth're chattering . . . Mind you, that could be the speed.

Thrust on-stage without any lines — him and me both. Although he must have some directions — 'cause he's moving, though he hasn't got that far — 'cause my senses are super-sensitive, and my mental processes super-fast.

He: reaches a second barrier — a collapsed drystone wall, with another sapling screen sprouting from it . . . While he's scrambling over this, I shouldn't be simply wondering why he's here, but strenuously investigating this apparition: an intruder in early-morning mist-strained sunlight, halfway up a remote valley full of Forestry Commission that slices into the bracken-shaggy hills.

Would be strenuously investigating it, if I didn't already know what he's here for . . .'cos I ain't no square with my corkscrew hair — *hair that spirals out from my scalp into multiple possible futures . . .*

. . . He: hides in plain sight, like a child, his breath smoking in the cold air — while I just go on . . . smoking.

And last year, early summerish, I would've been sitting in my room at Western Road when — silently, furtively — Edmond came in, his sparrow-like body wrapped in wings of dark overcoat. Yes, Edmond was thrust on-stage — just like this geezer — but he didn't need any lines, 'cause he never said anything . . . Polish — thin, dark face . . . Reminded me of the doctor at the corner of Brim

Hill – the one Mum said had been in the camps . . . Jon found him in the cemetery sleeping rough . . . another refugee from the Therapeutic State like all the rest . . .

Edmond had entered the room with a single A4 sheet of white paper in his hand and laid it on the bed, then retreated, shuffling backwards, from the presence of the Great White Spirit, who, as now, sat and smoked.

Sat and smoked while the flies revolved wonkily below the bare and dropsical-looking light bulb. Edmond placed the sheet of paper on the bed – Will hand-cranked his cigarette to his lips. The flies revolved some more.

Outside, in the hanky-sized back garden, Clive was walking round *annaround* . . . his starting eyes fixated on his beaten-up old boots. Round and around he'd gone, his head nodding so that his greasy black hair flip-flopped on the greasy collar of his shiny-grey suit.

Clive's lack-of-progress was the last thing Will had seen before closing the curtains – and the first when he'd opened them. It'd been a short night for both of them – and a revolutionary one for Clive. Will'd thought it might be time for his depot injection of Largactil at the Warneford.

Depot injection . . . Largactil . . . such heavy words – and turgid as the drug's effects. Will's shot up a lot of drugs – speed, smack, coke, Valium, phenobarbitone, methadone – but never Largactil. He did, however, once buy a chlorpromazine pill off of Ten Pence Tom, simply in order to experience what they did.

He'd spent that day with his mind as blank as Edmond's paper and – whenever he was able to struggle upright – wading through treacle, but Clive? He'd gone round and around, while Edmond came in and out. At the time, Will wondered if the two actions might be *causally related?* Part, even, of the same process, one involving the revolving flies as well? Could it've been that when he raised the cigarette to his lips he hand-cranked this man-mechanism into motion?

Will had thought this – then lifted the cigarette to his lips once again . . . *And yes!* The bedroom door immediately and soundlessly opened, Edmond sidled back in, picked up the sheet of paper he'd only just deposited and backed out again.

The flies continued doing circuits of the light bulb – while Clive went on revolving the garden. Will had considered then – and reconsiders now – whether the mechanism had a purpose? Was it perhaps a celestial model of some sort – a small-scale representation of the movements of far greater bodies?

Alternatively, could the blank sheet of paper have been a message – or a petition aimed at the Great White Spirit? Apart from the intelligence that he was a film animator by profession, and came from Poland, they knew nothing about Edmond, who'd remained mute the entire time he stayed at Western Road, communicating only via these gnomic gestures.

If the psychiatric diagnosis 'schizophrenic' had been in use at Western Road, then it might've been applied to Edmond as well as Clive, who were men-of-a-feather – fluttery, and troubled by captious voices – who did indeed *flock together* . . . However, Will and Jon took the view that psychosis was an entirely legitimate response to a society crazed with its own sense of power: it demanded THIS! And it howled THAT! Pushing you one way, pulling you the other, until it was no surprise if you began to walk round and around, or communicate using sheets of white paper.

It'd all begun with Oisin – whom Jon had picked up in the pub. Oisin was dependent on depot injections of stout rather than Largactil, and he was fey rather than psychotic – one of that international tribe of tambourine-bangers who followed fellow drinkers home *in the jingle-jangle morning* . . .

'He can,' Jon had suggested, 'join the band.'

Oisin did, and at the Abusers' next gig – a battle-of-the-bands held in Crystals, the cheesy nightclub in the concretised constipation of the Cornmarket shopping centre – he helped power their version of Da Doo Ron Ron with his manic drumming. A number that must've persisted for at least fifteen minutes until *some fascist cunt pulled the plug on us* . . .

At some point during the wild night that'd followed,

Oisin became detached from the rest of the gang, then picked up Siobhan, whom he'd brought jingle-jangling back to Western Road in the small hours. Will came downstairs in the morning to find her slumped in the living room, eating cereal dry from a saucepan.

Siobhan was thirtyish, with drip-dry skin and wrung-out features, save for glowing, coal-red eyes. She wore incongruously dowdy clothes: a brown nylon midi-length skirt and a pale blouse with an embroidered collar – incongruous, that is, until Will found out she'd recently been released from Holloway.

She'd been quite incoherent: an apparatchik of the Therapeutic State would've described Siobhan as *exhibiting florid tangentiality* . . . yet even hungover and first thing, Will had admired the raw psychic force emanating directly from those mineral eyes. He'd decided at once to accept her for who she was, and, so as to make her feel at home, fetched a saucepan, filled it with Rice Krispies and begun eating.

While they'd munched, Siobhan revealed her gnosis to Will: how she'd wandered far and wide – to Daventry, Chester and Oswestry – always searching, but that now, at last, she'd found him.

Who? Will had gently enquired.

Why, you, she'd replied – for Will was indeed the Great White Spirit she'd been seeking. It was Will, Siobhan sort of exulted, who controlled all the world's events, from the utterly inconsequential to the most momentous: he sat in the fifth dimension, with wires attached to his fingers, such that he'd only to crook a finger to pull the trigger of Hinckley's gun, or detonate an IRA bomb.

As she'd raved, Will became fixated by her close-cropped gingerish hair, which stood erect on her narrow skull . . . *an electrified crest*. By this, and by her picking at the scabs on her arms with nails bitten to the quick-*quick-quick* . . .

Obviously, in a curtained booth at the Warneford, a reality such as Siobhan's would've been rigorously tested – but at Western Road things were very different: it'd been, Will thinks, the local branch of the *League for Psychic Discovery* . . .

Not long after moving in, *tripping off our bonces*, Will and Jon had allowed their creative impulses to run amok: 'The lust for destruction is also a creative lust!' Will shouted Bakunin's rallying cry as they'd piled up all the shitty little sticks of furniture in the lean-to outside the back door: 'No more cubic, caramel-vinyl-covered pouffes! No more crappy occasional tables!'

Jon agreed, snap-dragoning the spout of a milk carton as he ventriloquised: 'Modern life is rubbish!' Then he'd poured the sour slurry into the sink, fetched some Blu Tack from his room, and stuck the carton upside down to the ceiling.

In the weeks then months that had followed, all sorts of other detritus joined it, until the entire ceiling of the kitchen-cum-living-room formed a demented and rotting collage.

He's a neat-featured young man, Jon – for the most part quietly inscrutable. Will knows him from London, and Jon was the keyboard player in the Abusers, until, quite likely tiring of Will's manic upstaging, he took the rhythm section with him . . . *to start a proper band –*

He: stands upright now on the far side of the tumbledown wall – and me: I open my mouth, but my only lines are smoky ones. If only I could live in smoke – warm and woolly smoke, or pale, blue-grey and interesting smoke . . .

Or mounting cumulus clouds of smoke – the vaporous battlements of my infant imagination, which had seemed so solid, yet which, I now know, can be breeched with a mere wave of the hand . . . He: makes a gesture midway between a finger-point and a wave — Will spots a flicker of red cloth as someone moves along behind the sapling screen on the other side of the garden: *They've surrounded the cottage!*

The idea strikes Will *clearly and distinctly* – a solid grounding in British empiricism can riddle a young person with scepticism, but he's more certain of this than he's been of anything . . . *in years.* Together with the red cloth – firmly attached, so as to be part of a *complex idea*, comes this: an absolute awareness of what's about to happen – a realisation so blinding Will adjures himself to *remember: you knew immediately what was happening* . . . And not only that: *you knew why, as well* . . .

Already, Billy's sheepy face and milky eyes are before him – already he could hear the crap actor bleat his apology: he'd fucked up – he knew that. But was this good enough reason to damn him forever?

Will has all the time in the world to consider this – and to ponder as well the weirdness of shooting up methedrine on top of Welsh mountains — 'Cause that's what he and Jeremy have been doing round the clock . . . *and round the clock again.*

He recalls *through a syringe – yet brightly*: the two of them standing beside the trig point on top of the stepped grassy pyramid that's Waun Fach, chatting away, while Will'd drawn off a chilly millilitre of methedrine-laced water from the spoon slotted in the brassy groove pointing true North.

Sleeves rolled – as if joining some cult at once masonic, outwardly bound and vampiric – the two had *bled together* . . . hearts struggling yet higher, as they'd stared along the ridge towards the subsidiary peak of Pen y Gadair Fawr. Seconds later, works stashed, cuffs buttoned, they'd *yomped on* . . . *and on* . . . until the entire world speeded up, to the point where days and nights flickered across the hills.

Had it been twelve, twenty-four or seventy-two hours since they'd walked down the valley in the twilight to the pub?

Whichever – it'd been a very dark night indeed by the time they'd staggered back up to the cottage. About halfway there the four of them – Will, Jeremy, his girlfriend, Sara, and a girl called Jean, who'd driven them from Oxford to Wales in her parents' car – had been overtaken by a vast delta-wing-shape of luminescence that swept up the valley from behind, then overflew them into the inky hills.

In its wake, the four dragged themselves from the ditch they'd tumbled into, tipsily elated, and breathlessly confirmed that, yes: *We'd all seen the same thing!*

Still incredulous, they'd got back to the cottage – where Sara, whose parents' place it was, had switched on the old Roberts radio in the kitchen, and they'd all heard the tail end of the news bulletin: throughout the evening weird flashing lights had been seen all over Wales, from Fishguard to Ross.

High on vindication and righteous anger – how dare the Pentagon violate British airspace with their spooky new aircraft? – they'd immediately sat down to compose a letter to Billy. Will had brought nugatory supplies of amphetamine and hash, together with a pack of Feminax to taper off his codeine habit. His objective was to cut everything down as he revised for finals – but, with weird shit like this going on, clearly it wasn't going to happen.

Compose a letter – or more precisely, design one. 'Cause Billy had told Jeremy – who was his mate – he could get anything.

'Anything?' Will had queried – and Jeremy confirmed: 'Yeah, I know the dealer – a seriously heavy geezer in Coventry. Billy means it – he can get anything.'

'So,' Will persisted, 'uppers, downers, twisters, screamers – ab-so-lutely fucking anything?'

Needled, Jeremy was indignant: 'Doth thou question me, quiz me, prick me most unconscionably?'

But then that was Jeremy: his sharp features and fierce expressions rendered parenthetic – if not exactly Shakespearean – by his round wire-rimmed glasses. Passionate, whether by cause of his own spirits or, more usually, bottled ones, he's an English scholar at Oriel, whose ambitions will be severely circumscribed, Will suspects, by his dreadful *chippiness* . . .

Not a word Will likes – chippiness. Chip E. Ness – it announces itself with a cheap printed business card and wears a C&A suit. Nevertheless, those who call others chippy are worse than the chippy themselves – being for the most part the silk-waistcoat-sporting members of dining societies. Alumni of the major public schools, who're the pig-ignorant beneficiaries of closed scholarship places at the University, and believe that anyone they deem déclassé must covet their privileges, the *dumb-fucking hoorays* . . .

Unfortunately, in Jeremy's case, this is undoubtedly true – he squirms in an enduring agony of chippiness – as if these chips have weighed heavily on his shoulders for so very long, they've begun to engraft with his wanting, middle-class flesh.

Will suspects he himself may not be entirely without chippiness – but he's good at not showing it, having long since realised that the key attribute required for social climbing is a good head for heights.

It was Jeremy who'd made the mistake of introducing Will to the ludicrously posh Caius, and now they're rather closer to each other than either is to him. Caius now lunches Will at the Sorbonne rather than Jeremy – and has also taken him to a new Michelin-starred restaurant in the country, Le Manoir aux Quat'Saisons.

Will doesn't like anything about these lunches beyond the fact of having been invited: the stiff white napery and sombre flock wallpaper, the weighty bœuf en croûte and spiky crème brûlée – not to mention the bottles of vintage Burgundy, and the balloons of marc de Bourgogne – it all leaves him with a fatty palate, meaty farts and a mid-afternoon hangover that can be fended off only with more of what caused it.

Caius – since he's usually withdrawing from smack – also insists on wearing his full-length velvet-collared 'crombie at the table, and addresses the waiters in French, whether they understand him or not. There's a French wing to his family, and since for him – as for so many aristocrats – consanguinity is primarily a matter of property, he complains often of the chateaus he's been deprived of, while Will envisions the royal palace at Fontainebleau, witnessed on a school trip many years since: its faded tapestries and creaking corridors. As the scion of cadet branches on both sides of the Channel, Caius's relationship with his family is complex, but Will gets this too: for the aristocracy the only ideology is genealogy itself. Gets it, 'cause he hasn't been revisiting Brideshead through a haze of dope smoke . . . *for nothing*.

Indeed, quite soon after he'd begun hanging out with Jeremy and Caius, he realised their trio bore an uncanny resemblance to that of Sebastian Flyte, Charles Ryder and Aloysius, the only debatable point being . . . *who's the fucking teddy bear.*

In December, Caius had tickets for The Winter's Tale at Stratford, which he and Jeremy had been vaguely studying. So all three of them went, by taxi – in fact, a black London one – that rattled the fifty miles there, waited a couple of hours for them, then grumbled all the way back to Oxford.

Caius paid for this, of course – but stupid Jeremy tried singing for his supper, with anecdotes of his own drunken excess which were received with chilly indifference by their host, who sat bolt upright in the middle of the back seat, taking swigs from a hip flask as the oncoming headlights made his sapphire-blue eyes scintillate.

A winter's tale, indeed – and Will dated his ascendancy over Jeremy to that evening: after all, who could possibly top Caius, with his stories of headlong flights to New York, followed by sallies down to the meat-packing district, where scoring wasn't just dangerous – but potentially lethal.

These grand dramas of drug kingpins, leather queens and exits during which Caius had been pursued – if not by a bear, then at least by the monkey ever ready to leap on his back – were far more dramatic than any Royal Shakespeare Company production — In New York, Caius stays at the St Regis, and usually scores from Laurent, an exotic Upper East Side dealer, who serves up near-pure heroin and cocaine, together with his visions of uterine existence: 'He tells me . . .' Caius drawls, 'that he will become human in a future lifetime.'

And when not sitting there, naked, *in a silk-upholstered chair*, the sweat lashing off him as he does speedball after speedball, Caius lets it be known that he associates with the bon ton on both sides of the pond – whether they be princes, philosophers or punk-rock stars introduced to him by his mate Johnny, who writes for the NME.

Will's at once enthralled – and appalled: he may well sit up in his room, or the library, late into the night, totally wired and filling page after page with fanatically cramped handwriting – he may also turn up for tutorials the following day close to fainting – but the important thing is that he does – moreover, he simply wouldn't dream of not doing so.

Is this scholarly conscientiousness – or simply fear? His very first week at Oxford Will was appalled to realise how much better prepared were his peers – better prepared, better informed, perhaps just . . . *better*. He'd resolved then and there to complete every assignment on time, and to shine as best he could. Speed had saved him from the humiliation of not holding his liquor, quite likely it'd help him to enquire – together with David Hume – into the nature of his own understanding.

Over pints in the King's Arms, Will's father told him about his own first few weeks up at Oxford, in the autumn of '39 – how they'd been marked by a terrible indecision: he'd received his call-up papers, but what should he do? Remain true to Dick Sheppard's Peace Pledge, which he'd signed two years before, and to his Christian faith – as he understood it – or heed the call to arms?

Round and around the town he'd bicycled – as if his rotating feet might make the world turn faster – and forty years later his younger son had followed in his flapping wake. Will's dilemma was hardly as weighty – neither was his gown: a commoner rather than a scholar like his dad, he was obliged to wear a ridiculous little shorty one when sitting exams or attending official functions, together with a dark suit, white shirt and impossible-to-knot white bow tie.

His father – not that Will admired him for it – had broken the most rigid of conventions, deciding that God-given laws were absolutes, while the claims of King and Country were only contingent. By contrast, his younger son's imperatives are hardly categorical: Will wants to get high whenever and sleep with whomever he pleases – trouble is, he's afflicted with this wheedling conscience, hectoring unmercifully.

Familiar already with Freud – has his histrionic mother not told him, numerous times, of how her analyst dissuaded her from aborting him? – Will finds it hard to identify this punitive voice with his father's gentle remonstrations. After Will had stolen the family car and wrapped it round a lamp-post, Dad could only manage his usual *My dear boy, must you be so wild and impulsive* . . .

While as for his more abrasive mother, her own neuroses made her a yet more unlikely candidate. Far from restraining Will, her internalised voice usually *eggs me on* . . . Waste not, want not may be a prudential injunction when *stocks are low and supply chains are poor*, however, under surplus conditions it becomes a recipe for . . . *excess*.

Caius and Jeremy can quote poetry from memory, and enjoy vigorously disputing the merits of this or that critical theory. Nonetheless, they barely function academically – and regard this as a badge of pride: Jeremy speaks airily of only having submitted two essays last term, and narrowly escaping rustication – while Caius is more disengaged still, referring to his tutors as if they were incompetent waiters.

Anyway, Will finds it hard to imagine Caius physically studying: hunched up over a library book, reducing fine poetic embroidery to homespun précis – and with a biro? A bourgeois-fucking biro? No. Caius has a slim, leather-bound notebook with NOTES gold-embossed on its cover. In this, Will imagines, he writes down nothing besides piercing aperçus and Wildean bons mots.

A smart kid . . . Will's mother is fond of saying . . . *will get an education in a ploughed field.* Will can't picture Caius as a child at all, such is the stench of corrupted innocence that enfolds him . . . *tight as his 'crombie.* Neither has he been raised in a field – ploughed or otherwise. Rather, his decadent parents – by his own account – dragged him from sad house to gloomier apartment, in a haze at once snobbish and alcoholic.

Naturally, as soon as he was old enough, they sent him away to school – and it'd been there he'd received a perfectly good education. From his family – presumably by osmosis – he'd acquired his cultured air, while with his dissolute public-school playmates, Caius became acculturated to getting high. Very high.

Will doesn't think he's ever met anyone who likes drugs

quite as much as he does – until Caius, that is. Caius sweating, the beads fat as raindrops on a glassy pane – Caius, lying back on the three stacked-up mattresses that serve as Will's bed, furled in his black wrapper, taking drags from Will's bong with one hand and swigs of whisky with his other: *Heart of oak!* he cries with each hit, and smites his chest with his fist, in the region of where *his own might possibly be* . . .

Caius has, besides his vast trust fund, untold reserves of built-in orphan power. Will's mother says what defines chutzpah is the ability to murder your mother and father, then claim clemency on the grounds you're an orphan. Certainly, Caius's parents seem dead to him – while his ability to somehow *walk in through your eyes, take a look round, and see if there's anything he can use* . . . is deeply seductive.

And he's funny – compulsively so. Will sometimes wonders if Caius's wit – which for the most part is mocking and cruel – is a further defence. But mostly he just laughs – then tries topping his friend's last outrage with one of his own.

Will's living in a tall, steep-gabled Victorian corner house in Jericho for this, his final year. Living with five fellow students – all women, but none of them his girlfriend. Chloë, a linguist, is away studying Russian in Leningrad. If he were a mouther of clichés – and outright fucking lies – Will might say, *When the cat's away, the mice will play* . . . The truth is, however, that he's pretty much . . . *always playing*.

Mabel, whose attic room is swagged with silk wall hangings, and who serves lapsang souchong in little china cups, is pleasingly plump and usually naked beneath her silk dressing gown. Freya, who has the large room over the kitchen, with windows on two sides, is a strapping six-footer – sex with her is . . . Well, with his eyes closed Will thinks, unkindly, of Giant Haystacks, and Eddie Waring mouthing off about *two falls and a . . . submission . . .*

Helen, who has spiky dyed hair and a druggie boyfriend called Freddy, is pretty, and for these reasons *pretty much off-limits* . . . while Will doesn't fancy Phyllis, a seriously bespectacled and vegan chemist, at all. Not that this makes any difference, because one drunken night or other, she'd knocked on Will's door and just . . . sort of . . . tumbled on to his mattress pile.

Another sickeningly predictable effect that'd nonetheless *preceded its cause* . . . Will wonders if he may be surrounded by some sort of zone, contaminated by radioactive lust – because three nights ago – *Yes, three!* – when they'd returned to the cottage, following their close encounter of the third kind – Jeremy's girlfriend, Sara, had entered Will's frigid little bedroom, up under the cottage's eaves, and also *lost her footing* . . . Will drew her into his arms, placed his mouth on hers, then reached up under her several woolly layers to feel her breasts.

Drinking the cans they'd brought back from the pub, together with a bottle of Red Square vodka, the four psychonauts had concocted their letter to Billy: Will drawing a table to function as a ready-reckoner, so that Billy could automatically adjust their order depending on what the heavy Coventry geezer had in stock.

Heroin, hashish, cocaine, grass and amphetamine – these, and in that order, were what Will desired. And when the table was completed, he felt he'd allowed for every possible eventuality.

Save this: the man's hand gesturing towards the red material shimmering between the saplings . . . No! Even if he had the table to hand, it wouldn't help him to deal with this, so Will sits out his last few seconds of freedom, recalling those flies revolving the light bulb, and Edmond entering his room at Western Road, putting the sheet of paper on his bed, then leaving – and Clive walking round and around in the garden. Meditates on this – hypothesising that, far from this being a model of some sort, it was rather . . . *a botched pantograph, which threaded the wires held by the Great White Spirit through space and time, and into this almighty fuck-up* . . .

Yes, that was three nights ago – and the following morning they'd returned to the village to post it.

Will may've only brought a gramme with him for reading week – but it's pure-white methedrine, whizz of great superiority, that, it's rumoured, is synthesised by clever graduate students in the University's very own labs. Whatever the truth of this, it definitely *reaches the parts* other amphetamines don't.

Will's wrapped the remaining speed and works in one hiking sock, the last of the hash in another – both lie coiled in a little chest of drawers tucked beneath the dinky dormer window in his bedroom. On top of the chest – which is covered by a white cloth with a beaded border – he's placed his ring-binders full of three years' worth of meticulously kept notes. The task at hand has been to somehow *snort all this gear up* off the page and into his hurting head.

Which was why he'd brought insufficient hash: plan was to halve the amount in each joint, then halve it again – in the process ungumming *my works* . . . 'cause it'd been a big mistake trying to fix this delicate mechanism by . . . *dipping it in tea.*

That was the plan, but they've only been in Wales for four days, and the joint he's currently smoking . . . *is the penultimate fucking half!* Billy's due to arrive tomorrow, but right now Will's convinced that the man in the leather car coat, while *thrust onstage without any lines . . .* is speedily acquiring a talent . . . *for improvisation.*

Whereas Will just carries on sitting and smoking, staring from the figures *odd-wobbling* now, through the distorting glass of the slow-flowing cottage window, to the worm's casts of roll-up ash in the tin ashtray . . . *ash-hash . . . hash-ash . . .* both quite elemental and . . . *certain things.*

A couple of years ago, in Tangier, where he and Chloë had arrived after a three-hour flight, a motley figure fell in beside them, as they charged – heads down to avoid constant hassling – into the medina to find a cheap room. Yes, Hassan had joined them, wearing a leather jacket covered in badges, sporting a tasselled shoulder bag, and using the thick paperback book he held open as a sort of cow-catcher, with which to sweep the beggars and other hustlers out of their way.

'Tell me, pliz . . .' he'd pleaded, 'tell me pliz – tell me!' He grabbed Will's elbow to detain him: 'Tell me!' And pointed at the text – one Will now recognised as Roget's Thesaurus – which was open at the entry for dance: *Caper, Cavort, Frisk, Frolic, Gambol . . .* 'Pliz tell me, what is this thing called . . . skanking?'

Will had laughed wildly – it was true then, what Brother Bill said: *You may wade through shit – but at the end of it you'll find a Johnson . . .* Hassan may not've been an initiate of his namesake Hassan-I Sabbah's secret order of assassins *but he knew where to score* . . . and once Chloë had been deposited in a tiny tiled cubicle of a room, off a yet tinier courtyard where a minuscule fountain . . . *piddled*, that's what they went to do.

'This one iz Sputnik,' Hassan had said, pressing a crumbly lump of tan hash into his hand, 'and this one' – he got out a clingfilm-wrapped bar – 'iz Zero-Zero.'

Aha! At last the legendary Zero-Zero – Will had had any old Rocky passed off on him as this, ever since he'd begun smoking dope – or Rocky, Leb', Red Leb', Turkish, Pakki Black, Pakki Red Seal, *Nepalese Temple Balls* . . . The Roget's had disappeared back into Hassan's shoulder bag as soon as Will provided the definition – one that was a demonstration: standing there in the alley, surrounded by shitty-arsed goats and clean laundry, winding up his legs and arms, to the rhythms laid down by *unseen Wailers* . . .

Hassan had only been an intermediary – the actual dealer wore a striped, floor-length and very dirty djellaba. He spoke no English at all, apart from these two synonyms: 'Sputnik' and 'Zero-Zero', and had drawn Will into a close huddle, in the soft right-angle between two mud-brick walls. The call to prayer crackled through loudspeakers, out over the crumbling old quarter, wherein everything smelled at once spicy . . . *and shitty*.

Will looked into the dealer's furtive eyes – their whites

were ... *a misnomer*, their pupils ... *pinned*, but he hadn't the nerve to ask for opium.

Instead, as he remembers it, he'd pulled the crumpled dirham notes out from his sock, and a dog-eared pack of Sports cigarettes from his pocket, accepted skins and rolled up. Then they sat smoking, in the bare roofless room of a derelict little house. Sucking on the harsh tobacco mixed with the sweet hash, Will abandoned his girlfriend still further – ceasing to obsess on their vexed relationship. He'd stopped thinking, as well, about these antinomies: West/East, north/south, up/down, in/out, God/not-God, Chloë/not-Chloë.

'Pliz,' Hassan had said, laying his hand on his heart, 'pliz.' He picked up the cigarette packet from the beaten earth between Will's outstretched legs: 'Me, Sufi ... and he' – he indicated the dealer – 'he Sufi too. For Sufi God iz allthings – allthings God. Cigarettes God, 'asheesh God, skanking God ... And you, my friend – God in you. You very tall. God is in the ... in the ...' He raised his hand up, and thrilled by this mystical turn, Will supplied the primary quality: 'The tallness? God is in the tallness?'

His companions then each seized one of his hands, and, high on fraternity, Will had contemplated this exciting new monism.

The monism that'd been Morocco: in the fast-fading twilight, and the still faster-fading *light of my own reason* ... Will studied those eroded walls: they looked to've been built using the same hash as they were smoking – as had those of the other houses piled up the hillside.

It'd seemed plausible that the dun surface they were sat on was hash as well – while the King, whose beige-Bogart features had blinked down from banners strung up along the avenue from the airport, was pretty obviously . . . *full of it*. Moreover, thinking back: as the plane banked down through the hazy cloud cover over the North African coast, Will had seen the dramatic up-thrusting of the Rif Mountains, with their friable peaks of Zero-Zero, and their *deep, resinous valleys . . .*

Stubbing this joint out in the tin ashtray, Will feels the fragmentary presence of the hash in the plastic bag, wrapped in the sock, inside the drawer, in the room upstairs. Feels it as if the crumbs were a sentient being – an abandoned girlfriend, perhaps – while all around is this hashless Godless Welsh waste. A waste across which the man in the leather car coat now stealthily advances, towards the back door of the cottage. Still, he hasn't reached it yet – leaving Will with plenty of time to rue his great love of . . . *dope*, which, in common with the man . . . *crept up on me*.

Speed, heroin – cocaine too: these had all been coups de foudre violently sundering the dull beforehand from the *vivid ever-after . . .* But dope – which had first come to Will in the form of shavings from older smokers' larger lumps – had

slowly pumped its way into every little cavity of his psyche . . .
progressively insulating me from reality.

There were the drug's effects – but there was also all the
know-how, which satisfied the hobbyist in him, even if he
sometimes despaired of his fellow *masters of whine* staring
at tacky ten-years-after wallpaper swirls as they mouthed
shibboleths about Thai sticks and *Durban-bloody-Poison*
. . . The handicrafts of deseeding, joint-rolling and roach-
clipping were entry-level enough for Will, who'd taken an
entire term in Design & Technology to make *a fucking string-
holder . . .*

As for the effects — certain moments were Gestalts: it all
came together, the tiny arrangement of tiny things on his
chequerboard bedside table – a stash box made from an old
Owzthat tin, a World Cup Willie figurine with a ball bearing
in its plastic base, a tiny lapel badge with YOU ARE HERE
on it – and the thrilling happenings out on Highway 61:
Will both wanted to give Brother Bill his big thrill, and
experience it himself. Where was this mutually masturbatory Calvary? It was right fucking here: he saw a snappily
suited figure chained between the rowan trees lining the
Suburb's Central Square, and *dying happily ever after.*

His mother's dictum that the English Jews were like the
English *but more so . . .* could be applied in this hazy context:
what Roget might term *the griff, the gear, the solid, the stuff, the
herb*, possibly by its very proliferation of synonyms alone,

rendered the entire realm of thought, feeling, rhythm and blues *more so*. That was it – no radical transposition to another plane, *ma-an*, or Übermensch fantasising *You lookin' at me?* Simply *more so* . . . Will's mate Hughie, with his wild curls and giggling eyes, is an expert at making more so out of less than: were he here, he could conjure four further joints out of the crumbs upstairs. Hugh's rubric is 'little and often': he'll drop by Will's room mid-morning, mid-week, and chop out lines of speed millimetres long – if you seem anxious, he'll offer you a quarter of a Mandy.

Will gets that Hugh – who, impressively, had to leave Sheffield University after a mental breakdown – is so *saturated in the potion* he only needs topping up from time to time, yet can't face this truth about himself: that at some faint, numinous, but for all that very precise point, *little and often* had fully combined with his mother's injunction to *waste not, want not*, such that the entire world became *more so* . . .

. . . *but, of course* — if the entire world is more so, with what can this comparison be effected?

And now? Gargling the last throatful, Will feels an aching need for more oily-black hash to be poured *on these troubled waters* . . . Brother Bill says weed is 100 per cent non-addictive, and, unlike junk, a kick rather than a way of life. Will, his bowels liquefying, damns him for such bullshit: for he craves dope as life itself.

On this sharp spring morning, with *the heat, the man, the*

people, the filth . . . closing in on him, he looks about wildly at the *nationalist* dresser with its *conscripted* plates, a stack of old Reader's Digests, and a lifeless two-bar electric fire with a striped flex wound round its mirrored concavity: ragged holes are expanding in the film of reality itself, through which he glimpses the insensible and mineral horror of raw existence.

They must be sealed up pronto! with cosmic Polyfilla – the stuff that makes all stuffs . . . *God*.

He'll have to unlimber his unwieldly body from its frantic mind and goad it upstairs, tiptoeing so as to avoid waking the others. He'll have to open the drawer, retrieve the sock, get out the bag, winkle out the crumbs of hash — And he will, just as soon as he's dealt with THIS: the loud knocking on the back door of the cottage, as some *cunt from Porlock* persistently punctures *the pleasure dome* . . .

When did it begin? Was he knocking last June, when Will was sitting in his poxy bedroom, in the little house on Western Road in Oxford? Of course, considered sub specie aeternitatis, the knocking's been going on *for-fucking-ever*, quite as much as *RIGHT NOW*. Just as little Edmond, with his wings of dark overcoat, is always hopping into the bedroom and laying his single sheet of white paper on the bed.

His traverse of Will's grotty fag-scarred rug represents,

Will now realises, both the arrow of time and the line of prose: as a bird might take its first hesitant steps across fresh-fallen snow, so Edmond had both carried the page and made a series of marks on it.

Edmond's story and Will's are the same: 'cause his hip-bone's connected to Will's leg-bone, while his backbone links to those invertebrate inebriates revolving the light bulb, which, in turn, receive their motive force from Clive, who, driven on by internal voices, strides round *annaround* the pool-table-sized back garden. *Yes . . . all connected . . .* Standing, Will peers down at his cold crumpled crotch *ash rubbings . . .* then creeps towards the back door.

During that long summer of Psychosis Considered as a Means of Psychic Liberation, Will's old schoolfriends Pete and Mike had come to visit him in Oxford. They were living together in a squat they'd opened near Hackney Marshes, Mike having dropped out of Bristol – much to his parents' distress – while Pete had wandered away from college in Swansea, following a rainbow trail of Psilocybe semilanceata.

Visiting them during the Easter vac', Will had been sort of amused by the cereal box adapted to read SUGARY SMACK that served as a repository for their works, a cannister of BP Pharmaceutical citric acid – even a bottle of distilled water. Sort of amused – but mostly appalled: they were jemmying the cash boxes in pay phones for smack money – but Mike's mother had been a nurse before her marriage, and he still respected antisepsis, if not the law.

At Western Road they'd walked in on a scene reaching a smelly crescendo: the rubbish glued to the kitchen ceiling had spread to the living-room one, and both rooms had a significant resident fly population. 'Dear, dear Drosophilidae . . .' is all Jon – who was studying molecular biology and relied on them a lot – would say.

The London lads didn't have any gear, but Pete had brought two big wet amps of methadone, and the long-needled, blue-collared five mil' works necessary for intra-muscular shots. They'd all examined the amps sceptically, together with an ancient strip of genuine purple hearts – the drugs had come, in a roundabout way, via Pete's fruit-machining father: 'Geezer owed him and offered this stuff up – old man didn't have a clue what it was.'

They'd nerved each other to do it – then did, and lay back, massaging their aching biceps as the methadone flowed thickly between their three minds, emulsifying them into a single sticky puddle of semi-being.

Then they splurged across the scrofulous carpet, staring blankly at the fly-blown heavens.

All at once – and afterwards no one would admit to having let him in – Ten Pence Tom was in the room with them. It was shortly after Oisin had told Jon and Will the reason why Siobhan had done time in Holloway: she'd murdered her aunt – with an axe.

Yes, they were sharing the house with a bona fide axe murderer – so there was a degree of nerviness in the air, together with the skittish flies. Ten Pence Tom had buzzed about the room, kissing light bulbs and caressing plug sockets – a Van de Graaff generator of a man, whose mingy features and raggy hair had been haloed with sparks – or so the stoned trio agreed later, when they compared notes on the incident.

'Got any jobs,' Tom deterministically demanded, 'small jobs . . . little jobs – tiny jobs, perhaps? I'll do a job for ten pence if you gotta job needs doin'.'

Forcing himself upright and towards the kitchen, Will felt he was wearing a tutu made of the Earth's crust. He'd an awful presentiment – though no real reason to believe Ten Pence Tom was violent, beyond the aggressiveness with which he sought gainful employ.

A week or so before that, another mate of Will's, Ben, had been sitting up late in his room on the other side of town, speeding his way through an essay crisis, when there'd come an insistent knocking on the window. Freaked, since his room was on the first floor, Ben gently drew back the curtain to discover Tom's wiry figure, kinked up on the narrow ledge outside, while his crazy face had been thrust up-and-under the flap window:

'Got any jobs,' he'd petitioned Ben, 'little jobs – tiny ones, even?' I'll do a job for ten pence – if you've gotta job needs doin' . . .'

As surreptitiously as possible Will gathered up all the knives in the kitchen – then, hearkening to Tom's insistent drone, the forks as well. Bundling all this cutlery into a plastic bag, he stashed it outside with the now rotten pouffes. Returning through quicksand to the fray, he'd nonetheless been in time for their visitor, who zeroed in unerringly for the kill: getting in the face of each of them in turn, he'd gurned, 'You're all libras, aren'tcha – I'm good at that . . . Good at guessin' people's astronomical signs an' that.'

Mene, mene, tekel, upharsin . . . They had been weighed in the balance . . . *and found wanting.* The flies spun, the madmen walked round and around, in and out, up and down – constellations *of pure flashing mind*, shining in the dark eternity of a human being, that Will, *the Great White Spirit* . . . controlled with the wires spiralling out from his fingers . . . *and still does*: wires attached to his scale-model puppet, so, with trembling fingers, he sends it stumbling to the cottage door.

Teetering on the threshold, Will's overwhelmed. First by the view: beyond the sapling screen the domed hillside rises up, its dense bracken seething in the morning breeze, while the sun strikes down through broken cloud *to shine its grassy pate* . . . Then overwhelmed again by terrible nausea – the cosmic sucker-punch, as the *First Cause* announces himself *long after so many effects*:

'Good morning, my name is Detective Inspector Budge of the Dyfed and Powys Drug Squad – I have a warrant here to search these premises.'

It isn't a warrant he holds up, but his warrant card, which features a mugshot of himself, grinning facetiously from behind celluloid. 'My colleagues,' he continues *a little portentously*, 'have the cottage surrounded, so –'

So fucking what? So resistance is futile or some other clichéd tough-cop bullshit? Well, it is futile – Will knows that: but it's not only because the other three are asleep upstairs, or that he's *utterly strung out* . . . it's because he's transfixed by this awful realisation: it all could easily have been avoided, if only he'd had the nous to snatch the sheet of white paper from the bed, ball it up and throw it out of the window . . . *before Edmond returned.*

Clambering down from the coach to the ground . . . *down to the ground.* And, *oh the feeling, when you're reeling* . . . Will shakes out his sweaty limbs, stretches, breathes in exhaust fumes, exhales fag smoke, and stares about him through the thick and distorting lens of a heavy hash hangover.

He hasn't been this sober since his last finals exam . . . *fractal elaborations of Paxton's cast-iron and glass architecture auto-assembling out from the superstructure of a Mini Clubman to line the banks of the Isis* . . . Fu-uck, that was stro-ong acid . . . *Meadows full of bovine-human hybrids, heavy on all bare fours, teats between breasts and udders – pink, distended* . . . and the bricky bulk of the Odeon looms, filling his ears with the frozen music of the Doors' *This is the end* . . . combined with the thick whiplashing of helicopter blades.

That'd been apocalypse, then – seen the first week he was up, a scant thirty months ago – and now it was all over: the movie of his university career. The screen blank, the projector yet whirrs: *self-flagellating with its celluloid whip* . . .

Like any arrogant artificer, Will had flown too high – now he's going down, *down, down, deeper and down*, to the deathly disco where failures with thumbs stuck in their belts rhythmically maintain *the status-fucking-quo* . . .

Setting off across the tarmac *paella of fag-butt and gum-gob,* Will savours the bitterness – then spits this out: it seems like fucking aeons since he first visited mustachioed Mark's older brother, Phillip, who'd been up at Magdalen.

Will, aged sixteen, maximally impressed by oak-panelled rooms, and a dissolute friend of Phillip's, who'd come by, drunk and eloquent at lunchtime on a Saturday, and spoke of how, as a demi, he was required to dine at High Table — The evening before, leaving the President's lodgings a trifle inebriated, he'd tripped, busted through a venerable wooden door and into the College wine cellars, where he had indeed *sported and struck some attitudes . . .*

Anecdotes about others' anecdotes – possibly this was the truth of it: turning up George Street, swathed now in polythene, Will strides straight . . . *into Honey's walk-in closet.* The Honey-run had begun in Oxford, continued down the motorway and ended when they'd pulled off the Marylebone Flyover and parked up.

Will – together with his then housemate, Henry – had outed a little coke in their second year, scoring quarter ounces off Honey, abstracting half, cutting the remainder with mannitol. Henry was the wheel-man, while Will: he was the passenger, *and he rode and he rode* – within minutes of arrival they'd be sitting with Honey on her drip-dry sofa in her wipeable flat. She wore ironed jeans and quite possibly ironed her taupe-coloured hair.

Coked up, they'd followed her pink fluffy back into the closet, where she pointed out to them curling tongs and irons, trouser presses and toasters, electric blankets and radio-cassette players – all of it *still in the boxes . . .* She'd got on the wrong end of her own product, had Honey: her monkey muzzle was puckering up, as she fanaticked her profits from consumables into what she stupidly imagined to be . . . *durables.*

By contrast, Will and Henry had *la-la-la-la-lalalalaughed* their way back up on to the flyover – they'd seen the city's ripped back sides — then the bright and hollow sky, as the car shot through the gunsight cutting in the Chiltern escarpment, and began bucketing back down into the rolling country of south Oxfordshire.

Puckering up – as shrivelled as her own *mucosa* . . . Yup, restricting her own *mucus supply* was Honey, which might've made her *dried up enough* for Keith Joseph, the then Secretary of State for Education, and one of Thatcher's henchmen, whom Will remembers being barracked unmercifully in the History Schools, then driven out on to George Street, and effectively chased, in a huddle of advisors and Special Branch pigs, to his waiting car.

Had such youthful idealism meant anything – changed anything? To the hypocrisy of attending the acme of the privilege they decried was added self-righteousness, as they hunted down the dries, reclaimed the night and lent the dockers support – all of it with a headful of Honey's *gross domestic product* . . .

Now, stumbling across the junction with the Cornmarket, Will sees the Martyrs' Memorial – specifically its mossy pediment – and with the plastic bag containing his shorty-gown and mortar board *softly slapping* his thigh, he makes for it, with a view to resting his head: *the coke-dust leaks out . . . dandruffy on my suit collar . . . Inside? A complex mechanism of valves, springs and sprockets – one that's ever-tightening . . .*

Yes, Will had fantasised about a glittering university

career – to be followed by glittering prizes – quite as much as he'd been a dreamer of a new dawn. But instead? He slumps down heavily and reaches for his fags – instead an open viva: *an open-fucking-viva!*

Confronted by his admittedly rather bizarre finals papers – the one featuring a cartoon of Jean-Paul Sartre next to a similarly proportioned hammer, and captioned ACTUAL SIZE comes sluggishly to mind – the examiners were presumably unable to decide which degree he should be awarded. It could be a mere pass one, with no honours at all – or an exalted first. There's everything to play for – and the player's due onstage, at the Examination Schools in half an hour's time, which is why he's wearing his subfusc, and his mind is also . . . *shrouded in gloom.*

Hugh had taken Will along to Joseph's speech, and they'd returned here, a few weeks later, to confront the pissed-up rugger-buggers who'd commandeered the Memorial in celebration of the British victory in the Falklands. One of them punched Will in the face, hard – and try as he might now to rescript the fracas so as to incorporate a spirited fightback – the truth was, they'd retired to the Balliol JCR. Where, after he'd sneezed out the blood, Will snorted up a minuscule line of coke Hugh chopped out for him on a windowsill in the bogs.

Then Hugh bought him a single shot of whisky: 'Little and often,' his friend had almost certainly intoned when Will raised a bloodied and quizzical brow – because this was Hughie's rubric, one equally applicable to drugs . . . *and political engagement.*

It's as if, by titrating both conviction and intoxication, Hugh hopes to prevent his own waxy wings melting – thereby ensuring his life remains *A-ma-zing!* His friend's joyful – and habitual – cry resounds in Will's ears, and he wishes Hugh were there to lend him a little support, because he's right: either use a drug little and often – or substitute another. After all, while any given intoxicant can modulate the full range of possible human experience – on a scale from coked-up paranoia to coked-up ecstasy – so habitual use delivers a sole outcome: a yawning gulf which must be filled with . . . *more coke.*

It's the same, Will believes, with alcohol and the other drugs: the effect of smack or speed is at least partly the wanting of more smack or more speed. Only with cocaine, or – Will ruminates bitterly, sucking on his cigarette – tobacco does the wanting fully eclipse all other effects, such that the hit of a line or a fag becomes *the desire for another line . . . and another fag . . .*

Sitting on mossy stone, feeling its damp chill infiltrate his thighs, surrounded by a three-dimensional Ladybird Book illustration of summertime Oxford on a weekday morning, Will feels an oubliette open in his dungeon of a stomach – down there it's colder still, and the torture is worse – *Awww, fu-uck* . . . a hash hangover is definitely not what you want when you're about to undergo the most testing examination of your life so far. Possibly ever.

Will remembers his interview at Keble: the long-haired don with the languorous manner, lying back in the armchair and drawling, *Do tell us, please, Mr Self, if you had to make the choice, what would you do: kill an adult dolphin or a human baby?*

He'd equivocated then and he's equivocating still: with the adult dolphin actually lying beside him on the plinth *wheezily whistling through its spiracle* . . . Or is it, perhaps . . . *a seal?* While as for the baby – this, Will carries inside him, a Numbskull . . . *mucking about with the controls.*

Which of them should die? His mother's amphibious imago or his own infantile one? Or were they in fact . . . *the same thing?* She's away in the States, visiting his older half-brother, and her friends – friends who remain hazily underimagined by her youngest . . . *her sweetie-pie, her Benja-fucking-min* . . .

Will's father's gone too – fled back to Australia, where he went for a sabbatical a few years ago. Why? He'd explained the previous autumn, when Will went to have Sunday lunch with him and his soon-to-be-third-wife, at her cottage in Brill, a hilltop village outside Oxford. Could anyone that old and frumpy possibly be a fiancée?

Over soggy roast potatoes and leathery lamb, sitting beneath a framed and non-ironic sampler *Bless this Louse* . . . he'd quoted Gore Vidal's quip regarding Australia: *I've seen the past – and it works* . . . Neither credulous Steffens nor Beatrice Webb, he, *oh no* – the ageing Professor is lighting out for a territory where he can still teach: all that's left for him in England is superannuation.

After lunch they'd gone for what the pontificating Polonius called *a gentle stroll*: three or four miles circumambulating the village, clambering over rotten stiles and striding across sodden paddocks. To distract himself from his father's gentle reproof: *I do think you might* . . . *It could be an idea for you to* . . . *If you could just be a little more* . . . *moderate* . . . Will scanned the cow-splatted turf ahead, stooping from time to time to pick an elegant mushroom and pop it in his mouth.

'Are you sure they aren't poisonous?' Piffled Pooter – and William Lupin had snorted derisively . . . *he's so fucking dumb – dumb and* . . . *useless*.

When Will had received the hateful letter informing him the Philosophy Panel wouldn't award a grant for his Master's, he got straight on to *the nonagenarian nepotist* – for his father did indeed know its Chairman from *back in the sepia day*: 'They can't do this,' he'd spluttered into the mouthpiece, 'they can't refuse me a grant, 'cause I haven't had my finals results yet – and I'm meant to get a fucking first!'

*

Perhaps – but was Will not forgetting his own demonstrable proof, worked out with Caius and Jeremy over many a weekday joint? Hume's scepticism had destroyed any certain knowledge of an external world for Kant, so he'd undertaken his laborious Critique of Pure Reason, thereby proving the existence of at least two *certain things*: his own existence, and that of God – but it'd taken another 150 years before Wittgenstein – having turned again, like some metaphysical Dick Whittington, from the Russellian linguistic turn – established that the universality of grammar itself implied the existence of not just two but multiple minds.

And with multiple minds came — *certain things . . . certain things a certain Philosophy Panel certainly seemed to know . . .* But how? How the fuck did they know them? The answer had come from Will's tutor – *a Johnson on the far shore of a lagoon full of liquid shit . . .* He'd written a perfectly good reference for Will – but also saw the one from *Dr K, the kunt who taught me Kant . . .* which was about as terse as possible, while demonstrating its own synthetic a priori truth: *I do not believe this candidate will complete any postgraduate course of study for which he's afforded a place . . .*

. . . *Really? Really?!* Will's tutor, whose soft and sandy manner was one of continual self-effacement – the erosion, perhaps, of the personal identity he increasingly viewed as merely contingent on consciousness – had got right to the point: 'There's very little point in applying elsewhere at this stage – not with this.' He'd waved the warrant for the arrest of Will's academic career. 'You'll need to get another reference – and that'll take time, so you may as well wait for your results now . . .'

Will had been winded and furiously indignant . . . *windignant?* 'What the fuck? He gave me an alpha for his course – why else would I have asked him for the reference?'

'Be that as it may – this is the situation.'

'He must know,' Will had said, sitting in his tutor's sixth-floor study, at the top of one of the staircases ranged round the back quad, and looking out over the buttery lawn, spread across the Fellows' Garden. 'But how?'

How indeed. In the weeks after the bust the savage come-down subsided into a manageable enough paranoia: they were indeed out to get him – but next time Will would see them coming, not least because of DI Budge:

'Look, Will,' he'd said in the interview room at Carmarthen nick, 'I know you're not a criminal, really – but there's this evidence . . .' He'd held up the letter to Billy, sealed in a plastic bag '. . . of clear intent to procure drugs – and unfortunately not just marijuana.'

So, at least there'd been this tiny fillip: Will had managed to express with his table all the possible permutations of Class A, B and C drugs the Welsh reading party desired. Moreover, unlike DI Budge, Will hadn't *repeated myself* . . .

Because Budgie's colleagues had not only surrounded the cottage – they surrounded it again *annagain* ... The red cagoul was accompanied, preposterously, by *several fucking anoraks* ...

And all the comings and goings of this vastly disproportionate squad made Will feel dizzy – so he'd sat back down in the kitchen, and stared out at the figures in bracken, carpeting the hillside.

Naff dressers or not, they'd still known how to *spin the drum* ... returning to Will soon enough, bearing the handicrafts he'd ... *prepared for them earlier.* It'd been a stilted affair, the bust – the participants exhibiting the chilly politeness to be expected when white-collar strangers – such as estate agents or loss-adjusters – are allowed into the home. The students were in shock – the cops bored and disappointed. *An hour's fucking drive for four grotty little punks, less than a gramme of hash and few smears of speed* ...

Their cars were parked a quarter-mile down the lane – Ford Grenadas slumped heavily on the verges, and *bright the sinuous rill* ... running beneath Will's feet, as he'd clambered into the back seat.

He'd remembered then – re-remembers now – his mother, on a Snowdonian holiday, gathering wild watercress in a brook, then having a Rachel Carson *crise des neufs*, because she was worried it was polluted.

Last into the car had been Sara and her escorting

officer – she'd had to hang back and lock her parents' cottage. Her face was pasty-white – drenched in shock, and with her ringlets she made Will think of a Pre-Raphaelite Ophelia, about to be thrust below the water . . . *with a Doc Marten's boot.*

But then there'd been Budgie – who didn't even consider Will a criminal, let alone the rest of them. He had the sort of face that went with the leather and mousey collar-length hair: big featured, with a chin like Jimmy Hill, and consoling, brown eyes:

'So, Will, there's these piddling quantities of actual drugs, and there's this' – again the evidence-fanning – 'which unfortunately means three possible charges of conspiracy to procure for everyone who signed it.'

However, DI Budge turned out to be a big tough narc, who'd wanted a big tough bust – on the drive to Carmarthen he told them he was one of the detectives who'd worked on Operation Julie: 'That's why they call me Budgie – we posed as birdwatchers when we were doing the surveillance.'

'Surely,' Jeremy chimed up from the back seat – and these had been, so far as Will recalls, his first words since their arrest, 'your nickname is a simple abbreviation of your real one?'

At this the cops had all laughed – and one of them said, 'Boyo, he's just meddlin' with you.'

*

It came down to paperwork rather than semantics in the end: in common with the students, the cops *just couldn't be arsed to do it* . . .

'Look, Will,' Budgie said, his brow furrowed, 'it's better and simpler for me – and obviously much better for your mates – if just two of you take the charges, and it's pretty obvious who those two have to be.'

Yes – poor Sara: their cold kiss under the chilly eaves had sealed their letter, and their fate. Sara would have to be charged, since she'd allowed the drugs to be consumed on a property she was responsible for. While as for Will, he'd been *caught bang-to-rights* . . . a line some stoners believed you'd only to utter at the moment of arrest for the case to eventually be dropped: since no court in the land would believe anyone, no matter how dopey, could come up with *such a fucking cliché* . . .

And now? Will hauls himself to his feet, head swimming, and heads on along Broad Street, staggering slightly to avoid oncoming tourists . . . *and memories* – although not only his own.

Yes, a fucking cliché – that's what his life is, was and presumably *always will be* . . . There's this viva voce to deal with, then, in a fortnight's time, he'll have another opportunity *to condemn myself out of my own mouth* . . .

He'll be travelling up to Wales with Sara by coach – they'll have to go the day before, and stay the night in a B&B, since the case is listed for nine in the morning. Sharing a room to save on costs, *obviously* —

He leans against the wall beside Balliol's gates. Last year there'd been no fewer than three suicides of students with rooms in the front quad. Two were jumpers – Will's fellow Icaruses, high-diving into yet deeper oblivion. One of the urban myths of this tinpot town was that they kept an entire ward freed up at the Warneford during finals.

Bring out your white man! The cries of Trinity hearties, gathered to shout racist insults over the party wall, echoed down the decades through his father's retelling: the old faker had been a Balliol man – albeit pink rather than black – and he never let Will forget it.

Would failure truly matter? The world could do without Will's conjecture of an accommodation to be made between Marxist epistemology and the later Wittgenstein. While as for personal progress, Will knew any dissertation would be a sort of papery nest, within which he might curl up, hopefully, for another year *hibernating from real life . . .*

Then there're the drugs — it's all very well blaming everything and one else, but Will has his moments of genuine clarity. Many of them. He knows he wouldn't've stopped using before his finals – even without the stress of the bust.

Hallucinogens were quite likely the reason why he'd drawn the cartoons on his papers – or possibly it's because the world as Will perceives it is so very *cartoonish . . .* Crossing the road diagonally towards the Sheldonian, and its *pop-eyed* heads ranged on encircling columns, he considers the way he can create a reality with a few black strokes on the white void of the page – then distort it.

Is it comforting that all this complexity can be reduced to such seeming simplicity – or is it, rather, that human understanding consists precisely in the ceaseless elaboration of nothing much? Memories of his first year rise up, wraith-like, from the paving stones. He'd had the room right next to the right-end head, and late at night there would come soft knocks on his window. When he raised the sash, one or other of his fellow collegians would clamber through, and, since his bed was immediately below, on a couple of occasions they'd stayed and had sex with him.

Et in Arcadia ego . . . such, such had been the joys . . . *her intense-smelling, almost faecal sweat – her Tupperware complexion . . . wipeable . . .* Or had the cartoons rather emerged, Etch-a-Sketched out of the white void of his own childhood?

Since his parents' final split, Will's past has been disassembling – an effect that really did precede its cause, since when he looks back now he sees . . . *nothing*. In which case Will's only trying to draw some lines where there'd been none: *Oh, Will!* His father's florid face in the doorway, wreathed in vegetal smoke. *It smells like an opium den in here!*

The stopped-clock was right on that occasion, as he'd also been when they'd discovered a deck of ten quarter-gramme wraps in his desk drawer: *Oh, Will, your mother and I feel you really oughtn't to be selling cocaine . . .*

Pivoting into Catte Street, Will nearly loses his footing, pitching forward from this white void . . . *into a far larger and emptier one.* He remembers punting last windy spring with Laura, whom he still sleeps with *from time to time . . .* coming back to her room in New College and going down on her . . . *esters of urine, strained through pubic hair* then coming almost at once – an effect miserably in advance of its rightful cause, although, that said, Laura was beautiful: a green-eyed and lan-guorous odalisque . . . *It could've been worse.*

Much. He could've done gear yesterday – in which case his hangover would be far, far *gummier . . .*

He's been gummed up quite a lot since finals, has *little Willy . . .* Genie's carried on being generous with the cool fifteen-fucking-grand she got, just to do the cooking and sup-ply some feminine front for a gang smuggling hash in by yacht from the Lebanon . . . *Hello, sailors!*

She invested most of this dosh in light-beige – and very pure – smack, and she likes to treat Will as her boy-toy, kiss-ing the crook of his arm as she *slides the needle deftly in . . .* then flushing the works to inject him *in mounting rhythms . . .* as she expertly . . . *rubs my cock.*

Genie's hair has been dyed so many times it feels like swarf – she wears gold-painted bovver boots and a motorbike leather painted silver. She fucks Will with deter-mination – but little conviction, and shares her brother Hugh's enthusiasm – although the things Genie finds a-maz-ing are far, far . . . *darker.*

Neither sibling thinks the Soho private members' club, where Hugh works as relief barman in the vacs, as the least bit remarkable – their mother's a regular, so they've more or less grown up in these two tatty rooms above a trattoria on Dean Street. But the first time Will visited, and Hugh introduced him to Francis Bacon – who was standing at the wincy dinky bar, his hair smeared back from his expres-sionless face – he'd known he was somewhere as exalted as any Fellows' dining room.

Which was where the third years had been entertained by the Rector after their final exams: going, in subject groups, *suited and fucking booted* . . . to this oak-panelled cubbyhole tucked behind the hall. Stewards in white nylon jackets served them with brown beef and mauve claret. The conver-sation had been at once stiff and jocular, as the dons tried one last time to . . . *only connect.*

Will, quickly drunk, had savoured this incongruity: a man on criminal bail, working his way through the cutlery in the correct order, while the Rector served up this conversational titbit: *We're very much looking forward to your remaining here with us next year* . . . For at that point they'd been *between courses* . . . certain things not having been communicated by the Dyfed and Powys Police to . . . *certain people.*

After the Stilton came the port, passed from hand to hand – then the Chief Steward had borne in an ornate silver ram's horn that turned out to be a snuff box. The other students all passed: *silly fuckers* . . . the only thing they'd ever snorted was . . . *their own snot.*

When the horn reached Will, he made a point of pouring out a generous mound of the pale-beige powder on to the skin webbing his thumb and index finger. The snuff was very strong – it burned itself out in Will's nose, pain fading to . . . *dull ache: Smack-U-Like* . . .

In Soho, Hugh serves up drinky-poohs under the jaundiced eyes of Ian, the Club's proprietor, who sits on a stool by the ornately engraved old till, his swollen nose a fiery beacon of broken blood vessels in the dappled gloom of an alcoholic afternoon.

Hughie says Ian is *all right, really* – but he's taken an instant dislike to Will, who, as soon as he'd walked in the door – which is covered in green baize, like that of the Fellows' dining room – Ian dubbed *the lanky cunt* . . . Will's the lanky cunt – and Genie's the junky one. Eschewing drinky-poohs, they *repair to the in-house* . . . a tiny karsi partitioned off from the Club's main room, and here Genie chops out generous lines of her pale-beige smack on the surround of the dinky sink.

Will finds it difficult to imagine what Hugh and Genie's childhood must've been like in this arena of high-bohemian pomp and squalid circumstance – but no harder than he does picturing the secure backgrounds of the well-scrubbed, ex-public-school boys and girls he's been at university with, who, however wildly they may have behaved during the past three years, have done now with *sowing their oats* . . . and are instead getting ready, with every appearance of happy anticipation . . . *to do their porridge.*

They talk of jobs in the City – or with management consultants. The more bohemian ones have internships lined up with newspapers or publishers – whereas Will has had no plan whatsoever beyond staying put: lingering here on the threshold of the straight world, with one eye roving . . . *the outer darkness.*

But, while Will may've been Janus-faced *for bloody years now* . . . Hugh and Genie have never been allowed . . . *in from the cold.* After school in some Hertfordshire shithole – Berkhamsted? Hemel Hempstead? – Hugh did get to university, but during his third term at Sheffield he'd had a nervous breakdown.

Recovered, he'd applied to Oxford by sending in an a-maz-ing essay on Historical Determinism. It must've been, since it'd secured him a place. Will thinks the most a-ma-zing thing about Hugh is . . . *Hugh,* who, with his eager golden-brown eyes, wild brown hair and nervily elegant fingers, has a gentle yet powerful charisma.

Will unashamedly adores Hugh – but then so do many others, since, despite his own foul-mouthed and alcoholic mother, he possesses in abundance that power more usually ascribed to . . . *orphans*. Hugh plucked at the strings of his acoustic guitar, while Will sang, *The best things in life are free* . . . which was how the band had begun. And, given their overlapping proclivities – Will for lots-and-more-or-less-continuously, Hugh for little-and-often – the Abusers had been no misnomer.

On his third or fourth visit to the Colony Room Club, Will and Hugh had been drunkenly whiling away the afternoon with its potty-mouthed clientele, when Ian announced to the entire bar, 'Johnny, here, is opening a fine new e-stab-lish-ment around the corner, aren'tcha, lover-boy?' And Johnny-boy – a brick shithouse in a grey suit and tan trench coat – had grudgingly concurred.

'Sooo,' Ian whined on, swirling the ice in his gin and tonic, 'we'd better wet the cunting baby's head, eh . . . Fran-cis, you're standing the 'poo for everyone.'

The painter, whose hair is the colour of shoe polish, and whose eyes have the hue and apparent depth . . . *of a muddy puddle*, didn't demur.

They'd all stumped downstairs and around the corner to Old Compton Street, where, behind a whitewashed plate-glass window, and white polythene covers, cocks were being vigorously sucked and buttocks precipitately parted. The clubbable members disported themselves between the shelves, while Francis filled all their glasses. Ian gave a charming little oration about cunts and cocks and how *n'er the twain shall meet*, so as to welcome into the world this new-born purveyor of sadomasochistic gay pornography,

Raising their glasses, they'd toasted 'To Janus!', which was the name of the shop – everyone, that is, except Francis. The painter stood by the counter, zipped up in his Belstaff jacket, toying idly with a small bottle of Rush! Air Freshener, and utterly inscrutable.

Will's never heard him say so much as a word, let alone the benediction he feels he deserves: for if Bacon is Soho's genius loci, then Will's *finally arrived* . . .

Although he's not exactly sure where. Turning into New College Lane, the mid-morning hubbub falls away as he strolls between ancient and flinty walls. Yes, every time he'd been to the Club with Genie, she'd dobbed him out a line or two of gear – and a couple of weeks ago she'd gifted her boy-toy an entire gramme.

Will surfed up to Clacton on its thick flood tide – taking the tube as far as Gants Hill, then a coach on across the Essex flatlands. It was the fourth or fifth day he'd been using – the longest continuous period yet – and, fully immured in its syrupy reality, he'd gouched out on the coach – then come to,

feeling an alien hand gripping his own. A hand he only realised belonged to him, as he'd prised its unfeeling fingers open
one by one . . .

The friends were staying in some grandparents' holiday
bungalow, and they'd all been taking healthy walks and tossing together salad lunches. His gramme gone, Will claimed
a dicky tummy – but this fooled no one, least of all himself.
He'd lain in the curtained-off cubicle allotted him, staring
at a shelf of light holiday reads: *Two Sams at the Chalet
School* . . . his eyes so heavy he couldn't look away, and med-
itating on the modulations of his emerging habit.

When he'd first begun using smack, what'd a-ma-zed
Will most was how, out of its strength, had *come forth such
sweetness*, as he'd swooned and roused, the ecstasies of the
high gradually *treacling away* . . . until, at last, he'd slept —
and plummeted down, through dynasties of dreams, back to
the very crucible of his imagination: the little boy, curled up
in bed in his uncle's loft, and controlling the sunbeams
solidified with golden dust motes, by squinting then relaxing, *squinting then relaxing* . . .

But this sweetness had been only another feint – followed
by . . . *bang! another sucker-punch.* The bells of St Mary sing
out over the vaulted domes *and the dreaming-fucking-spires*
as Will scuttles along. Now, when the opiated tide ebbs
away, he'll be stranded for a day or more, lying on gravelly
sheets, eyes full of dust that can't be rubbed away. Then

there's the depression – a horrid counterpoint to febrile arousal: miserably he tosses – and tosses himself off in the spare room of his mother's new flat in Kentish Town, nauseated by the smells of fresh paint and rubbery carpet underlay, sickened by the blubberiness of his *soft cock* . . .

. . . *Yesss*, the tide goes out and the seabed's exposed, littered with Will's dead thoughts and dying ambitions – which flop about in brackish pools of his own sweat, while outside oceanic London laps away, wave-upon-wave of roof-crests and gutter-troughs – a grey-slated and leaden zone, where the ceaseless movement of all-in-relation-to-all results only in a terrible stasis.

It's this awful feeling – that nothing ever can or will change – which torments Will the most. It's this that drives him from his salted bed, frog-marches him to the station – where he takes the train to West Hampstead – then urges him on, down through streets lined with *Victorian mausoleums* . . . while all the time . . . *the vultures circle overhead.*

Genie's opened a squat of her own at the end of Hemstal Road. It's a gaunt, detached three-storey house that looks out across a quiet corner of a dull little park. Will can score nearer home, off of Terry, Kentish Town's own *king of kiting*, but Genie's more reliable: summoned by a string threaded with little Indian bells that tinkle against the top window, her wild curls will soon enough appear.

Will thinks of an archangel, for the wide sleeves of her Chinese silk dressing gown dangle down ... *broken wings*, and when he's climbed the three flights, crunchy with fallen plaster, he finds further confirmation in her black track marks and zombie pallor: Genie's no longer sitting at God's right hand, but falling.

Two kittens currently share the top floor of the house, which is where Genie mostly hangs out – and, as she moves about in her Chinese dressing gown, concocting her fix, they cling, mewling, to her silken skirts, while the garish dragons embroidered in gold thread writhe, as she bends to siphon off the solution.

'Here's the list,' she'll say, passing Will a bit of paper upon which she's itemised the kinds and numbers of syringes and needles she wants him to buy at Bliss, the chemist's on Willesden Lane. Works, citric acid – plus the antiseptic creams and fluids needed to combat the career junky's most aggressive enemy: sepsis.

As Will sees it, Genie and her brother, with their bohemian background, haven't had to kick against any moralising pricks – which is why, he suspects, she understands intuitively that doing exactly as she pleases *is the whole of the law* ...

Genie applies the same conviction to dealing smack as she did to the smuggling venture – and to her part-time whoring as well. If he comes late in the afternoon, Will sometimes finds her *all dolled up* ... her pallor masked with expert make-up, her track marks covered by long sleeves, her breasts thrust forward by high heels, about to embark on what she calls *a date* . . . her objective being, Will suspects, not money but to maintain a sense of being . . . *still desirable.*

Will's never been to Lee Circle, or to the junction of 103rd Street and Broadway – but he strongly suspects these locations must have the same ambience as Genie's part of *County Kilburn* . . . Clutching her list, he'll limp across the park, past the playground where dossers slump on the roundabout and piss-artists dangle from the swings – then through the far gates and on to the High Road, where sons-of-the-Irish sod stand about outside betting shops, crazed by booze *and their immemorial losses* . . .

Brother Bill describes 'junk territory': certain dreary areas on the fringes of Skid Row harbouring dubious businesses – *taxidermists, makers of false teeth and purveyors of quack cures* – and bearing the impress of addiction.

Stumping beneath the stucco façade of the Odeon Cinema, Will often sees street junkies shuffle-limping ahead of him towards Bliss – a suitable enough name for this, one of the handful of chemist's in London that'll sell you works without a prescription.

Now, emerging into the clamour of Oxford High Street, he slumps down on a bench directly opposite the Examination

Schools, and gets out a final cigarette . . . *before I face the firing squad.*

Yes, Will's beginning to share the street junkies' distinctive gait – but why? It isn't as if he's fixing in his groin – a dread expression, conjuring up vile images of *phallic hypos ejaculating blood . . .* and a *Final Solution* to the problem of lust. Which is how he sometimes thinks about his burgeoning heroin addiction – for, smacked-out, he feels none whatsoever, whereas straight he's . . . *a fucking dog – led by its own turgid nose.*

Will's fond of La Rochefoucauld's maxim: *God invented sex in order to place Man in embarrassing positions* – yet none, surely, are as shameful as his own, for he lurches across town, hobbled by his half-masted trousers and underpants, from one impulsive liaison to the next.

Why? Is a question he'll pose *again annagain* while actually lying prone between thighs, fiddling with another of the mucus-slick beads on this *fleshy abacus* . . . Why's he compelled to pursue an experience he seemingly values so little? And, at this juncture, his eyes will slide from this rictus, or that taut neck, to some inconsequential thing: a batik scarf looped round a pier glass, or a poster of the White Rabbit, *peeling away from the peeling wallpaper . . .*

Will sucks mournfully on his fag, and considers his grandmother – *a Tenniel illustration of a woman,* who, with her ivory perm, adipose body and permanently rug-swaddled lower limbs, resembles a creature caught in mid-metamorphosis from upper-middle-class Englishwoman to . . . *sheep*.

He remembers her getting out the old wooden box, unfolding the linen-backed board and passing round the ivory counters, so Will and his brother could choose ones *to be synonymous with* . . . She'd played the game as a child, and faithfully preserved this element of her own late-Victorian childhood, just as she holds fast to her simple piety. Yes, Granny believes in a sky god – a Great White Spirit who crouches in the cloudy fifth dimension, spinning a teetotum to decide who will be saved . . . *and who damned*.

The teetotum still spins in Will's muzzy head – and, when it slews to a halt, on he'll go. Willy's Walk to Grandmama, the game was called – but now the destination has changed, and it should be called *Willy's Stagger to the Smack Dealer* or *Willy's Pants-Down Hobble towards the Next Compliant Girl* . . . and away from the conscientious one.

He'd left Chlöe time and again, to go and smoke dope with Sufis in Casa, in Fez and in Marrakesh – finally, in Ouarzazate, he'd abandoned her altogether.

Abandoned her beneath a bloody blue sky, in a huge and dusty square – a flimsy *batik scarf* of a girl, her pale hands gloved in henna tattoos. Abandoned her saying he couldn't take it any more – the dreadful friction between them, trapped as they were on a hairpin emotional bend. She remained determined to head south, into the Sahara, where she'd be at the mercy of the Tuareg, with their indigo skins, and the Polisario Front, with their *camouflaged ones* . . . While he – he'd been resolved to return north, to Tangier, to lose himself in the medina, and opium.

But then, piloting his hysterical head through the souk, smelling the cochineal and cantharides, seeing sunlight dappling skull caps, headscarves, *kinking kif smoke* . . . he'd tried himself in the courtroom of maternal censure. She sat, wigged in her own hairy helmet – she advocated, in her pink Terylene dressing gown, a cloned dozen of her deliberated, muumuued as the blue men of the desert are robed. Her verdict was unanimous, her judgement severe: if this slip of a girl were to be in any way hurt, he'd be damned eternally.

So Will ran – faster then faster still, his mouth full of sick-sour guilt. Ran back to the dusty expanse where he'd left her, his frantic eyes wide, scanning the dusty tumult: camels furiously flobbing and screeching, trucks backing and filling.

Will sits on the bench beside the bus stop while a bread van's exhaust pants against his exposed ankles. He takes a drag on his *bum-sucked fag* . . . and the greige superstructure of the Examination Schools re-emerges from this *local weather system* . . .

*

Chloë had still been there – sitting, looking fatally vulnerable on her little metal suitcase. He'd spluttered out heartsick apologies: he'd meant nothing of what he'd said – a moment's madness. *Would she forgive him?*

They'd returned north – neither very happy. Will had, he felt, at least made the pragmatic decision – nay, the utilitarian one. That night, on the train jolting back towards *Nous ne sommes pas des tourists, nous vivons à Casa . . .* while he'd fitfully slumbered, Chloë somehow managed to solicit a marble-sized ball of opium from a man who pestered her *jameela . . . jameela . . . ghazala . . . ghazala . . .* as so many had for the past three weeks in the streets, on buses and in cafés – quite brazenly, sometimes right in front of Will. Her boyfriend – who, when he woke, fetched small cups of muddy coffee and muddied them further with the opium. He'd gulped down this paradoxical brew – and she declined it.

Will had loved Morocco – apart from the shits. By the time they left he could hold a banana-shaped wrap of kif and kif pipe in the one hand he simultaneously employed to fill and tamp. Wafting the little clay bowl with a flame, he would draw deep, exhale to one side then blow back down the stem, propelling the comet of embers in an arc *across the sheltering sky . . .*

*

Will sighs – sags. This is hardly the culture the panel assembling over the road will wish him to display familiarity with. He's early for the viva – but late for this party, which ended *before you were born . . .*

Fuck adult dolphins and human babies: Will's dilemma is Brother Bill's: the existential choice is between being and feeling – good, that is. Brother Bill undergirds his amorality with talk of junk's profanity: it's the Ugly Spirit who sits in the fifth dimension and controls everything with wires . . . *not the Great White one . . .*

Besides, Will's beef isn't with morality – or knowledge for that matter – but with reality itself. Tackling this vexed question with his ever-wry tutor, he'd proposed the Argument from Hallucination as a necessary corrective to Berkeley's one from Illusion: 'Say you take an extremely powerful hallucinogenic drug . . .'

'Okay, ye-es.'

'One with well-defined and very obvious effects – such as distorting your vision so you see geometric patterns, something like that.'

'All right, yes . . .'

'Then – and this is crucial – while you're actually under the influence of this very powerful psychotropic drug, you either take – or, more likely have administered – a second extremely powerful psychotropic drug, one which has entirely different, but just as dramatic, effects.'

'Okay, so where does this get us to, precisely?'

'It gets us to reality, because the different effects of the two drugs could be experienced by the person taking them only if there exists an ulterior, non-drug reality.'

Will's tutor had remained seated in the underlying, non-drug reality, his slate-grey eyes limpid behind the oblong lenses of his rimless spectacles. He didn't ask his tutee for concrete examples – although Will could happily have provided them, both positive and negative: the three-in-the-morning alarm, followed by necking a Mogadon and an acid blotter – the objective, triumphantly achieved, being to wake up tripping.

Or dropping a black bomber immediately after peaking, so the subject feels like *kicking all that oneness to fucking pieces* . . .

During the climacteric of last acid-drenched summer, Will was in the pub at the end of Western Road, when Siobhan's features had swum out of the barman's face, and her mouth told him to go to the Lamb and Flag. When he'd arrived in the middle of town, she was standing at the bar with Oisin . . . *raving.*

And why not? You don't have to be a Piranesi to fabricate such darkly fantastical visions out of reality itself – all you need is a red microdot, and the necessary head for heights, as it winches you up the hallucinogenic hill, which transmogrifies into a rollercoaster, whipping you down into a satanic cathedral, the *blood-red and pulsing* walls of its inverted spire lined with an infinity of mouths, all open and screaming the Bad News of your *own utter annihilation* . . .

Will's standing in front of a porter or beadle of some sort, who wears spongebag trousers, a tight dark jacket and a bowler hat crammed down on his jug head. Meanwhile *scores of paratroopers, fresh from Goose Green, abseil down the neo-Gothic cliff face behind him – 'cause it's just one damn hallucination after anoth–*

'Self? First floor, third door on the right – you can't miss it.'

Any more than you can a head-on collision with a *fucking cliché . . . a proctor!* That's right – a proctor, *not an arse doctor*, although he quite likely also knows some *shitty things about me . . .*

Mounting the wide treads of the staircase, eroded by generations of student soles into *surrealistic lips . . .* Will's stomach begins to churn.

'Mr Self?' The Chairman of the panel occupies the Messiah's place at the very centre of a long and highly polished, dark wooden table set below three of the Examination Schools' high and many-paned windows. Summer sunlight streams all over the place, soaking into and splashing up from every surface – while the Examiners, all men, all black-gowned, sit perfectly still.

'Yes.'

'Please take a seat.'

The indicative finger is quite unnecessary – for the *thing-in-itself is quite sufficient*, standing as it does, ten feet in front of the table.

And when did I last see my father? Will thinks, having eaten another hearty breakfast . . . *of my own facetiousness.* He squeaks across the highly polished parquet and takes his place . . . *Yes, when indeed?* Both his parents know about the bust – but neither has expressed much interest in the trial date.

Mr Self . . . the Chairman begins, sounding amused, *Mr Self* . . . he reiterates, quite likely savouring the suitability of the candidate's name for his course of study . . . *your finals papers were . . . interesting to read – and embellished in an . . . unusual way, but we found them rather confusing, which is why we've asked you to attend this viva* . . .

No! None of this at all – the responses Will's carefully rehearsed to the questions he'd like to be asked are quite useless – for what the man has in fact said, with no pre-amble whatsoever, is: 'Can you tell us, please, Mr Self, what were the principal influences of Montesquieu's thought on the development of nineteenth-century French liberalism?'

The question still hangs, *buzzing*, in the grand, beeswax-scented void, such that Will's automatic responses, *What the fuck!? What the fucking fuck!?* seem to flit about it, *willing to wound, and yet afraid to strike* . . .

It is indeed lunchtime, and Will's altogether naked –
while, for a long and frozen moment, the viva panel members
stare at what's *on the end of their forks* . . . . Long enough
for Will to remember another chilly one spent in the wind
tunnel of his room on Juxon Street, back in the early
spring.

He'd tipped the wardrobe on its side as soon as he moved in,
and Blu Tacked a scale reproduction of a miniature of Kleist
to one of the walls – this was their sole decoration. He piled
his books up in the nook beside the chimney breast, and
spent his days – when not in the library – dealing hash and
watching whatever was on a four-inch black-and-white TV
he'd bought for fifteen quid in a junk shop. That particular
lunchtime, he and Jeremy were watching Land of the Phar-
aohs when *the drugs began to take hold* . . .

A blotter printed with the three names of God in Hebrew, Arabic and Aramaic: *Tetragrammaton, man* . . . said
Tim, who'd sold Will a sheet, along with his weekly quarter-
weight of Leb', which came wrapped in the canvas it'd been
sewn into in the Beqaa Valley.

Will hadn't felt like correcting him – simply stashed the
blotters and the dope away, then trick-cycled back from
Eynsham: a high-wire act, indeed, given he'd be straight
behind bars if he was nicked again.

It might've been enough to make anyone paranoid – but

then it's impossible to be that scared when you're watching James Robertson Justice, tablecloth wound round his prominent gut, pretending to be an ancient Hebrew architect. They were convulsed with laughter – and Will, who's preoccupation with them is self-evident – probably quoted Lévi-Strauss's aperçu: *alterations in scale always sacrifice the sensible in favour of the intelligible* . . .

Quite possibly, it'd been at that exact moment Caius entered the room, fresh from Heathrow and another New York jaunt, the heroin and cocaine rapidly leeching from his system, and intent on oblivion. Caius, despite its being *the merry month of fucking May*, had still been wearing his full-skirted 'crombie and high-waisted corduroys – and, although Will found his friend's fashion sense to be *a standing fucking joke*, it hardly mattered once he'd slumped down on Will's mattress and snatched up Will's weird water pipe.

Which was a Blue Peterish object, fashioned from lengths of plastic tubing, a cork, a thimble, and an old catering jar that once held mayonnaise *waste not, want not* . . . into which Will had poured first tap water, then a platoon of toy plastic US Marines, complete with their landing craft. Drawing deeply on this sensibility-sacrificing instrument, Caius's bright blue eyes began sparking with entelechy – greenish smoke piddling from his pale lips, he'd first pronounced their sin: 'You two're tripping, aren't you?' Then his anathema: 'You see that knife?'

Will and Jeremy had indeed seen that knife – how could they not? It was the large, isosceles-bladed and wooden-handled one Will used to carve the hash up into retail quantities – and it'd been lying on the plastic chopping board Caius suddenly lunged towards. Snatching the knife up, he swished it about, slicing ribbons of smoke . . . *into threads.*

'You're tripping, aren't you?' he'd reiterated – as the moon eclipsed the sun, the room darkened and started *to stink of ozone* . . . 'Fine, trip if you fucking want to – but I shan't, in my current condition, be joining you. And understand this,' he'd continued, 'at some point in the next hour or so, while you two are actually peaking, I'm going to stab one of you to death with this knife. Thing is, you won't know which of you it's going to be . . . until it happens.'

With that – *that!* he'd lain back against the mattresses and taken a huge lug on the hubble-bubble, *so confounding the Tonkin Resolution* . . . Will looked at Jeremy – and Jeremy parried his *light sabres* . . . with more radiophonic effects, *more ozone* . . .

The tiny, bewigged fabulist of the real looked down on it all from a great way away: had Caius really just said that he was going to murder one or other of them? *HAD HE?* More to the point, has the Chairman of the viva panel really just asked that question? *HAS HE?* The one about *Montesquieu* . . .

influence . . . the nineteenth century and French liberalism that hangs, sparkling, in the limpid air between Will and them.

There are certain things – and they entail . . . certain other things . . . nineteenth-century liberalism being very much one of them – although now Will tries focusing, the concept blurs then disintegrates into *yellow journalism . . . Constant . . . Thiers . . . people frantically j'accusing one another, and history being doomed to repeat itself, farcically, again annagain . . .*

As for Montesquieu, he shape-shifts through the decades, his fleshy features bi- then tri-sected, appearing in the form of assemblies, quasi-dictatorships, demagogueries and absolutisms . . . *fucker must've been cranking pure meth' . . .*

Was it for sixty minutes or six thousand years that Will and Jeremy had been transfixed by Caius's death threat? Whichever the span, it encompassed dynasties of dreams — collective reveries during which entire civilisations rose and fell, including the one ruled over by Jack Hawkins, in a pharaonic headdress, who'd been intrigued against by Joan Collins, in anachronistic harem pants, even as James Robertson Justice doggedly continued to build his monumental tomb – one measuring a half-inch on Will's wincy television screen.

Will and Jeremy were interred in this massively compressed moment, together with their pathetic funerary goods: empty fag packets, wadded pages from exercise books, empty Feminax blister-packs, very small change, a half-inch of cold tea in a stained mug. Caius had lorded it over them, wearing his *jackal's head* . . . and although at some point he'd disappeared as abruptly as he'd manifested to begin with, Will knows his heart remains . . . *on his fucking scales* . . .

Maybe a week or so later the phone exploded late at night in the vestibule outside Will's room, and when he reached it, the voice of Caius's friend Johnny crackled out of echoic pay-phone space: 'Caius . . . Chelsea Hospital . . . Overdose . . .'

Arriving in London the following day, broke, Will cut from Victoria through wedding-cake terraces to Caius's opulent pied-à-terre, where there'd been an atmosphere of near-death déshabillé.

The flat's main room was painted blue and furnished with large, square-backed chairs and a sofa, upholstered in a lighter-blue fabric. An oval mirror hung above a marble mantelpiece lined with engraved invitations – in this, while he rolled a fag, Will watched the jolly toss of the trees in the private square outside. He'd been buzzed in downstairs, and the flat's door was ajar, but there was no human presence save for the smell of sex — and something *still more sexual* . . .

A pretty girl – although not Caius's impossibly soignée girlfriend, Ann – had come, blinking, furtive, from the maroon recesses of what Will assumed was the bedroom. Apologising, she adjusted last night's cocktail dress. Pretty, louche and well-mannered – Will's heart was full: but, true to her class, having made her superfluous sorries she'd left.

A few minutes later, Caius emerged – and then Johnny. The former had been dry and desiccated – the latter sweaty and nervy. Parachuted into the aftermath, Will for a moment glimpsed them with adult objectivity, so was appalled by these dissolute children, who, having gambled with their lives, now gaily related Caius's kiss-me-Hardyisms – how he'd cried, 'Careful with this jacket, it's fucking Savile Row!' as the boorish ambulancemen manhandled him back to life.

At least they'd had a little gear left.

It was the first smack Will had taken with Caius – and he felt bad about it. Up until that moment, he'd felt he was, if not exactly a positively good influence in his friend's life, at least a less profoundly awful one than Caius's parents, who, by his own account, were useless and frigid figures – his mother, the heiress, having exchanged dipsomania for religio-mania, was in competition with her son to see who could fritter more efficiently: her with her dippy charitable projects, or he with his profoundly selfish ones.

As for Caius's much older father, he seemed in awe of this ancient, absent figure, who had had three careers. First, a dissolute tea planter in Kenya's Happy Valley, then a spook in wartime London, and finally a Liberal Member of Parliament – Caius muttered that he'd been *very liberal* . . . But that was in the late-fucking-fifties! – Since then, the old libertine had resigned his seat and undertaken conservatoire training.

According to the son of his dotage, the old man was now as proficient as any concert violinist – but played only for an audience of one: himself, in a shuttered and airless room, in a dusty white box of a villa, in a gated estate, somewhere on the Riviera.

Yes, Caius's parents had left him, dangling, and now the poor fellow was trying to belay across the rock face of the English class system. No wonder he's in permanent crisis – one Will admires, because Caius seems as fractured as the 'schizophrenic' Warneford outpatients who followed in Siobhan's slipstream. He's a bird man, like Edmond, *like me* . . . who'd flown too high on his blood-splattered linen wings.

Caius's money comes from a vast American dry-cleaning fortune – which explains how very personally he took it when the one in Carfax sent the constabulary round to question him, after Caius had despatched them a dozen shirts covered with blood stains. Will could've told them: Caius was no murderer, only a potential suicide *with malice aforethought* . . .

Caius had worn a wax death mask as he concocted the fix: 'There isn't enough,' he said, 'unless we share the works.'

His mother's hypochondriacal son, Will was usually careful about disinfecting works – and fanatically so if they were to be shared. But he'd been flattered as Caius passed him the hypodermic, filled with a solution of water, heroin and *his own blue blood* . . . Handed it to Will rather than Johnny, first, with the intimate gloss, *It sucked me first, and now sucks thee. And in this works our two bloods mingled be* . . .

. . . *O, Grandma, why do you have such heavy and raw-boned fists?*

Why, all the better to clout you with!

And clout him she'd had to, because one nothingy afternoon, when he got back with the shopping from Willesden Lane, Will used one of Genie's sterile sets of works to scrupulously administer an overdose. To himself.

Willy's walk might've ended right there, and for good. Instead, he'd come to, soaked to his spotty skin, with Genie astride him, punching him in the face – first with her right hand, then with her left.

The blows had been so very regular – metronomically so – that at the very moment of regaining consciousness, Will realised this was going to happen again *annagain* . . . He heard her screaming, *You fucking idiot!* as his eye plopped from its socket to roll across the bare boards – coming to rest where one of the kittens was dabbing with its paw at the blood-engorged hypodermic that'd fallen from his arm.

You fucking idiot! is Will's own version of Honi soit qui mal y pense. It should, he thinks, be written across the lintel of every door *the lanky cunt* stoops to enter – lest he forget, as he does so much else. Why did he draw the dumb cartoons on his finals papers? Possibly because he too is a cartoon – if by this is meant a series of lines scored on the blank expanse of the hungover day, which, looked at together, are laughable, if not exactly amusing.

At long last Will croaks, 'I'm afraid I haven't actually read anything by Montesquieu, so I'm not able to give a very author –'

'Thank you,' the Chairman smiles – the tight little smile of someone who's proved their point, 'that will be all.'

ALL. A universal rather than an existential quantifier: *That's ALL she wrote* – she being not the cat's mother, but the fat lady who sang out Will's degree result a week later – screamed it for ALL to hear *FOREVER*: a third! A miserable fucking third. It ought, Will feels, to be some compensation that Caius has only scraped a pass degree, so this punctilious snob will – in the intellectual arena at least – have to endure the rest of his life with no honours at all. But it isn't.

Will carries his third on his forehead – the mark of *that thicko, Cain*. It would be easier to bear, he thinks, if he hadn't been so very diligent, completing every essay he'd been assigned – albeit his one on Spinoza's Ethica was a single long sentence, spiralling out to fill an extra-large sheet of paper, thereby expressing the simultaneously labyrinthine and indivisible character of the great monist's thought.

Will had sat there, turning the sheet round and around as he read the essay aloud to his tutor, who'd remained predictably . . . *wry*, although Will must've looked like a codeine-addled fool, who, having snarfed an entire sheet of period pills, was trying to operate some heavy machinery *that simply wasn't there . . .*

. . . *or here* on a plastic stacking chair, next to Sara, who occupies one the same — whereas Caius, buoyed up by his *inexhaustible-fucking-trust fund*, has embarked for the South of France, on the first leg of his luxury cruise through life. They took the coach to Abergavenny, then yesterday evening a local bus on to Carmarthen.

They're now sitting in the room allotted to defendants, awaiting their fate. The duty solicitor they spoke to when they were arrested isn't available – instead, his colleague popped in a couple of minutes ago to tell them: 'It's pretty straightforward, really – the only question is what the arresting officer'll say – in cases like this the magistrates tend to take their lead from him.'

Pop in. What a revolting expression: *I've just popped in . . . Pop that in your mouth . . . I'll pop the cork . . . Pop-goes-the-fucking-weasel . . .* Will sits staring at the posters pinned to the scuzzy wall: WATCH OUT, THERE'S A THIEF ABOUT! Which seems a little unjust – true, he may be a drug user, but he's never stolen money to buy drugs – only dealt them so's to get *a little personal* . . .

Detective Inspector Budge materialises on the far side of the Formica-topped table, as if he's been hatched from its cracked-eggshell surface. There's been no sound of door opening, or heavy plod – yet here he is: *thrust onstage*, although this time with a script in his hand.

Budgie gives Sara the once-over: she's wearing a brown monstrosity of a suit, borrowed from her Marks-and-Spencer mother – and a cream-coloured blouse with a pie-crust collar. Next he scans Will, who's suited, booted, shaved and sober. Budgie nods, smiling and flicking back his collar-length hair as he rustles through his paperwork.

'All right, Sara? Will?'

'Good morning, Detective Inspector,' Will replies, without a scintilla of facetiousness, for, *waste not, want not* . . . Waste not the accident of your birth – which has bestowed upon you good manners, even a certain charm – and you'll want not for.

'Budgie, please – I told you that already . . .' He smiles, an abrupt fissuring of his honest, ruddy face. 'This' – he flourishes one of his pages – 'is a written statement I've done for the court, see, and it doesn't say anything you don't know already – fag?'

He's retrieved a box of Benson & Hedges from the lower depths of his leather car coat. Will accepts – Sara declines. Joined in fire and smoke, they might be conspirators – Budgie says, 'I've only repeated what we agreed to together back in April, yeah? That the drugs Will was in possession of – and those you asked Billy to get for you in Coventry – were entirely for his own personal use, while you, Sara, cooperated fully with me and my officers.'

Budgie sits back heavily in his plastic stacking chair, takes a drag on his fag, then, rocking slightly, exhales. 'The important thing for you is that I'm not giving evidence in person – I only stopped by to drop this off. Tells the magistrates I don't consider the case to be of any real significance, that I'm not seeking any kind of exemplary sentence . . . Anyway, should count in your favour.'

Will says, 'Thank you, Inspector, we really appreciate it.'

While Sara, who's been fairly taciturn for the past twenty-four hours, softly concurs: 'Thank you, Inspector.'

'Budgie!' Budgie guffaws. 'No need for that Inspector malarkey with me, couple of young scholars like you – give it a few years . . . put this sort of nonsense well behind you, and it'll be me calling you Doctor, or Professor, or . . . whatever.'

He rises, so do Will and Sara, who half bow as they shake his hand. Then Budgie's gone – *fluttered from our lives* . . . leaving Will to consider the differences between this chirpy Welsh bird and the oily corvids of the viva panel.

Yes, Budgie's flown – and he's left *our cage door open* . . . outside, in the body of the courtroom, there's shuffling . . . rustling, *plaintiff calls*: 'You bloody well ought to, boyo . . .' 'Seen her come down on Ioan like that . . .' 'I can't pay that . . .'

The courtroom is housed in the Town Hall – a four-square building, the neoclassical façade of which boasts columns, and exaggerated fanlights that radiate *conformist nonconformity* . . .

Peering out into the high-ceilinged space, so brightly illuminated he can see the cobwebs smearing the plaster mouldings, Will thinks of Renaissance depictions of the ancient world: naked babies sporting at the sandalled feet of Ciceronians, cattle feeding from wall-mounted mangers . . . *empty horns of plenty . . . their grapes rolling away . . .*

Will thinks of last night – and the sex he and Sara had, much as they'd also had biriyanis in a small and smelly Indian restaurant close to their bed and breakfast. Will remembers flock wallpaper – and the dense pile of her pubic hair. It'd been another guilty entanglement – his ejaculation, given he was mildly junk-sick, as unpleasant and unexpected as a hangnail caught in a Terylene sheet. Hers? *Nowhere to be found.*

A small, harassed-looking man, his pale-blue tie loosened, and wearing thick-lensed glasses, sticks his head in the door: 'Fulton, Sara Jane, and Self, William Woodard?'

They nod and grunt.

'You're up now,' he says, swinging it wide open.

The bird, Will thinks, perches on the windowsill looking at the fresh-fallen snow – snow that makes the oblong garden smooth and white as a sheet of paper. The bird has the face of a destitute Polish film animator and bedraggled black clothes-for-wings. It'll hop down off the windowsill, Will muses, then hop away across the snow, making deep cuneiform prints telling its own picaresque – how it tried for a worm, here, how it stopped and cocked its head to listen, there.

Once the bird hops down, the die is cast – there's no way back, and, no matter how crazily circuitous its route, the deep, dark finality of those prints will make this seem quite inevitable.

Does the bird decide for himself which way to go? Does he – in a word – will it? Or is it either flighty chance or weighty fate that ruffles his feathers?

Perhaps the Great White Spirit will intervene – he sits there, in the void of the fifth dimension, days and nights flickering by – sits there, a whippet-thin joint pinched between the fingers of one hand, while from the other extend taut wires, one of which is tied in a noose around the poor bird's soft and vulnerable neck.

4

April 1984

'. . . And at the sixth hour darkness was coming over the whole land entirely . . .' The voice worms its way into his consciousness. '. . . and this was continuing right up until the ninth hour . . .' Summoning him to ungum this dully geometric vision: the black shadows cast by a Venetian blind ruling a white-tiled floor. 'Because it was then that Jesus cried out in a loud voice . . .' He'd arrived at this place in daylight – that much he recalls – and fallen across this narrow, iron-framed cot in a swoon. There's a loud click, a squawk of feedback, a hiss then: 'El-oi! El-oi! La-ma sa-bach-thani!' The weird words, amplified by some sort of public-address system, force him up towards the bright, salt-smacked surface of consciousness. 'Which has the meaning . . .' The first voice – female, unamplified – resumes, '. . . or so they say, of God, my God, why have you forsaken me –'

'No, no, no!' A third voice – male, angry – breaks in: 'No! That is not it at all, Rohan – that is not it at all. These are the final words our saviour was saying in his earthly existence – no, actually! Not even that – these are the final words he was shouting out, beseeching his father who is God in the most high. Give it some of the oomphing, man.'

'Oomphing?'

'Passion, man – passion!'

There's another click-squawk-hiss then, 'El-oi! El-oi! La-maaa saa-baach-THAAANI!'

Dreams, Will thinks, are narratives we assemble retrospectively, at the moment of waking, in order to account for the recollections of the previous day, unspooled in the fluid, greenish suspension of the unconscious. But educated Indian voices pedantically hot-gospelling? These he cannot remember at all – they'd played no part, surely, in his yesterday?

India, however, definitely had – and it's continuing to do so now.

Will's arms and legs lie, leaden, in a pool of cooling sweat. A motionless ceiling fan hangs overhead, and, turning his head on the soggy pillow, he sees a small wooden table and a metal-and-canvas chair.

That's all.

'Okay . . . okay, that's better, Rohan – now, script, please.'

'But you said these were my final words?'

'Final plea – final plea! Damn it all, man – look at the script.'

'Oh . . . yes. Okay . . . I am thirsty.'

'Again, please – and louder.'

A click, a squawk, a hiss – and: 'I am thirsty!'

Will's thirsty too – his throat grates as he swallows

involuntarily. He pulls his hand from beneath the damp sheet and sends this numb probe in search of a plastic water bottle he has a distinct memory of – his only one just now. Poppy-old inconsequences wheedle through his hurting head . . . *Church full of singing, out of tune . . . Everyone's gone to the* –

'Okay, that is much better, Rohan. Now, we don't have the centurions here just now, so I'll do the next action, which is this passing of a gourd full of water up to you.'

'And will it?'

'Will it what, exactly?'

'Will there be a gourd of water, man?'

'Yes, yes, of course. Why is it you're always doubting me, Rohan – we will be having proper props, costumes and everything like that – loin cloth, crown of thorns, the whole bang-shoot. Now, please . . .'

'I am thirsty!'

'No, no – not that, the very last line, the one down the bottom of the page.'

There's a pause during which Will feels the last dreamy images and sensations draining from his mind . . . *a swirl of blood round a plug hole* . . . then Rohan screams the line through a hurricane of feedback: 'IT IS FINISHED!'

He may not know where or when he is, but this is a tocsin that fully awakens Will to this reality, which is *pain* . . . the pain of a sentient skeleton that's been assembled from mismatched bones: balls rammed into sockets and ribs forced into cages, which is why *everything fucking hurts* . . .

Especially when he moves – and Will is moving . . . *has moved!* And now stands by the blinds, perfectly aware he's a fifty-fifty chance of pulling the right cord – as he yanks the wrong one, so revelating this: a dusty concrete courtyard about which are strewn the usual inconsequences – a green plastic water butt, some cardboard boxes and an old metal sign with Sanskrit lettering unfurling across it.

There's a five-storey building surrounding the courtyard, its serried windows either striped or shuttered by their own Venetian blinds, below which are tiny balconies fronted by bright, pastel-coloured panels.

On one of these balconies – more or less opposite him, on the fourth storey – a large wooden cross has been erected, to which a young man in a pale-blue shirt and jeans has been lightly lashed with a length of clothesline . . . *Rohan?* While another young man – thicker set, with a chin-strap beard – is standing on the adjoining balcony, together with a short girl wearing a white dress and a stormy expression.

The bearded young man reads from a play script attached to a clipboard: 'Surely, he was the son of God.' His delivery toneless, as if recording a formality for bureaucratic purposes.

The casual Christ replies, 'I'm telling you, Amit, this is no way to say this line – you are being converted in this very moment from heathen mind to God-consciousness. Put some conviction into it – really, man.'

'Oh, for goodness' sake, Rohan!' Amit, who sports the regulation black-framed glasses and pocket protector of the Indian knowledge-worker, smacks thc balustrade with his clipboard. 'I am not playing the centurion! The centurion cannot be here – which is why I'm giving . . . giving . . . Why it is I'm to you giving . . . giving –'

'A cue,' the lowering girl interjects. 'It is called a cue, man – that's what you're giving to him.'

A cue – that's right. Will shivers – which is the wrong one, since he knows what this betokens: the beginning of a dreadful performance, during which he'll wind up into a foetal ball, shakily uncoil, wind up again . . . *annagain for fucking days*.

Weird how cold the subcontinent's been – cold in Nepal, where he'd had to supplement his skimpy cotton clothing with yards of indigo scarves. And cold in Srinagar, where Will had arrived three weeks earlier, and wandered through the muddy streets, crunching iced puddles. Men had been roosting on the warped boardwalks, eyes watery with the smoke from the earthenware charcoal burners tucked beneath their brown burnouses.

It was also cold when Will awoke earlier today – roused on clammy vinyl, in the air-conditioned and aseptic second-class compartment he'd treated himself to after the fiasco in Chandigarh.

Roused by this: 'Ah! You're awake – for which I am glad. I have been observing you this past hour, approximately, and I deduce from the condition of your clothing and your luggage and so forth, that you have been travelling in our country for some time now – weeks, possibly months. While from your reading matter – which I took the liberty of retrieving from the floor, where it must have fallen during the night – I can tell that you are a sincere student of our customs, culture and so forth . . .'

The thin man's ascetic mien was further caricatured by glasses with thick, black frames – while he too sported a pocket protector, although his shirt had been long-sleeved, freshly pressed and very white.

He'd been all angles – the man on the train – elbows, knees and gesticulating fingers that belied his fluency: '. . . and I am wondering if I may make a small request? Which is to ask you for your impressions of our country, whether general, or gathered under various headings – to wit: politics and society, religion and cultural traditions, the treatment of animals – both working and domestic, not forgetting temple ones, such as cattle, monkeys and so forth, which I believe particularly exercises our visitors from the West . . .'

The man ticked these categories off with his nervy fingers while he spoke – his strong Indian accent, together with his pedantry, making each phrase sound as if it were being simultaneously enunciated *and choked back down* . . . He must've entered the frigid compartment sometime during the night – a small mystery to set against this great prosaicism: he'd immediately worn out his welcome.

Struggling upright on the slippy seat, Will had croaked, 'I . . . I've just come from Kashmir.' And left it at that, choking back a speech that now *repeats on me* . . .

. . . I've just come from Kashmir, and I'm as sick as a rabid dog rootling in the garbage heaps of Srinagar . . . Smack's only two bucks a gramme up there – and I've had a fucking skinful . . . Virtually pure too . . . I tellya, mate, I thought I was gonna fucking die . . .

True enough – but then Will had also thought he was going to die when he arrived in Srinagar, and the wind from the Himalayas simultaneously slapped him in his spotty face, while gripping his balls through the thin cotton of his jeans. Death was also uppermost in Will's mind, as, in Varanasi, he'd watched the bodies, waiting at the burning ghats for their fiery consumation.

And before that, as well, in his room at the Star Hotel, on the shores of Lake Phewa, after being sent to bed, Death had lain beside Will as he'd listened to the mosquitos come whining in to feed – to this, and to the soft blows of his decelerating heart as they'd *beaten the retreat* . . . Indeed, *back-and-back* . . . as he ranges over the weeks he's been travelling in India, it occurs to Will that Death – and the fear of death – have been his constant companions.

With him from the very beginning, as, mindful of his budget, Will haled a tuk-tuk outside the arrivals hall of Delhi Airport, then folded himself inside.

Head bowed, canted awkwardly – and feeling the sharp angles of his Commonwealth Bank of Australia passbook digging into his meagre rump, he'd jolted along the dusty road into town. The tuk-tuk's two-stroke engine pounding all this in through his wide eyes: tens, hundreds, thousands – lakhs, seemingly – of dusty, whey-faced men and women, who clustered in gutters and beside culverts.

Down had come cradle and baby, and all the mucked-up macramé of power lines, through which Will saw a toxic-yellow sky full of vultures, hanging by their tattered wings. What was the gospel according to Brother Bill? That a vulture in a London sky would be a sort of cosmic solecism? London – which he'd cordially despised when he'd lived there, saying of the city *it drags on me like a sea anchor* . . . Something his disciple understood, while not altogether knowing what this might be – because he'd also had to escape the cold and greenly heaving city, lest he go under.

On the flight out to Sydney, last August, there'd been a re-fuelling stop in Bombay. In the terminal, in a stall in the gents', Will unfolded the wrap, tapped the last beige granules out on to the toilet seat, then hoovered the smack up through a rolled-up pound note. *A windy nag* . . . he'd been, knock-kneed, ribs ridging his mangy hide – like the ones leaning in the shafts of the gharries the tuk-tuk had buzzed by, skittering over potholes, slithering through cowpats.

But the Will who'd arrived back on Indian soil after a six-month sojourn in Australia was a different proposition altogether: his complexion clear, his hair neat, his clothes clean – and his blood yet cleaner. At least, that's what he'd assured Caius, via airmail.

His friend had remained caught up in his own narrowing gyre: flitting between London and Manhattan, shooting up speedballs, puking up cordon bleu cooking, trashing hotel rooms, and gouching out in cabs, only to awaken on the hard verge of the Van Wyck Expressway, hours or days later, his 'crombie pockets turned inside out, his wallet and passport gone.

India hardly seemed a suitable destination for a trust-fund junky with a hazy – but, for all that, desperate – desire to get clean. Which was where Will came in: Will had been clean for months already, and understood the lie of this strange and sterile new land. Will-the-snivelling-smack-head had been laid to rest out in the wilds of the Australian desert – while, phoenix-like, a new Will has arisen. It's this one who arranged the rendezvous with Caius in New Delhi, promising his friend they would travel to see miraculous sights – and discover new insights into their miserable dependency from the wise and ancient sadhus who sit, cross-legged, at the source of the Ganges.

Yes, that'd been the plan – one formulated in the pale-blue aerogrammes that had flapped between them.

Standing now, forehead pressed against the windowpane, listening to the passionate players' voices echoing round the courtyard, Will can't prevent this slogan ticker-taping behind his eyes: TIMMS' EXCELSIOR FOR SUPERIOR SMILLING . . .

He'd seen the toothpaste advert stuck to a rotunda, around which swirled tuk-tuks, Ambassador saloons, oxen and myriad multi-occupied motorbikes. It featured white smiles in brown faces, together with this: TIMMS' EXCELSIOR FOR SUPERIOR SMILLING . . . a Cheshire cat's grin of a slogan that's stayed with him throughout the intervening month – and may well remain after all his other memories of India have gone. *Smilling . . . yes!* Because smilling is what Will does in the face of his friend's anger and snobbery: smilling being misspelled – and therefore insincere – smiling.

Staring hard at the fat back of the tuk-tuk driver's neck, Will felt the flies settle on his lips and eyes – then creep up his nose, dragging exotic diseases behind them. The truth was, all these months, Will had nursed two incompatible desires: to be with Caius, and to be back on smack. His cleanliness really was only skin deep, and he could hear his hunger for drugged dissolution ... *the banshee*, howling around inside of him. But he knew this much: it was too late for Will and Caius to be carefree drug-addled buddies, en route to find the Indian Dream – whatever that might be.

No, there's nobody who's carefree any more: Caius's friend Johnny is attending these na-na meetings now, and preaching a weird credo of complete abstinence from all – all! – drugs. Last year, before he'd set off for Australia, Will had gone along with Caius to one at a community centre in Chelsea. He'd then spectacularly undermined Johnny's evangelism by chopping out lines of skag in the gents'. Three of them – and Johnny hadn't needed any further encouragement to . . . *shit all over his fucking clean time.*

Rattling towards the Oberoi Palace Hotel, where he'd arranged to meet Caius, Will had also been preoccupied by another slogan – the one scrawled across the final flap of the last aerogramme his friend had sent: *I MUST GET CLEAN. THIS TRIP TO INDIA IS ALL ABOUT GETTING CLEAN . . .*

Then the driver – who, judging by his full beard and dingy turban, was a Sikh – had reached up and pulled down the poxy little sunshade, releasing a plastic bag full of white and lumpy powder, which he'd deftly caught then immediately tossed straight over his shoulder.

It'd fallen right in Will's lap – and, after examining it with wide eyes, he'd asked, 'Is this . . . heroin?'

To which the Sikh replied – at once brazen and disengaged – 'You want?'

In the weeks that'd followed, Will heard this indifference whenever he scored drugs off the natives: because the Indians don't really give a shit about this stuff, only the profits to be gained by selling it to stupid Westerners. But, on that first occasion, he'd just sat there, goggling at this mother lode – perhaps as much as half an ounce of smack.

It'd been this he'd yearned for *tragically* . . . six months earlier, the very instant the last particles pinged into his mucous membranes, and he faced a smack-free future on the far side of the world.

Will's eyes had begun watering over the South China Sea – and he was nauseous by the time they touched down in Sydney. He'd pay for it later, he knew – but still the condemned man ate a hearty lunch of steak au poivre, washed down with most of a bottle of tannin-heavy Australian red.

Ate it – and sweated as hard rays struck at him through the tinted glass, while jets taxied in the orangey mid-distance.

Yes, it'd been hot enough in Sydney – but when the prop plane clattered to a halt on the runway at Canberra Airport, its windows snaked with raindrops, the never-ending autumn of heroin withdrawal had swept into Will's body, bringing its own cold downpour . . . *of pain.*

Sanskrit looks like a fringe . . . or a border of some . . . sort . . . Will's eyes, sunk deep in their sandy pockets, grate upwards to meet those of the stormy-browed girl on the balcony opposite.

'You are almost at the exact point of humiliating me, Samreen,' says Amit, his fussy hands on his wide hips. 'We must be making it perfectly clear, here, who is doing the directing, and who the props, the stage managing, etcetera.'

Samreen says nothing – only stands beside him, her fists on her slimmer hips, while Will smiles sympathetically in her direction. Her eyebrows also form *a fringe . . . or a border of some . . . sort . . .* but they're just as illegible to him. The fringed canopy of the fat Sikh's tuk-tuk had jiggled *jollily . . .* while the plastic sword stuck to its dashboard *swiped at the flies . . .* as he pulled off the airport road and into a muddy and mud-walled compound.

And now, feet slapping the tiled floor, Will hies him to the bathroom, while thinking *feet slapping the tiled floor, Will hies him to the bathroom . . .* Where, squatting down on the two corrugated foot-plates, he smells again the dung and woodsmoke – sees once more the bitch lying in the mud with the puppies *sucking greedily at her teats . . . Yes,* he remembers that compound in some detail, because up until then he'd wondered if he and Caius would ever meet: their rendezvous having been so long in the making.

As he'd motorcycled south, from Darwin to Canberra, then flown from there to Sydney, and on to New Delhi, Will felt as if he were halving the distance between them, then halving it again *annagain* . . .

But once the tuk-tuk slewed to a halt, so this interminable division had ceased.

Soon after, junk time was reinstituted.

And at that time, Will managed to convince himself he was acting responsibly – humanely, even. He'd hefted the big bag of smack, wondering if he'd enough cash to *buy the fucking lot!* – then passed it back, saying, 'No . . . no, thanks – but can you get me some opium?'

The Sikh left Will in the tuk-tuk, under the indifferent gaze of poor women, whose noses had been expensively chained to their earlobes – and when he'd returned, it was with a lump of sticky black goo, wrapped in cellophane.

Caroming on towards town, Will had rehearsed what he was going to say to Caius . . . *just a little bit . . . hardly as bad as actual smack . . . just a taste – been a long time . . .* while only too aware of Brother Bill's tart dictum: *It doesn't matter if you smoke it, shoot it up or shove it up your ass . . . the results are the same.*

Yes . . . the result is addiction, which in turn results in . . . *withdrawal* – that colossal ebbing away of all the vital fluids:

Will's eyes swim – his nose drips, while every breath, no matter how shallow, *bubbles* . . . as his insides *liquefy* . . . All prevarication is purged from his mind, to be replaced by a single pressing dilemma: *Will I shit first . . . or vomit?*

At least he's in the right place: Will slumps sideways, so his head lolls over the shower surround, while his tail remains aligned with the lavatorial hole . . . *never, ever 'toilet' – not even in extremis* . . .

'Well, then – that's that . . . then!' Rohan's petulance crackles through the public address system, provoking:

'For heaven's sake, man – why're you undoing your own bindings, we are by no means finished here, you know?'

Will can only picture the angry Saviour-substitute, shirt-sleeved and unbound – but he hears him perfectly: 'If you cannot manage this simple business of the centurion's action, how will you be able to . . . to' – and hears pages shuffling – 'play the part of Nicodemus, who has to wrap my body in these linen bandages – and not just any old bandages, it says here these ones are all smeared with myrrh and bloody aloes, man!'

Will's body isn't wrapped in linen bandages smeared with myrrh and aloes – rather, it's blotchy with Band-Aids, which were smeared with antiseptic cream before being applied, some thirty-six hours ago, on the Houseboat Ceylon.

It was a poxy act of prophylaxis – and Will can sense

every little nick and abrasion on his scaly hide *fizzing with purulence* . . .

'We are simply organising all of these movements today, Rohan – so you must be patient. The final results will be very dramatic, you see . . .' Will sees only the rubber mat that might stop him slipping, *if I could only stand up* . . . but he hears: 'You will expire on that balcony, see, and disappear altogether . . . Only to reappear over there, on that balcony – which is where the fellow playing Nicodemus will be waiting with the bandages to do the embalming business.'

There's no privacy for a traveller in the populous cities and towns of northern India – unless it's paid for. Even then, the Indians seek you out – their faces impassive despite their vigorous entreaties. *Where does it all end?* Embalmed in bandages smeared with myrrh and aloes, or, wrapped in an old length of sari material, its tattered fringe barely covering your putrid features – like the corpses at the Manikarnika Ghat.

He'd drawn deep on the soapstone chillum, while the untouchables chanted Ram naam satya hai . . . Ram naam satya hai . . . then, handing it back to the sadhu with the Ginsberg beard, he'd adjusted his lunghi and waddled down into the water.

Will convulses, and yesterday's dhal rises up into the back of his throat . . . *eternal recurrence, indeed* . . . He feels the cool tiles beneath him . . . *far more culturally appropriate than a sandalwood pyre* . . . and longs for a recent past within which he was clean, healthy . . . *and completely isolated.*

For click-after-click-after-click his gaze had been fixated on the *tattered fringe* of the road's metalled surface. Every hundred or so that surface disappeared altogether, and the bike began shuddering over the muddy corrugations baked rock-hard by the desert heat.

The vast Gulf & Western skies, with their geometric patternings of lenticular clouds, were separated from the ruddy earth by horizons at once definitive – and weirdly arbitrary. For here was *too much of nothing* . . . for it to be apportioned to this earth or that firmament.

About a hundred clicks out of Three Ways, Will became aware of another vacuity at his back – and, twisting awkwardly on the bike, saw that his petrol can, which he'd strapped on to the rack, together with a pinstripe suit jacket he'd bought in an Oxfam shop on the other side of the world, had gone.

Backtracking for fifteen minutes, he'd found the can, ruptured and empty. The jacket was fine.

After that, Will had nursed the bike on, crouched low over the handlebars to cut wind resistance. There was only one roadhouse between there and Camooweal, over the border in Queensland – if he ran out of petrol, he'd be reliant on other drivers, and there weren't many of them. Anyway, it was madness trying to flag down one of the road trains, which could have as many as four semi-trailers coupled behind its house-sized cab – high up in which sat some Ocker trucker, in sweaty stubbies and a wife-beater, higher still on amphetamine, as he *miled away the whiles* . . .

Vance and the other doomsayers back in Darwin had warned Will: when he saw a road train approaching he should slow right down – so as not to shred his tyres as he pulled off the metalled road – then get as far as possible away from the track: 'I tellya, mate, there's ten, twenty sets of double-bogeys on those fuckers . . . Come down hard on a rock and it'll shoot out sideways faster than a rifle bullet . . . Happens all the time – and they find bikers like you stone dead, with a hole clean through their helmet . . . and their fuckin' skull . . .'

Will took this saltiness with a further pinch: if he'd learned one thing during his time in Australia, it was that its white inhabitants mostly feared their own homeland – feared its great gravelly expanses, its wave-battered beaches and its minatory hanging rocks. Feared the great vacuity their forerunners had created when they and their diseases wiped out the Aboriginals, so erasing also their knowledge of every dry wash, salt lake and thorny scrub.

The whites crouched on their patios, behind their bungalows, barbecuing beef – they huddled close to the heat, because out back it's cold: the absolute zero of infinite space. White Australia was cold cul-de-sacs and frigid ovals – chilly boulevards running for click-upon-click along frosty bluffs battered by brilliant white and horribly cold surf.

The white Australians might advertise their country as baked and golden – but the truth was they shivered as they pulled up their knee-socks so as to conceal the warty excrescences of their melanomas: they shivered – feeling this *terrible frigidity* at their backs.

Lying in Room 421 of the New Delhi YMCA hostel, with his cheek against the shower surround, and his buttocks against the squat toilet, Will's gripped by an ague, so begins to *sh–sh–shake out the sh–sh–shits . . .*

The roadhouse had finally appeared plunked down by the turn-off for the Tablelands: a shack with a fly-screened veranda and a couple of petrol pumps. Will hung panting over the Super Dream's handlebars, while a doughy, freckle-faced girl made heavy weather of letting the screen door spring shut behind her – then she flung one leg in front of the other until she stood before him, unwrapping a Violet Crumble.

'You're fat,' the girl had said – a statement so surreal Will was struck dumb, so he simply sat there goggling at her, as she demolished the frozen chocolate bar with two savage bites.

Then he'd dismounted – and she filled the tank. Will paid her with a twenty-dollar bill – and she made change, groping in the marsupial pouch slung beneath her dropsical belly.

Then Will went on ... *and on.* Ahead was the longest stretch of his journey without any human habitation: three hundred clicks – while dusk was only a couple of hours off. Will had his swag, though, and a firm resolve to sleep out in the bush. He'd been sleeping under the stars since he left Darwin, but was within shouting distance of others – whereas this would be *Le Buisson profond*, one might almost say.

Indeed, would say, if one had been spending a considerable portion of one's time standing at the bar of the Hotel Darwin, knocking back schooners of Victoria Bitter while pouring over À la recherche du temps perdu.

Will had his swag – and ten litres of water in the *hairy bollock* of a hessian bag. He had cheese, crackers and apples for a frugal supper, to be washed down with fiery draughts of Bundaberg rum – after which, he'd curl up into the Dreamtime, allowing his troubled thoughts to become nothing more – or less – than the reverie of the Earth itself.

Five months earlier, when the prop plane clattered to a halt, Will's father had been waiting for him: a great dolmen of a man draped in layers of flannel, tweed and Gannex. A man whose love for his adopted country seemed less that of an emigrant for some brave new world than that of a nostalgist for one hazily remembered, which probably never was.

He'd driven Will along the rain-dashed avenues, past giant crescents and alongside massive hedges – for this was suburbia on a monumental scale. Bolt upright at the wheel of his Ford Escort – not so much a car as a *wheeled lectern* . . . Will's father had seamlessly resumed his world-girdling seminar: 'Go on, have a guess – no, really – you'll never accurately estimate what the population is . . .'

No – nor could anyone. A crack team, equipped with sniffer dogs and Aboriginal trackers, would be hard pressed to hunt down live bodies in this waste of urban space *everyone's gone . . . to the moon . . .* The Escort had rounded Civic – as the civic centre was tersely abbreviated – then set course for Brian Lewis Crescent, on the shores of Lake Burley Griffin.

An artificial lake only two years younger than Will, with a fake shoreline of hand-picked boulders, that he stood staring at from under the dripping eaves of his father's bungalow. What kind of fucking cosmic solecism had that been? For when he'd left, London was griddling – and it'd been hot in Sydney as well, but the temperature in Canberra was only in the upper fifties, while the leaden skies were cross-hatched with drizzle. He stood there, smoking passionately, while marvelling at this pebbledashed fact: he'd travelled halfway round the globe, only to find himself in a suburb called Acton.

*

Skin-crawling, thoughts . . . *lagging*. Will hauls himself up high enough to yank the chain – then stares down at the shitty little maelstrom between his feet.

He remembers the avocado-shaped and avocado-coloured sink in his father's bungalow, the water draining paradoxically away – taking him with it, anticlockwise, back to his autumnal London go-round. The silvery leaves with their sooty smack-trails lay in drifts behind the paperbacks in the brick-and-board bookcases. Will had moved from a squat, to a temporary share, and eventually into a narrow, cell-like room in his mother's new flat.

It was en route to her garden . . . *I love my garden* being one of her mantras during the year she'd been establishing herself in Kentish Town.

She'd stomped through his cell several times a day, but never seemed to notice anything untoward. He lay on his bed, scheming and reading – then went out into his . . . *exercise yard* – which he walked alone, or with Damian, round and around – from debtor, to creditor, to dealer, again *annagain* . . . You wouldn't have thought it possible for an adult son to maintain a clandestine heroin habit – even a poxy ten-pound-bag-a-day one like Will's – under such supervision, but somehow *we managed it* . . .

One morning his mother had returned from a trip . . . *I love my little trips*, to find him gouched out on the floor of the main room, cigarette burnt down to the filter between the blistered fingers of one hand, the other lightly cradling an empty syringe.

She'd screamed at him . . . *true enough* – but what was maternal distress? Only a weak sort of magnetic field – lines of force, radiating out and through objects . . . *bodies*, yet quite unable to *effect attraction* . . .

The enigmatic mounds appeared alongside the track – radiant cities of them, either eroded sandcastles or Modernist slabs. Some were aligned with the Earth's magnetic field, and seemed to whisper to sun-struck Will, as he wandered among them sucking on a spliff, his bare legs scratched by the thorny scrub.

Vance and the others had tried frightening him with tales of desert highwaymen who'd stage a breakdown, flag him down, beat him up, and bugger him relentlessly before smearing his piggy flesh with honey then tying him across one of the termite mounds. Whereupon its inhabitants – who practise a clever combination of little-and-often and waste-not-want-not – would eat him alive.

'Come the fuck off it!' Will exclaimed whenever one of the Darwin mob came out with another of their scared stories – and he'd respond with this observation: how, for all their drawling assurance, these bong-sucking, beer-swilling rock 'n' rollers were just another smear of alien Vegemite *scraped off on the edge of the Great Southern piece of toast.*

Although, to be fair, Vance wasn't exactly your standard bullshitter – he'd been candid about what brought him to Darwin: 'Fuckin' hammer, mate.' This being Ocker rhyming slang: hammer + tack = smack. A teacher by vocation, who haled originally from small-town Victoria, Vance had found himself gouching out in front of the class – so lit out for the Territory on a major geographical, and ended up on a remote cattle station teaching the employees' kids.

As the monsoon decanted on Darwin, Vance scratched his bollocks through his sarong, and spoke of still danker days down in the Gulf, where the rain had been so heavy it penetrated these stockmen's already booze-sodden minds. Predictably, they went troppo – beatings, rapes and murders were born of their unbearable propinquity, suicides of their desperate loneliness. Vance had found one man strung up in a corrugated-iron shed, still alive, his saddle boots beating a retreat against its resonant walls.

He had a way of recounting these episodes – at once disengaged and oddly reverent – that connected him, Will sensed, to deeper narrative currents and ancient mythopoeic landscapes. Vance was a jolly swagman, all right – but for the most part his good humour was a function of Emu Export and the local weed, which was plentiful.

Will bought a couple of ounces to sustain him on his epic southern progress – but the flowering heads were still green, so he'd spread them about on top of his stuff, then buckled up his saddlebags. As he'd hoped, the sun was hot enough to cure them, and after a couple of days he was able to stop every hour or so, skin up, meditate on these *insect people of Minraud* . . . then bucket on through the dust.

Will shivers – tears a couple of shiny sheets from the holder and does the disgusting necessary. Through the open door of the tiny bathroom, he can see a half-smoked joint lying in a metal ashtray underneath the bed. There's no point in fighting anything any more – gravity included – so he drops back down to all fours, then crawls unsteadily towards it.

No – there's no point in fighting, because withdrawal is just this: an incremental and inexorable retreat, as, milligramme by milligramme, the warmly supportive waters slip down the beach, leaving the castaway on the abstinent island to feel his full and penitent weight. *Stranded* . . . Will is: stranded in Room 421 of the New Delhi YMCA for the foreseeable future – because it is indeed as he'd silently screamed at the man on the train that morning: the gear up in Kashmir had been profanely pure and evilly cheap. Beneath the ramparts of snow and ice lay a veritable Canaan, flowing with heroin: this was the promised land Will was searching for, as he'd dragged his wanting body across the wastes of North London, from suicidal squat to despairing council flat.

No wonder, once he'd reached it, his habit rose on the tide, until, thirty-six hours ago, he'd come to in the main cabin of the Houseboat Ceylon on Dal Lake, and realised *if I don't get out of here immediately, I'm gonna die* . . .

How long will the brown tide take to ebb? Will's no idea – this is a true terra nullius. All he knows is that yesterday afternoon, when the Srinagar bus reached the railhead at Chandigarh, after eight hours straining and switch-backing over the mountains, he'd panicked, feeling intimations of paralysis in his jellying arms, dissolving legs and belly *full of melt water* . . .

The dusty maidan in front of the station was unbearably raucous and colourful – Will's peeled senses were confused by smelly sights and stinking sounds, such that everything his gaze alighted on . . . *hurt*: a Dalit woman leisurely beating a donkey with a gnarled stick, a naked infant howling as its bemerded buttocks were dashed with water, vivid flobs of paan juice on the gritty ground, glossy-black oxen backing-and-filling between the dirty-yellow buses – while over it all were strung bare wires through which the baby-blue sky . . . *screamed*.

One minute Will was full of resolve – the next utter desperation. Checking his watch, he saw he'd forty minutes before the Delhi express departed, and, picking up his clunky metal suitcase, staggered over to the rank of waiting tuk-tuks. The driver spoke no English, Chandigarh being only a way-station for the few Westerners en route to Kashmir. A dumbshow of shooting-up, smoking and snorting had been met with equivocal head-wagging.

They picked up a sidekick, who propped one meagre buttock on the minuscule front seat, and as they bucketed through the potholes and swerved around the goats, his body swung out . . . *into the Heraclitean flux.*

Up the trio in the doughty little three-wheeler had gone, its engine dry-heaving. Each twisting lane was narrower than the last, as they pursued the final crumbling compounds and collapsing shacks fleeing before them, up into the parched hills.

Not only pale – Will had a *bloodless* view of them, as head spinning he watched the sidekick scamper in through metal-worked doors, then reappear between breeze-block piers. No one was *holding* . . . a stupid enough euphemism, for which there must be *some Punjabi equivalent* . . .

Will had kept checking his watch: the time until departure seemed to pass in sudden increments of five minutes: *thirty-five, thirty, twenty-five!* At last, the sidekick came back with a garishly labelled tin box: four Ganeshes, one each side, the elephant gods' trunks rising up to lift the lid – which Will did: inside had been moist and brownish . . . *snuff.*

'Not snuff! Smack – he-ro-in!' he'd groaned – then performed again, for them, the feral dogs and the wormy kids: the tapping of the powder into the spoon, the heating of that spoon, the drawing off of the solution, the tying of the tourniquet.

Will hadn't expected plaudits – let alone applause. But, rather than the anticipated indifference, these men's expressions had been sombre . . . *and contemptuous*. Will had travelled for weeks in India and Nepal, without troubling to learn so much as a salutation in any of the subcontinent's many languages . . . *but he got their drift*: drugs are a dreadful thing – a scourge of Indian youth. But at least the misery of their countrymen was comprehensible to these men, in their grubby shalwar kameezes, staring at the snuff box – but the despair of the blue-eyed Westerners, with American dollars stashed in their jeans' pocket, was deranging.

What could their drug-taking be, save a sort of psychopathological slumming – in line with their affectation of local dress?

And is there anything less alluring than *pale skin in a bright sari* . . .

'Well, then . . . that's the whole of that . . . then.'

Back at the window, Will exhales, and the thick smoke is sliced thin by the blinds. One of his mother's homilies – about how the truly inventive conjure just about anything out of a ball of string . . . *and a couple of Venetian blind slats* – magics the imitation of Christ out of this cinematic haze: *he's slipped his bonds* . . .

'For heaven's sake!' Amit exclaims. 'We are by no means finishing up here, Rohan.'

'How now're we going to do this scene, man?' He rubs his sweaty sleeves. 'You can't manage the simplest stuff – like the centurion's passing of the gourd.'

'Ach! Have a little patience, Rohan – this is a play. We have to sort out the actions first with the leading actors . . . then introduce the minor ones and put it all together. It will be so very dramatic, you see – you'll give up the ghost there . . . then reappear over there –'

'Ye-es,' Rohan scoffs, 'you've said that already – and I can't wait to be embalmed, and to be put in the tomb, and so forth – rolling away the stone, you know, just you, me and little Samreen here . . .'

Peering at them through the smoke, Will wonders if he should offer his services – after all, he'd make a far more convincing three-day-old corpse than Rohan, and it would be the *Christian thing to do* . . . Then he cackles, coughs, and reels away from the window to collapse back on to the narrow cot, where he grinds his leaden head into the hard bolster.

Will did as he'd been told: slowing down to below twenty before pulling off the Barkly Highway. It was a couple of hours since he'd left the fat girl at the roadhouse eating her Violet Crumble. The sun was setting, casting *violet shadows* . . . from the low scrub the bike brushed through. Lurching into dry washes, and working his way around the miniature ravines created by once-a-decade cascades, Will headed north, the land falling away before him in a series of wide, shallow terraces.

His first few weeks in Darwin had all been about waiting: the inexorable build-up to the monsoon – followed by a monumental pressure drop: semi-trailers of tepid rain falling from the rumbling sky – followed by the rot, and the silverfishy seething of microbial life, boiling up between *cracks in reality* . . .

It'd been a sodden Christmas and a waterlogged New Year. No one without a four-wheel-drive attempted Queensland much before March.

Will had left Darwin under spongey clouds, the track ahead streaked with long, gunmetal puddles — but here, far to the south, the dry air rasped exposed flesh, and there were no eucalyptus any more, just the low and thorny scrub.

About five clicks off the track, Will halted on a bluff and made camp. He got out his provisions and unrolled his swag. Before pulling off he hadn't passed a vehicle going in either direction for about an hour. To the north, it was hundreds of kilometres to the Gulf coast, where there were a few Aboriginal outstations and mining settlements. To the south were the great palisades of mulga that had turned back the first European explorers, and the wide plains stippled with spinifex that gave way, in turn, to blinding saltpans set in the stony wastes of the Simpson Desert.

Out there, only months since, Xavier Herbert's dead body had been found in his ute, hundreds of clicks down the Birdsville Track towards Lake Eyre. Will had Herbert's *Capricornia* tucked in his saddlebag – five hundred pages of rampageous prose, limning the queer contours of the racial divide in outback Australia – but that *wasn't the half of it.* Herbert, who'd rejoiced in the job title 'Protector of Aboriginals', also factored his time in the Territory into *Poor Fellow My Country,* which was twice that length.

Puffing on his joint, swigging his rum, Will meditated on the old writer's suicide: all those words, flooding out of him – and these images, perhaps: the stick figures of the blackfellas who'd remained uncontacted – and who, as the whites invaded, withdrew, walking deeper and deeper into the outback.

I tellya, mate . . . Vance had said . . . *they gather out there and hold enormous-fucking-corroborees . . . Hundreds of initiates, doing their dances, performing ceremonies . . . See, it's blackfellas' technology that makes this place – and that technology is . . . magic.*

From violet, to mauve, to a full and ruddy purple – the shades had slipped over him, as the sun dipped down to the west, disguising the Earth as a series of alternative planets, before plunging it altogether into utter and otherworldly darkness. Will's heart beat heavily as the night sky pulsed into being overhead – the weighty array of the Milky Way, scarcely visible in the light-polluted northern hemisphere, hung over him: massive clusters of stars, inconceivably remote . . . *frighteningly close*. So far as Will was aware, the nearest human to him was at least fifty clicks away – up the turn-off to a cattle station he'd seen back on the Barkly Highway.

For a while he'd lain, feeling the planet roll through the heavens beneath him, tossing up entire nebulae with each revolution – but then a cloudy cover was pulled into place and tucked under the horizon. As the final illumination was blotted from the sky, Will had been gripped with a mortal terror: it was his own mind – this small and wavering ember, which glowed faintly, then disappeared altogether, *ground out beneath the great heel of the night* . . .

And then the bush had come alive.

A shock.

Since he'd seen little in the way of major fauna as he drove around Australia — sometimes, in the distance, a silver-grey rivulet running along the horizon would resolve into leaping kangaroos, and a couple of times Will ran into small mobs of feral camels, which would scatter, spitting, as the Super Dream spluttered towards them.

*

It had been livelier back in Darwin, where Will slept on the Heinzes' veranda while they were down south, avoiding the wet season. The pool was a few steps from his bed – and he'd enjoyed late-night soaks: lying in womblike gloom, everything but his eyes beneath the surface, smelling first the salt winds soughing in from the mangrove swamps – then feeling *the black bat night!* Vectors of teeth and fur, borne on leathery wings, that swept in so low they brushed his face — before the flying fox rose into the mango tree, elbowing its mates aside as it manoeuvred *to hang upside down at the bar* . . .

Later yet, Will would listen for the ratcheting, followed by the definitive 'click!', that heralded yet another guest checking into the roach motel underneath his bed. Surviving Darwin in the wet without going troppo was all about acceptance – accepting the ceaseless sweating in the one-hundred-degree humidity, accepting yet another five-ounce glass of ice-cold beer, and nodding dazedly as the twenty-two cents were abstracted from your pile of change on the bar.

Life – at human scale – continued sluggishly: the mangrove swamps were heaving with salt-water crocs – the leaden sea teemed with lethal box jellyfish. There was nowhere to go but another pool, in another backyard, where there was another beer, and another bong, and another fat white nutter in a sarong, who'd say something like, 'Jeezo, you can feel those termites' magnetic activity, mate – feel it humming in yer fuckin' brain . . .'

For it was at this much smaller scale that everything . . . *seethed*.

Turning world-girdling somersaults through jet lag and withdrawals, Will had slept fitfully in the spare room of his father's Canberra bungalow. But he soon recovered sufficiently to be ravening – so found himself, in the linoleum hum of his stepmother's kitchen, with her pious tea towels, and her religiose knick-knacks, frying everything he could lay his hands on – then stuffing it into his mouth, as he stared blankly at the black pane . . . *without form or void*, willing any spirit there was available to *move upon the face of the waters* . . .

For he'd been alone – horribly so: with no Chloë or Caius – even his mother's ever-presence felt subdued. He was alone, eating breakfast in the long, dark night of his soul – but then everything was topsy-turvy here at the bottom of the world, where the leafy suburbia of his childhood was writ ridiculously large – while he'd never imagined late summer could turn . . . *so quickly into spring*.

Night after sleepless night, as soon as dawn fingered the vertical textured louvres, he put on trainers and went out. Drizzle would be falling on the Antipodean Acton – *pissing down* on Lake Burly Griffin as well. On the far side of its slate waters there was another beach faked from quarried boulders – and beyond this rose the futuristic finial of the Australian Parliament: a huge and beautifully clean hypodermic needle . . . *injecting democracy into the very crook of the Southern Cross* . . .

It was the closest to jogging Will had ever come: limping down concrete ramps and along smoothly tarmacked bike tracks, he lugged his leaden limbs through all this uncanniness. In an underpass, sprayed along a weeping wall, he'd seen this graffito: THEY TOOK THE DREAMTIME AND TURNED IT INTO A NIGHTMARE . . . then limped back to Brian Lewis Crescent, where he'd sat drinking coffee and reading the suicide helpline advert on the milk carton again . . . *annagain*, while he listened to the fridge.

Eventually, the frowsty elders would show their bed-heads.

It had been to escape this that Will headed north – this . . . *and hammer.*

The job his father secured for him was a four-month contract working as a consultant economist for the Lands Department of the Northern Territory Government. On a salary equivalent to a Grade 11 guvvie employee – not bad for a pommie chancer, who'd in fact abandoned any study of the subject after his first year at Oxford, roundly declaring economics to be *a pseudo-science under conditions of late capitalism* . . .

His first few days in Darwin, Will waited to be found

out – creeping across the Department's nylon carpets, whispering more quietly than the air conditioning. How long would it take his colleagues to realise the absolute inelasticity of his understanding of . . . *price elasticity*?

But then he'd got to know his colleagues: Kurt, the Department demographer, who moonlighted as the Honorary German Consul, and looked *like a peasant, shitting in the corner of a Brueghel*. Kurt manifested his sophistication and acculturation . . . *or so he thought*, with his *ripper* Australian English: wrapping his arm round Will's shoulders and chortling about how, when he was involved in a single-vehicle rollover (in one of the Department's utes), he left *skid marks in me jockeys, mate* . . .

Then there was Brian, whom their colleagues derided as an Abo-lover, who walked with a limp, and who'd thrown over his secure civil service job in Croydon, bought a Honda C90 motorbike and underpowered his way around the world, only to end up in another secure civil service job. So far as Will could make out, Brian spent most of his time at work reading old copies of the National Geographic, and dreaming of . . . *pastures new*.

These were the men Will had to convince he wasn't malingering: a representative sample of the Territorian administration, which seemed for the most part to consist of eccentrics and ne'er-do-wells, either on the run from trouble or attracted by the generous allowance paid out to those prepared to live in this remote tropical hell, with its pyramidal – and marmoreal – casino, and its long grass people: blacker shapes in the black shadows beneath the pandanus trees, sitting there in a litter of tinnies . . . *living the nightmare.*

Besides, what'd been the precise nature of Will's job? In theory, he was contracted to write a report on the demand for residential building land in the Territory – presumably a component part of the boosterism that had led to the 'construction' of Palmerston: Darwin's very own new town development. This might be a sight to gladden Will's father's heart – what with its graded roads, backhoed subdivisions and, as yet, no residences whatsoever – but it brought home to Will the utter spuriousness of his own task, given the Territory was six times larger than the United Kingdom, yet had only a hundred thousand inhabitants.

Be that as it may, the Crown – in the form of the Federal Government down south in Canberra – had to release parcels of land in fifty-year leases, so there was at least a bureaucratic requirement for a forecast of some sort.

It took Will a few conversations with Kurt, and a couple of sessions mugging up in the library, to arrive at a suitable metric. Normally the demand for building land could be factored from the rate of household formation, taken together with a bundle of economic indicators – such as employment rates, gross domestic product, and so forth. But the Territory

was an environment too artificial even for this approximation –
at least for its white population. What determined their rate of
household formation was the guvvie compo' pure and simple:
if this 'troppo allowance' went up, so did the numbers. If it
fell, people put their units up for rent and hired a U-Haul.

When Will had arrived, in November, Darwin was swelter-
ing beneath a dirty cloud-dome. Vaporous threads snaked
down to smudge the pale knees of the colonialists, as they
hurried from one air-conditioned capsule to the next. Steam
rose from the sidewalks. The monsoon was due – but it was
taking its time . . . *pumping up the troppo volume.* And, as the
pressure mounted, so the rioting vegetation grew sombre,
while the air crackled with humidity and electricity.

The Darwinites sweated it out – newer arrivals attempting
some simulation of normal life on this alien planet, while
those who'd been around since before the cyclone favoured
houses built to cope with the climate, which had wide teak
verandas, pitched corrugated-iron roofs and slatted walls
through which the soupy air . . . *slurped.*

Lying on his bed at Larrakeyah Lodge, Will watched the
ceiling fan whip one way, then slow . . . *and turn the other.*
Perception, he knew, was a slippery business, but *on the
whole* . . . – a typical paternal expression – he felt he was *going
in the right direction* . . .

*

Which was just as well – because down south in Canberra Will had been doubly mired: a junky, fleeing his native fleshpots – only to find more expensively damaging ones.

'What does Canberra mean?' he'd taunted his father, as the two of them sat in the spring sunshine, listening to the gallus parakeets scream at the galah cockatoos, while companionably milking the silvery udder of another wine box. 'I'll tell you: it's an ancient Aboriginal word meaning "Milton Keynes".'

At which the insufferably tolerant old man would chuckle. His indulgence, Will's aware, had been *pretty much limitless . . .* and he'd said nothing about his son's real reason for being there, sedated, in the great southern suburb.

Said nothing, save reiterating from time to time his own version of the maternal homily: *Omnia moderatie et moderatio omnibus . . .* Not that there was much moderation at Brian Lewis Crescent, once Will was in residence. With no paid work to do, he sat at their dull dining-room table, grinding out cartoons and comic vignettes, that he then despatched to magazines and newspapers, both in Australia and England.

There were no replies.

He wrote to perfidious Caius and faithful Chloë – and the former didn't reply much, while the latter did . . . *copiously.*

Will took driving lessons in the mornings, followed by fluid lunchtimes. Late in the afternoon, once he was a little more sober, he and his stepmother would go for practice drives along the burgeoning boulevards, and between *hissed upon* lawns.

In return for her assistance, he taught her how to drink more heavily: after looping out through Belconnen and Giralang, they'd return via Civic, where they'd buy a bottle of Polish vodka and one of Rose's Lime Cordial. *Exactly at five, someone would bang a tin pan and yell, 'Drinking time!' and the others would jump up like fighters coming out at the bell . . .*

Will could feel a deep cellular change under way, as his junk-sick tissues grew accustomed to their new and spirituous substrate. Three weeks after his arrival, he was lying flat out on his bed in the spare room, smoking Pall Mall after Pall Mall: drawing deep, savouring the smoke when *the imp of the perverse . . .* stirred within.

How they'd laughed at the motto on the Pall Mall packet when staying that summer at Caius's mother's house in Provence: *Wherever particular people congregate . . .* And these particular people had been very particular indeed: Caius had introduced him to a princess, and a famous philosopher, a youthful Oxford don and a beautiful American who'd already published a novel at the age of twenty-two. The ineffably lovely Ann – about whom Will entertained the most ignoble fantasies – had also been in attendance. It'd been bewildering – because at one moment Caius would be deriding all forms of snobbery – intellectual, social, financial – the next, exercising them with a calculated ruthlessness.

'What single thing do you find most evocative of Paris?' he'd enquired of the philosopher – who was famous for his illogical positivism.

And the philosopher replied, 'A road sign, with the word PARIS written on it.'

There are certain things . . . Wherever particular people congregate . . . Waste not, want not . . . Synonyms and homonyms expose the semantic instabilities that homilies try to paper over – but if you gallop away . . . *the pantomime horse tears in half.*

It'd been this body part that lay smoking in the spare bedroom at Brian Lewis Crescent: the headless horseman of this *sleepy hollow . . .*

For there were no particular people at all in Canberra so far as Will could see – at least not among the academics his father and stepmother consorted with, who'd appeared painfully unsophisticated as they sipped the gimlets Will taught her to mix, and discussed what costumes they'd wear to the Lamington Ball, a forthcoming anniversarial celebration of the nomadic whitefellas' arrival during the 1920s.

They'd pitched up on this isolated tableland, bringing with them *hostess trolleys . . . sponge cakes . . . and vertical textured louvres fastened together with what appear to be lengths of plastic-fucking-keychain . . .*

*

Will thought a plausible acronym for the Australian National University would be ANUS. Because the campus spreading out behind the parental bungalow felt like *the arse-end of the universe* . . . scattered with low-rise modern buildings and eucalyptus trees, from which magpies swept down to peck at the exposed heads of unwary pedestrians.

Not that there'd been many about – since it was the vacation. Will moved from one patch of cover to the next, until he reached the Student Union bar, where . . . *as fate would have it*, there'd been the particular person he sought . . . *standing by the jukebox . . . and I caught his eye several times . . . He looked at me with special recognition . . . like one queer looks at another . . .*

Bob was wearing a black leather jacket, black Levis, black wraparound shades, a white T-shirt and black winklepicker boots. His black Holden Falcon had been parked outside.

'I've seen the past . . .' Will remarked conversationally, climbing into the passenger seat, 'and it works.'

But Bob was no student of post-war American literature – only another fifties revivalist, farcically repeating its tragic history of premature death. Half an hour later they'd been sitting in the cramped bedroom of a kitchen off the Tuggeranong Parkway, and Will was feeling both nauseous . . . *and suicidal*, as Bob chopped out fat lines of amphetamine sulphate on a copy of Elvis Costello's My Aim is True.

Will had seen the past, all right – the very recent past: for, staring at the powdery pieces added to Costello's quiffed hair, he'd realised this was no déjà vu, but a genuine recurrence: three weeks previously, in a squat on the other side of the world, he had sat and watched as a Bobalike did exactly the same thing . . . *on the same fucking album cover.*

Bob could get hammer as well – but, given the tiny local market, and the five-hour drive from Sydney, prices were extortionate. Or so Bob and his sidekick – a girl called Valerie – claimed. The smack was South-East Asian . . . *part of the White Australia policy, no doubt* . . . and, dissolved in tap water, it shot up . . . *pure and sweet.*

But it'd been four hundred bucks a gramme – twenty a hit. Within days, his paltry savings all gone, Will reverted to childhood: rifling the change from the top of his dad's chest of drawers, then getting a cab down the Tuggeranong Parkway, to another cul-de-sac and another bungalow.

Valerie lay, a little opiated lump in the middle of her parents' broad bed – and he'd curled around her Winceyette back, gently sobbing.

A thief! A fucking tea leaf! Transported not to a fatal shore, but an artificial one. Will stared out over Lake Burly Griffin: the savage conditions of the old world had been replicated in this new one within three short weeks. Australia was a warped obsidian mirror: its religion officiated by raucous matrons in floral prints, and a Labor Party financed by mafia money garnered from protection, hammer and weed plantations up by the Queensland border – everything in the Antipodes was huge. And corrupt.

A dead lizard on the lawn, sprinklers scattering the swarming flies, they stream back again, more watery . . . *than water.*

A colleague of his father's had a map distributed by the Australian Broadcasting Corporation pinned up on his office wall that showed the extent of their radio coverage: arcs radiating out from Canberra, Sydney, Melbourne, Adelaide, Perth and Brisbane, which then rippled away into nothing. Entire swathes of the island-continent didn't receive so much as a perturbation.

Four months later, sitting on the low escarpment, the Super Dream cooling beside him – its metal convexities contracting . . . *ticking* . . . *entropy meters* . . . Will had looked out over the dry seabed of the red centre and sensed it: the great yawning vacuity White Australia always feels nipping at its heels, as it scampers, laughing, into the Southern Ocean.

Holding his transistor radio to his ear, Will heard the rising and falling of these distant seas, while his cock-eyes called forth radio waves, breaking on the sandy dirt at his booted feet. *Too much of nothing can make a man* . . . As he'd prepared to sleep, Will grew more and more . . . *ill at ease.*

If there were any particular people in the vicinity at all, they'd be the ones particular to a knees-up, to a boomerang clack, and, very especially, to a subcision: the urethra of the initiate pulled from the transected shaft of his penis and flayed with a stone knife. His femoral artery would then be plugged with beeswax, so blood for particular ceremonial purposes could easily be obtained . . . *in the future.*

And what might that look like under a smoky moon, with the pointillist-painted limbs of the dancers another constellation altogether? No matter the glass-and-concrete futurology of Sydney, or the iron certainty of its bridge – when you looked into Ocker eyes, you saw a terrified evanescence: they were fading away into their own inner-wilderness, even as the skin surrounding them *shrivelled up into melanomas . . .*

When he was teaching down the track, Vance would take the elderly traditional owners out in his cockroach-infested old Ford Taurus – take them tacking across open country, cruising through the spinifex, singing it up again. Making it solid and real, *like Paris . . . with words.*

But when Will had asked him if he'd ever considered being initiated himself, Vance shook his head. 'Nah, mate, it's gotta be a mistake – whitefellas get initiated 'cause it's the only way to get along in these communities. If you don't have a skin, there's a sense in which you just don't exist. But if you do exist – you're someone's uncle, someone else's son – everything that's yours is theirs: they basically exploit the fuck out of you . . .'

Vance smiled often, and made wild claims with true Aussie understatement. In the local slang he was *true God . . .* not . . . *gammin.* But, for all this, he still seemed already verging on the non-existent to Will – proud of his white, working-class heritage, but hearkening to the desert mystics. His dusty unit bare except for a mattress, a boomerang and a bundle of hunting spears. Vance seemed always to be leaving.

On a weekend trip down to Katherine, with him and Corinne, his leggy girlfriend, they'd seen cruising police utes operate as snatch squads – scooping up blackfellas *for no fucking reason at all . . .*

'See that,' Vance had spat, 'the genocide was over years ago – these're just mopping-up oppos.'

Why wouldn't he be confused? Darwin was a confusing place: forty thousand colonists from Planet Earth and a few thousand of the remaining indigenes – amongst whom trachoma is endemic – playing out a deadly game of mutual incomprehension among the saltwater mangrove swamps and the 'pop-pop-pop' of pedestrian crossings designed for the partially sighted.

When Will left town on the Super Dream, the headband of his Walkman worn as a chinstrap, and Little Walter singing reedily through its earphones, *My girl don't stand no cheatin', my girl* . . . Vance had been teaching at Berrimah Prison, his prize English pupil being Lindy Chamberlain, the infamous dingo baby killer.

Nearly four years into a life sentence, Chamberlain stolidly maintained her innocence – while Vance claimed the whole thing was a fit-up: an Ocker secular revulsion against weird wowsers like the Chamberlains, who'd called their daughter Azaria, meaning *helped by God* . . .

Chamberlain said her baby had been taken from their camping ground near Uluru by wild dingos: 'Which is probably the truth,' Vance drawled, 'this bloody country's full of domesticated creatures that've gone fuckin' feral . . .'

It could have been dingos that kept Will awake throughout that long and deeply isolated night. Dingos – or, more likely, goannas. He knew he was within the range of the perentie – the largest species, which could grow to six feet in length. They weren't known to attack humans, but they had teeth, claws, and moved at speed.

Unless you were in a big vehicle – or one with big 'roo bars – the advice was not to drive after dark. Anywhere. In the Great Southern Suburb itself, talk among the washed-up academics and puffy-faced politicos often turned to those stupid so-and-sos who'd been KO'ed by a wallaby, which, dazzled by their lights, leapt through their windscreen *right by Civic!*

Yes . . . night must fall on the great collective hallucination of civilised Australia – imprisoning its inhabitants wherever they might be. And that night *had a thousand eyes* . . .

A lanky princess, laid out on his skimpy swag, Will felt specks of mica swell into . . . *artificial boulders*, as the bush exploded into life around him. Scree pittered – stones click-clacked . . . *stone knives were sharpened – while claws and teeth moved at speed.*

So he sat up, and remained like this for the rest of the night, working his way through the bottle of Bundaberg and a packet of Temple Bar — a strong, filterless Virginia cigarette, its paper packet bearing an image of the celebrated landmark, once the gateway to the City of London, long removed from Fleet Street to some sodden corner of *fucking Enfield.*

And what would the existential difference be, exactly, between being ripped apart by some Mokoi – a child-devouring demon, spun into being out of weird blackfella–whitefella psychotic syncretism, and merely having your head kicked in by a gang of lads in a park in one of the outer spiral arms of the London galaxy?

At dawn, he'd brewed up a billy of tea on his camping stove. The light welling up from the horizon leeched the land of colour – it wasn't a new day, *just another absence.* Packing up the saddlebags, strapping on water bag and swag, humping the Super Dream back through the *shrubberies* . . . Will pondered the twelve hours ahead: he'd have to ride safely but swiftly – a second night in the deep bush was unthinkable: *Fuck windmills* . . . the wilderness howled through his little mind, picking up the shreds of resentment, and the febrile nostalgias he calls his self, and evacuating them.

When Will got to Brisbane, Vance had been there already: he'd plane-frogged over Will, and was already partying hard with his old mates. After he'd heard Will's tale, his mentor had laughed darkly: 'That's bad country, mate – lotta bad vibes. There were massacres thereabouts as late as the thirties – 'course, no one acknowledges that in the white world. I wouldn't've camped out there with a big mob – let alone on my fucking own.'

Black Australians spoke a stifled English: a communicative sprite, trapped in the cage of some far older and more expressive language, so it emerged flat and percussively punctuated with smacks and clicks. The disaffected white strangers in this paradise were as deadpan and ironic as any Londoner – but the patio-dwellers yelped and yipped: *wrinklies drinking stubbies pulling sickies* – as if scattering their diminutives to the wind was a sympathetic magic of their own, capable of reducing the awesome scale of their uncanny homeland.

There'd been this maddening inflection to Australia all along – together with the interrogative swoop with which so many sentences ended – including some of Vance's: . . . *on my fucking own?* Why question this fundamental

286

solitude, when no matter how matey you may be *every man's still just a fucking island, yes?* Or yairs, as Australians pronounce it: yairs, Will hadn't slept a wink — and after getting back on the track, he'd had to ride for a couple of hours before a car passed him, heading west, its driver's face a paler blur in the great and grey nothingness of the overcast desert.

A click . . . a hiss . . . a whirr . . . a squawk:

'Then one of the Twelve – the one called Judas Iscariot – went to the chief priests and asked, "What are you willing to give me if I hand him over to you?"'

Will must've swooned again – and in this collapse his body has betrayed him: he's shat himself.

Tumbling off the narrow bed on to all-fours, he sees the joint stub, extinguished by folds of dank and smeary sheet.

Then he's on his feet, in the bathroom, shaking uncontrollably as he holds handfuls up to the guttering shower rose. This isn't the sort of thing you can simply *wipe away . . .* Night has fallen outside in the courtyard, lights have been switched on, and a full rehearsal convened.

'They offered him thirty silver coins – and from then on, Judas watched for an opportunity to hand Jesus over . . .'

Betrayals within betrayals: a moral . . . *mise en abyme.*

Will's arrival at the Oberoi Palace Hotel had been a

287

particularly black and gooey instance of this. But then Caius hadn't really been that clean – as he'd soon admitted, while dissolving a lump of the tuk-tuk driver's opium in a balloon of Courvoisier. This he'd swilled in one hand, as he lay back against the striped silk headboard, crossing his ankles.

His feet had been clad in velvet slippers with leopard's heads embroidered on the uppers. Outside the vultures were still there, revolving in the dung smoke on their tattered wings.

As junk softened the contours of Caius's grievance, it'd been Will's turn: why the fuck did they have to stay in this expensive re-creation of the West's air-conditioned nightmare? Besides, it was way beyond Will's budget – and, although Caius, as ever, had offered to pay, this only made things worse: Will was determined not to be beholden to him and his sadistic caprice any longer.

The bickering continued, as, nursing new-born habits, they'd headed for Nepal, flying up from Delhi on a bumpy prop plane full of sliding sunlight and excitable returnees. Without any announcement, the pilot angled the plane through the thick cloud cover – and skimmed between two of the savage peaks encircling Kathmandu Airport. The spine-jarring set-down inaugurated a truce – but, in true Dostoevskian fashion, their eternal gratitude for their deliverance evaporated by the time they got into town.

*

What had they bickered about? Will rinses the sheet – and rinses it again. Then he squats down – but he's too weak to maintain this posture, so slips sideways to lie athwart the foot-plates, with his head in the shower. A happy accident – because an acidic bile rises up, while the flow of watery diarrhoea resumes *at the far end* . . .

He thinks first of his father, who'd jocularly . . . *such a Pooterish word that*, refer to him as 'Bilious' – then of his arse-hole, at once so very far away and so gripingly present.

'If I want to wipe you,' he hectors it between retches, 'I shall have to write you a letter, inviting you to rendezvous with me somewhere between the shithole and the plug one . . . How should that be addressed? "To Will's Arsehole, In the Bathroom, Room 421, the YMCA, New-fucking-Delhi . . ."'

Outside in the courtyard, it's Samreen's voice that emerges from the static: 'Then came the day of the unleavened bread on which the Passover lamb had to be sacrificed. Jesus sent his disciples Peter and John to do this, saying unto them –'

'GO AND MAKE PREPARATIONS FOR THE PASSOVER!'

Yes, Will thinks, Rohan's definitely putting some oomph into it.

Idly, smelling his own corruption, he wonders if it's the darkness that's freed the captious Christ into such fluency.

'I have eagerly desired to eat this Passover with you before

I suffer – for I tell you this now with complete seriousness: I will not be eating anything at all – not a single little bite – until I find my fulfilment IN THE KINGDOM OF GOD!'

'No, no, no!' Amit interrupts – and in his watery reclusion Will cackles, smellily. 'No, no, no!' The director reiterates, 'That is not the line at all, man – the proper line is, "I shall not eat it again until it finds fulfilment in the kingdom of God." There's none of this single little bite nonsense, Rohan – where are you getting it from?'

'I am improvising, Amit – adding in more words to make my speech sound more realistic, see. There's so very much of this script that is altogether unbelievable.'

Amit shouts through a small typhoon of static: 'There's no call for any improvising, man! This is not some experimental thing, see – these are the very words of the Gospel! This is a passion play, man! A BLOODY PASSION PLAY!'

Will and Caius had bickered with a genuine passion: arguing about how they should travel, where they should go, and what they should eat. Standing in smoky, muddy Freak Street, they goggled at the hash-addled old hippies wolfing down cherry pie . . . *and fucking rösti!* in grotty little restaurants. They'd journeyed this far not to satisfy spiritual yearnings, only their . . . *dumb munchies.*

But soon enough, for the want of any other suitable cuisine, the taste of fried potato and onion had begun *eternally recurring*... Will drapes the drenched sheet over the flimsy shower stall and staggers back to bed. Rohan and Amit must've made a truce, for:

'Now that I, your Lord and teacher, have washed your feet, you should do as I have done for you. I tell you the truth, no servant is greater than his master ...'

Will had won a bicker, so left Caius in a whitewashed room at the top of three flights of stairs in a two-star-rated guest house on the edge of the old town. The room featured no mod cons at all, and was furnished with five tightly made-up beds – one of which Caius fought his way into, still wearing brown corduroy trousers, two thick pullovers and his 'crombie.

The warnings in the guidebook were stentorian: hepatitis was RIFE in Nepal, and Will had neglected to get a gamma globulin shot before he left Australia. He'd gone in search of this – and heroin.

There'd been pools of greenish water – or was it some purulent discharge. Flies clambered over the miniature Himalayas of dirty and discarded sheets. A dead-end corridor was the destination for a family of tiny Nepalese, who'd gathered round a still tinier form lying motionless on a trolley. The men were openly weeping – the women quietly wailing. Will hadn't savoured such a stew of virulence and poverty since the Darwin bus pulled off the track, and crept along the unmetalled road to the camp, where kids with flies in their eyes and open sores on their bow legs crawled out from corrugated-iron humpies.

In a side room, empty except for a metal examination table and some posters showing baroque skin conditions, Will paid twelve US dollars, then stood with his trousers down while a buck-toothed fellow sank the thick and suspect needle deep in his wanting flesh, then *oh-so-slowly* pushed home the plunger. *Nobody paid us any mind . . . sitting there on the couch with our sleeves rolled up . . . probing for veins with the needle . . . Anything can happen in the office of a . . .* Nepalese doctor.

Junk had been considerably cheaper than this in the land of the living God-King – not that Will's personal despot gave a shit: 'I think it's morphine,' he'd said, tweaking the bloodless tip of his imperious nose with his spatulate fingers.

Horrid fingers – with deeply recessed nails. Will sees them now, wavering in the gloom – and also sees that contemptuous face, sneering at him. Is it love he feels for Caius – or a yet more absurd emotion? For, while Will wants none of the obvious attributes his friend possesses – birth, wealth, sophistication, utter insouciance – he nonetheless fervently desires that elusive quality of 'being Caius'.

What might this be like? Well, despite all evidence to the contrary, Will yet maintains his illusion: that Caius's inner-space is no loveless vacuum, but warm, secure, and full to bursting with self-esteem.

'Ye-es, fucking morphine . . .' Caius had drawled – and carried on drawling, as for the next few days they dragged their increasingly feeble bodies from one pagoda of smoke-blackened beams to the next. A citizen of hotel lobbies and airport lounges – in his mother's mansions the many occasional tables are covered with thick glass, and the drapes tied back with velvet ropes – Caius suffered from Weltschmerz rather than homesickness. But Will, hearing Cockney glottals in the grotty streets, felt once more the near-mystical intensity of that dull spondee: 'Lon-don'.

Now, lying . . . *clucking*, in this little coop of a room, Will sees before him the statue of the Red Indian on the glassy prow of East Finchley tube station, his bow taut, ever ready to loose his arrow . . . *at Highgate*. Will thinks of the tube roundel – a homely target he's carried before him for thousands of miles, and which, in his feverish mind, is wreathed *in Beltane fire* . . . much as he imagines the cross propped in the balcony opposite, whose occupant now gives voice:

'The one who has dipped his hand into the bowl with me WILL BETRAY ME! The Son of Man will go JUST AS IT IS WRITTEN ABOUT HIM! But woe to that man who betrays the SON OF MAN! It would be better for him if HE HAD NOT BEEN BORN!'

Ye-es . . . fucking morphine . . . When what they'd needed was heroin. Be that as it may: *waste not, want not . . .* so they'd honked up line-after-line of the stuff, which Will went out and obtained, wrapped in scraps of newsprint, from this tuk-tuk driver or that chai wallah.

Ye-es . . . Caius was immune: a crazy redneck colonel, screaming at the dense shot and shell of this *War on Drugs . . .* who nonetheless would *never be hit . . .* Whereas Will recognised the tube roundel he saw floating before him to be a harbinger of his own death — Seen in Darwin, dangling in the mango tree the flying foxes hung from. Glimpsed in the desert skies he scudded beneath – then observed hovering offshore above the Barrier Reef, as he'd lain in a tin-roofed mansion on Magnetic Island, listening to the tail-end of the monsoon . . . *binging and bonging.*

With each line he snorted Will had felt another soft-but-firm blow: the muffled drum-beats keeping the time of *my own cortège . . .* Caius, for all the thinness of his blue-veined skin, *would never die . . .* but the second he'd stepped from the main doors of the arrivals terminal Will felt bacteria and virions winging in from all the dusty and dank corners of this great and grotty land – felt them settle on his lips, nostrils and eyes, as flies do in the outback.

And with each day that passed, as he'd followed Caius's pearl-grey fedora through the mucky streets of Kathmandu, Will grew sicker and sicker – as if he were receiving regular transfusions *of contaminated blood* . . .

Ye-es . . . *fucking morphine* . . . Once the parboiled days in Darwin melted into weeks, and Will grew acclimatised, so he began to feel the parts that Emu Export refreshed calling out for . . . *more!*

He'd made friends with Vance – and through him a gaggle of white Aboriginals, who revolved from poolside to bush camp, bonging and boozing. It was all perfectly congenial – but the screen door in the back of Will's foggy head kept on *clacking in the wind* — He could sense it out there: the hideous never-never of *never, ever experiencing junk again* – never subsiding into its sensory deprivation tank, and feeling . . . *nothing*.

At Christmas, he'd flown south to Canberra, straight across the red centre, staring down at this, the bed of an ancient sea, but en route for . . . *an antediluvian cliché*: fossilised turkey and petrified potatoes – all mounded up on plates, beneath which Will's stepmother had tucked collection envelopes for a Third World charity, so brown faces suffered beside the white sauce congealing in the forty-degree heat.

Sweating – and damning the poor woman for her crazed hypocrisy, Will had listened as she read out her latest piece of doggerel: *Can God survive in Australia? / It depends if Christianity is a fail-i-ure* . . .

Sitting in their living room – his stepmother's pretensions stopped at the point of drawing – Will stared towards the false horizon of Lake Burly Griffin, and the hypo' of democracy. Old junkies in London claimed that the trouble began when you stopped shooting up – it was then that all the crud they cut the gear with, which had been held in suspension, descended into your lungs. The tedium of his father's bungalow was like this: *finer than flour, alive, more dangerous than silica* . . . and Will did indeed feel it . . . *sift almost invisible, through the long afternoon of bloated tedium.*

The captious child accused them of hypocrisy – of sliding into the New Year on a slick of blackfellas' blood. Then he'd cracked – and wrote to Genie . . . *back in the Smoke*, enclosing enough Australian dollars for it to be worth her while – just possibly – to hobble to a bureau de change, take a tenner for herself, and use the balance for a half-gramme of smack *including post + packaging* . . .

Then he'd waited – and waited some more. His final fortnight in Darwin – when he was saying his goodbyes, buying the Super Dream and organising his supplies for the big drive south – had been overhung by this dark cloud: waiting for the monsoon to abate . . . *and the smack to come.*

The Heinzes returned from down south, and, appalled at the damage Will had inflicted on their Veedub Passat, exiled him from the veranda. Another couple lent him their little pre-cyclone teak box of a house, up on stilts in an otherwise empty lot on Mott Street in the middle of town. Will sat on its shiny front steps, screened by bougainvillea and grevillea, and waited — and waited some more.

From time to time, the frill-necked lizard that lived in this pocket wilderness crept out of the undergrowth. Up on hind legs, its reptilian snout questing, its eyes starting, it looked like a miniature dinosaur, hunting for . . . *tiny human prey.*

And still Will waited.

Waited at the Nightcliff Hotel, where Bo Diddley and his band's dum-b'dum-dum, dum-DUM! Dum-b'dum-dum, dum-DUM! bludgeoned the multiracial crowd into Corybantic ecstasy – and waited back at Mott Street, later that night, with Naomi in his arms . . . *a slip of a girl*, with skin that had been glossy the night before – but at dawn was a dusty and *matte black* . . .

Will waited anxiously – although his fear hadn't been that Genie's letter would be intercepted and opened, so that his father – who was the moral guarantor for his felonious son – would be deported. Rather, he feared the gear *wouldn't arrive at all* . . .

His report on the demand for building land in the Northern

Territory unfolded drily from the daisy wheel printer – Will sat at his desk, the blotter in front of him empty save for the crumbs from a cinnamon swirl. He waited – taking little sips of iced coffee from a waxed-paper carton, and painstakingly picturing Genie, rolling over in some soiled bed, getting up, getting her get-up, laboriously shooting up – including probing painfully . . . protractedly . . . for a vein – then, sitting there, staring at the gutted blue envelope and its slew of dollars, while deciding again *annagain, not to fucking bother!*

The big men of the red centre could point the bone, or otherwise rain down juju, but Will only had this ironic magic: thinking *what is not*, in order to summon supernatural gifts. Each trip to the post-boxes in the 'nade was a walk down a shit-smeared alley into a run-down London council estate – he didn't hear the companionable chatter of the long-grass people drinking their morning tinnies, or the popping electro-corn of the pedestrian crossings, only the Cockney whine of a thousand skag dealers . . . *I ain't 'olding.*

Then, one morning, his post-box was holding – a well-worn manila envelope, much franked. Will had ripped it right open, and a plastic baggie of white powder fell between his flip-flop feet. He didn't hesitate: but scooped this up, pocketed it and walked straight to where his motorcycle was parked: he drove to the pharmacy in Nightcliff, where they knew him, and blagged a bag of ten disposable one-millilitre hypodermic needles, by claiming the vet had prescribed a course of vitamins for his poorly dog.

Which was really the ravening monkey, climbing up his back. Although there was some substance behind this tissue lie: throughout the monsoon Will had been running the Heinzes' Dobermans out on the dull sands at Lee Point. He'd stride along beside the sea that couldn't be swum in, beneath the weeping skies – the two big dogs running away from him towards the smudged horizon, their pawprints parenthesising this nebulous void – making of what barely was . . . *nothing at all.*

Will loved running the dogs – he'd felt a deep sympathy with them, for, off smack, coke and all other hard drugs for months now, he'd attained a never before experienced vigour: big, sweaty, glossily muscled, as he ran, kicking up the sand, he felt his own body to be a Doberman, racing forward into the future . . . *and quite impossible to control.*

Back at Mott Street the atmosphere solidified as Will went first to the kitchen to get a glass of water and a spoon, then sat down companionably with the baggie, at a low coffee table: junk time had already been reinstated, the adrenalised tick . . . tick . . . tick . . . that slows ev-ery-thing . . . right . . . down, even as the addict frenziedly concocts his fix.

And all the time he did this, Will cursed himself for – not a fool, but something far worse: a prophet of his own becoming, who staggered, zombie-like, around Jerusalem again *annagain* – who died on the cross again *annagain* . . . who became re-addicted to heroin again *annagain* . . .

'It is the one to whom I will be giving this piece of bread.'

'So, give it to him.'

'To Jayesh? It is to him I should be giving it?'

'Yes!'

'And saying the line?'

'When he gives you the cue, "Surely, not I, Rabbi?" Then you say it.'

'It?'

'The line, which is, "Yes, it is you." '

The cool sharp evening shadows have punctured the day – and the pressure's dropping in Room 421, while, outside in the courtyard, the young Christians are preparing for their Lord's ascension, Amit's voice crackling through the wood-smoked darkness, 'Yes, it is YOU!'

Queequeg . . . had been confused by the *whiteness of the powder* in the baggie, as he left the Nightcliff pharmacy *harpoon in hand* . . . Had Genie got hold of some pharmaceutical gear? It wasn't until the needle penetrated his virginal mainline, the red rose bloomed in the hypodermic's barrel, and he smelt it rising up his gorge that Will realised: *It's coke! It's c-c-c-coke!* A frighteningly Real Thing in the surrealism of

Darwin — On his feet, he'd jittered out on to the teak veranda: the world was singing along with the ringing of his ears, the blood hammering in his temples and the sweat coursing down his flanks. The wind chimes were playing the ghastly jingle – while the entire sky *creaked* as a great dirty-purple cloud of monsoonal rain waved slowly back and forth over the pandanus palms and squat office blocks of downtown Darwin.

It was 1984 – but it was the Rainbow Serpent who'd been keeping Will under surveillance. It came stalking from the undergrowth, its Elizabethan ruff lying limp on its narrow shoulders, its police cap with its chequered band set askew. Where'd the fucker come from? Probably busting blackfellas – *Oh, ma-an!* It was a hard world out there, full of pain and suffering – was it any wonder Will needed some sort of anaesthetic?

So he'd had another hit of the coke – which was very pure indeed.

Then another.

And another.

Each time he bisected the little pile, Will swore this would be his last hit: he'd promised Vance some of whatever came in the mail – if it ever did.

Still, Vance'd been in Darwin so long he'd probably forgotten what real coke was like – if he ever knew to begin with.

So Will went on bisecting and bisecting, that *bear of very little brain* – making sure it was cocaine, *right to the bottom of the jar* . . .

What was fixing cocaine like? Fixing it with no downers to hand save a few stubbies of Emu Export? It was as if the raft of the Medusa were . . . *a fucking pedalo*, so he'd to pump his thighs as he piloted his dying hopes and futile dreams between the bodies *floating, face down* . . . Thighs Will now feels if he makes the slightest movement on the sweat-damp ticking – thighs and buttocks, *sung up* into pained existence, with their sores either scabbed over or rawly open, and covered by Band-Aids *smeared in Savlon, myrrh and fucking aloes* . . .

'Ach!' How disgusting is this? Isn't this the worst it's ever been? Although Will knows he's as yet only in the foothills of withdrawal – the great yawning chasms of discomfort, and the glassy peaks of pain *lie ahead* . . .

Worst of all: hadn't he foreseen this, sat on the rattan settee in the teak box on Mott Street, his labouring heart *shifting shingle* in his *shell-likes?* Anticipated his fall from any grace, as he'd watched the frill-necked lizard retreat into the undergrowth.

And now? Silvery medallions are flung across the bare walls of Room 421 as the spotlights dally round the dark courtyard, and settle – Will assumes – on the Saviour-impersonator, since he yodels: 'My soul is over-whelmed with soooroooow to the pooooint of deaaaath!'

On clear days in Kathmandu the sacred mountains could be seen glinting evilly in the distance. But weather conditions were of little importance for these particular mountaineers, whose most perilous ascent had been up the three gyring flights to their eyrie of a room, where, wrapped in his nappy of 'crombie, Caius lay back in one of the coffin-like beds and picked up his book: a luridly jacketed paperback filled with tales of eccentric Indian rajahs and princes. This was in fact preparatory reading: through a posh Indian friend, Caius had secured introductions to a number of the regal courts that still hung on, preserved in the aspic of their own historic irrelevance. And, as the milky ambience of the opiates . . . *curdled* into rancid addiction, he began planning his itinerary, while making it perfectly clear Will would not be accompanying him.

The end had come abruptly: driven out from the guest house by the conviction that a Montecristo would improve his mood, Caius went in search of an upmarket hotel with a humidor, only to run into Holi.

The festival that is, which was being celebrated by urchins, dashing through the streets and chucking paper packets full of powder paint at passers-by – bombs that burst most impressively, for the most part causing an explosion of jollity, although when the young sahib returned he'd been in high dudgeon, with his shantung silk suit spattered blue, green and red.

He declared Kathmandu to be *Too bloody much!* And while Will lay back on his bed and laughed, threw his clothes into his Samsonite suitcase.

Minutes later, Will was out in the muddy alley, watching the twin peaks of Caius's fedora, outlined by the rear screen of the Ambassador taxi driving him to the airport. They'd arranged to meet again in Kashmir, in three weeks' time, a rendezvous Will thought it unlikely either of them would keep.

For he'd been delighted to see Caius go – *the pretentious prat*. He'd be better off with his own kind, perfuming their beards and petting their *fucking peacocks* . . . Will was made of more robust stuff: a combination of middle-class rectitude, proletarian vigour and Aboriginal guile. Vance had told him all about Nepalese treks he'd taken, up into Himalayan valleys choked with rhododendrons, to the lairs of isolate mystics, and the vertiginous villages inhabited by sexually inventive animists – Will would follow in his footsteps, arrive at some distant Shangri-La *and fucking stay there . . . fucking.*

*

The following day he'd taken the bus to Pokhara, brown-bagging a bottle of opium-laced brandy: the plan was to taper off, regain his strength, then head for the hills.

Three days after that, Will came to standing, looking out over the moon-kissed ripples of Lake Phewa. Could there be anything lovelier than this? The muted chittering of the insects and the gentle wash at his sandalled feet, as Selene pulled everything hurting to her *soft and cratered belly . . .*

He'd been puzzling out how he arrived at this precise point – smoking a fat joint of local weed and black hashish, his head tipped back, his boudoir mind hung about with the velvet night – when he felt a sharp tug on his sleeve.

Will looked down into the face of the eleven-year-old boy who, so far as he could establish, was managing the Star Hotel – at any rate, whenever a guest wanted something they would ask the serious, single-eyebrowed Bishal, who, if he wasn't at the makeshift reception desk, would be mopping floors, scrubbing bathrooms or changing beds.

Bishal looked up at Will. There'd been no rancour in his expression – while his tone was entirely matter-of-fact, which is perhaps why Will, even in extremis, recalls his words ver-batim: *It is late*, he'd said, *and you have taken too many drugs. Now it is time for you to go to bed.*

In that bed, snorting another fat white line of morphine from the lid of his tobacco tin, Will had a moment of piercing clarity: there was a boil on the sole of his foot, he had a half-gramme-a-day habit . . . *and rising*. He wasn't trekking up into any mountains – but, rather, had been sent up the wooden stairs to Bedford-fucking-shire by an eleven-year-old boy! One far more competent and responsible than he was.

He returned to Kathmandu the following day – and, the day after that, boarded an eight-seater minibus. Its destination was Varanasi in Uttar Pradesh, and for two days Will had sat listening to an Australian hippy wearing a Victorian nightdress, as he glossed aloud a volume of Shakespeare's sonnets, *Thus have I had thee, mate, as a dream doth flatter . . . In sleep a bloody king, but waking no big deal . . .*

Will had wanted to strangle the man with his own thick, blond tresses, but the Indians on the minibus – a family of six: the father in an immaculate white shirt, the mother elegant in her bright sari, the children, in their Aertex shirts and grey school shorts, perfect little models of hygiene and deportment – smilingly tolerated him. Every few hours the mother would get out Tupperware and tiffin boxes, and serve her family with rice and curry. Will had marvelled at the way the children deftly balled-then-popped the glutinous food, leaving not a trace on their fingers or their lips – while the flies never seemed to lift off from Will's eyes . . . *to land on theirs.*

Stopping for the night at a cavernous caravanserai, they

were allotted loosely strung charpoys – Will bounced from his several times in the night. The clock had been running down – junk time giving way to the shitty revolutions of his own body clock. The latrine had been unspeakable – so he'd greeted the dawn by the side of the road, together with the other exiguous figures . . . *fatalistically shitting.*

The sun rose not just on the nothing new – but on everything that had never been renewed: a landscape saturated in humanity for millennia. Whatever the Aussie hippy declaimed, there was no comparison between this and a summer's day in Elizabethan rural England – here, every handful of dust had *already been handled . . .*

It had lasted another couple of days: the minibus bumping along the road, the hippy giving voice – and Will's bowels *howling . . .* At one stop, in the middle of everywhere, they'd coincided with another minibus. This one was full of Japanese tourists, and Will felt as if he were witnessing the first contact between humans and aliens, such was the Indians' astonishment at the sight of them. The Japanese had gathered round a stall at which a huge man was deep-frying some jalebi – coiling the dough into the sizzling oil through a paper funnel. The locals had, in turn, gathered about them.

Trapped by the crowd, Will felt the very worst claustrophobia – that of time: dynasties might come and go, millions would live and die, but still he'd be stuck here, at the dusty crossroads, by the stall, watching the avid Japanese, their camera lenses gobbling up the scene.

A man on an adjacent stall was serving up lassi: pouring a milky stream into aluminium beakers then adding spoonfuls of ice shavings. *Mmm . . .* it'd looked so refreshing, so cool – and so deadly: those ice shavings would've been made from contaminated water, seething with dysentery. *But it looked so refreshing and cool . . .*

So Will slurped one down – then went on, arriving late at night in Varanasi, and heading straight from the coach park to Vikram's uncle's carpet shop, where he lay on a pile of them while the uncle rootled about for some heroin. Yes: it was past his bedtime in Pokhara – and past it in the holy city on the banks of the Ganges as well. It'd been past the Dalit woman's bedtime as well – Will saw her, sweeping up outside when he arrived at the Tourist Bungalow – and a while later, glancing out the little window hacked in the cement wall of his austere room, he'd seen her preparing for the night too: settling down on a nearby pile of dung and covering her face with a lappet of her dun sari.

A few days on smack – a few days off: again *annagain . . .* Will's halting progress across northern India had been a strange figuration of his bowels, as, opiates ebbing and flowing, they'd clenched and unclenched, propelling him on . . . *the little shit.*

He'd tried to do the sorts of things he thought he ought, if he were to salvage this grandly pathetic tour: visiting the temple dedicated to Hanuman, or cycling at dawn down to the burning ghats, where he'd sat, smoking a soapstone chillum with the Beat sadhu, who, when Will hitched up his lunghi and readied himself for sacred immersion, made every effort to dissuade him.

Because he'd kept getting it wrong, this perverse pilgrim: the sacred monkeys sprayed him with their liquid shit – while Will's ill-advised baptismal swim had ended a hundred yards offshore, when one of his windmilling fists struck a putrescent water buffalo, swollen twice life-size, that'd been revolving lazily downstream. Down he'd gone, into the sacred and heavily polluted water – and up he'd risen, spluttering bacteria.

The following day he'd hied him to the railway station to buy a ticket for the Himgiri–Howrah Express. A chitty needed to be obtained at Window B and taken to Window F, where it was to be exchanged for a second chitty – this was required by the cashier behind the grille at Window A, who, once the required rupees were handed across, gave Will a last chitty, which he'd redeemed for a ticket at Window C. A ticket that – when he stepped into the blinding light of the maidan – he realised was not for the following day but a week later.

Will simply shrugged and accepted this delay. What did

it matter? He was only another fatalistic incarnation, lying by the side of the road on a pile of dung and *watching the world go by* . . . He'd celebrated his acceptance of India's Heraclitean flux by squatting down right there, in front of a man armed with a cut-throat razor, who'd shaved him deftly, then rubbed his nicked pimples with a lump of stinging alum.

At the Tourist Bungalow Will fell in with Yuri, who claimed to be the son of a high-ranking Soviet apparatchik. Yuri also maintained that he'd been exiled due to his heterodox beliefs – so condemned to wander the world. His canvas rucksack was carefully lettered, in biro, with the names of all the countries he'd visited . . . *including Swaziland.*

Will put him down as another dumb fantasist, the kind Brother Bill decreed *a terrific bore once he's spotted you as a man of intelligence* . . . But on the days Will wasn't using, he'd sit with Yuri in the Bungalow's clattery canteen-restaurant, sucking down quart-bottles of Stag Ale, and listening to his tales of global conspiracy, which seemed only shoddier versions of what credulous Westerners believed.

Yuri's hand shook as he raised his glass to his bloodless lips. Will had looked into his parboiled eyes and seen there the silhouette of the man who was murdering him: *John-bloody-Barleycorn* . . . Who'd also appeared to Will, in Granada, on a trip he'd undertaken to Spain a couple of years before – on that occasion in the guise of an old Englishman, shivery and white-haired, who'd been queuing in front of him at a bank.

Leaving riot-torn London behind him, Will had headed for the Algarve via Lisbon – on the Magic Bus, face down in a paperback all the way there, a lump of hash concealed in the toothpaste tube in his washbag.

He'd looked up to see revolutionary graffiti on bullet-pocked walls, found the railway station, boarded the train and buried his head once more. At the coast, he left the railway station and strolled along dull bluffs, looking for somewhere secluded for a smoke – but as he'd lit up a German hippy emerged from a bush, and suggested they sing Stairway to Heaven together.

Will had slept out on a golf course, curled up in a bunker – and in the morning was chased off by a club-wielding English retiree. At the clubhouse, where he'd sneaked in for a wash, he met a couple of English girls – and ended up staying with them in some parental ranch-style bungalow, in a five-bar-gated community. Quite possibly overwhelmed by this cornucopia: lying between Jane and Fiona on the sunburst-patterned cushions they'd removed from the swing-seat, he may've tried it on with both at once.

Expelled once more, he wandered over the land border to Spain, and entrained for Seville, where he spent a bad night in a mosquito-ridden hotel, dreaming his friend Hughie had died: fading away slowly, leaving only his doe eyes and lopsided grin *a-ma-zing-ly* shining in the stuffy darkness.

Will went on. In Granada he'd been too depressed to go to the Alhambra – too depressed, and too independent a traveller to surrender to mass tourism: the myriad flip-flops rubbing the aura off everything, thereby turning it into a copy of itself. Instead, he'd wandered the streets, looking for somewhere he could smoke some hash, and avoiding the Guardia Civil in their tight tan breeches and shiny origami hats, who patrolled in homoerotic pairs.

In the bank there'd been workaday Granadans, Will with his tenner's worth of Thomas Cook traveller's cheques to cash – and the remittance man. For that's clearly what he was: the Spanish equivalent of Canada's Uncle Martini, but with no transpontine nephew to bear him his libations. Rather, the poor old soak trembled in the bank queue, and the BOAC flight bag full of empty wine bottles slung over his shoulder chinked. Will had been shaken: there was the ghost of his own future, exposed in full daylight, his muzzle grizzled, his eyes . . . *full of white rheum.*

Yuri was another. Will grew reckless – chopping out lines of smack on the wall outside the post office: if he didn't get out of London – out of Canberra then Darwin, Brisbane then Delhi, Kathmandu – and now Varanasi, he'd die there or here, lying on a dung heap, a lappet of the blue-cotton scarf he'd bought in Nepal covering his fucked-up face.

But no: it was still wrapped round his scrofulous neck, when he finally arrived in Kashmir. Yes – wrapped in blue cotton hemmed with silver thread, Death trailed after Will through the muddy streets. He heard it whistle through the weasel words of the houseboat owners touting for business at the bus station: *Pleeease, sir . . . You come with meeee pronto . . . You are finding first-class accommodations . . . All good meal service and planning the travel itineraries . . .*

Rashid had somehow managed to force his face from the pack fanned out before Will – and they'd haggled mightily. By this stage in his journey Will had no compunction – a cheap holiday in other people's misery it may've been, but it was early in the season, while Kashmir was fast becoming an undesirable destination. There'd been recent terror attacks along the Pakistan border – word was the valley might be barred to tourists altogether.

So it was Will closed on two US dollars a day for everything. Every-fucking-thing: bed, board, laundry – and most of all: heat. Because it'd been cold – oh, so fucking cold! Cold like when it's winter, and you're sick, and you're stumping down the Holloway Road towards some rancid block where you hope a poor excuse for a man will sell you a poxy ten-pound bag, and the chilly dankness seeps up through the flobbed-upon paving stones and into your fried-chicken bones.

So cold.

The town had shanties and a frontier aspect. Men sat on the steps of the boardwalks, hunched up in their woolly burnouses, beneath which smoked little earthenware charcoal burners. Will envied them their non-addictive hit of warmth – *a kick inside* . . .

The H. B. Ceylon turned out to be high of poop and stern and fretworked all over. It wallowed in the shallows of Dal Lake, a substantial vessel, with several cabins, a galley and a well-appointed bathroom. Although, as far as Will could tell, he and Rashid were its entire complement. Not that they'd cast off and set out for anywhere – the Ceylon, together with scores of other such craft, remained limpid and picturesque, its superstructure mirrored by the placid waters, just as were the great icy ramparts of the Himalayas.

If you wanted to go anywhere, you haled one of the skiffs darting about on the lake – boats not unlike the punts in Oxford. Lying back, listening to the suck and swish of the sweeps, Will summoned up wind-tossed afternoons when he'd cycled to the College's boathouse and taken one out on the Cherwell – stretching up, crouching down, again . . . *ann-again*, the trailing pole a long rudder slowly swept, so that the prow swung under the concrete bridge carrying the ring road.

Would you, sir, be desirous of visiting the world-famous floating gardens? Would he fuck – this free-wheeling and free-floating traveller. *No . . . I'm not keen to visit them at all. In point of fact, I'd like to buy some heroin – might you be able to assist?*

Will lay in the huge wooden bed, with its ornately carved head- and footboards. He never saw anyone but Rashid – although he heard female voices and the steady flap-slap of Indian laundering. Rashid turned out to be beyond conscientious when it came to earning his daily two bucks: a mummyish presence, he'd creep into the cabin and remove Will's dirty clothes while he slept, then return to take breakfast orders. Immobilised by smack – and modesty – Will lay there, listening to the invisible women and the thud of his torpid heart. He felt so very negligible that he half expected to see this insistent organ inside his chest, as the skin and the flesh peeled back, and his ribs dissolved.

What had it all been for – and how long could it possibly endure? Will sucked the spicy smoke up through a tin foil tube then lay back, primed for revelation. But there were no dynasties of dream any more – only a terrifying sense of foreclosure, as, looking to this bright future or that shining prospect, he saw them closed off and shuttered up.

He replayed, again, the long motorcycle ride south from Darwin to Canberra – specifically the last eighty clicks or so, the road undulating ahead of him over the high, windswept bluffs above the Murrumbidgee River. The landscape was so very wide: a vast panorama resembling nothing so much as hypertrophied Yorkshire moors. Pulling the Super Dream off the road, Will had rolled a cigarette and sat smoking. He could go there, or there, or way over there – the world presented itself as infinitely receding possibilities, as his eye skipped from hill crest-to-crest.

But in fact he was going to fly to India and start using smack again – this was more certain than starry wars or starving Ethiopians. It was *a self-fulfilling prophecy* . . . another of his mother's damning and damnable phrases.

Only schadenfreude prevented Will from taking all his misery out on Caius the moment they met – because, before he could get going, Caius had vented his own.

They were standing on the steps outside the post office on another freezing Kashmir spring day, and Caius – who, while absent, had reacquired a certain élan – appeared utterly preposterous: a toffee-nosed ephebe dressing up in a raw silk suit and pearl-grey fedora, expelling great gouts of condensed indignation.

Who did he fucking-well think he was, *the unseasonable man from Del Monte?*

He liked to say 'no', did Caius: the maharajas' palaces had been no fun at all – worm-eaten and verminous, with antechambers full of ghee-greasy retainers, slobbering pan juice on silk-striped cushions. Miniature trains carrying cruets and port decanters notwithstanding, the anecdotage remained thin on the hard-packed ground. At night, listless, dehydrated after too many atavistic measures of spirits – pegs, chargers, *even stirrup-fucking-cups* – he'd despaired of his Hindoo holiday, but at least, unlike feeble little Willy, *he'd kept off the smack* . . .

Kept off it in Srinagar as well, where, having arrived like Will, early for their rendezvous, Caius had been correctly identified and captured within seconds: one of the bus station touts leading him to quarters he described to Will as 'a sort of narrow boat marooned in the town's sewer outfall'. When the pair went to retrieve his Samsonite suitcase, this turned out to be no hyperbole at all. It was hut-boat rather than a house one – cramped quarters Caius had been sharing with an extended Kashmiri family that included several vocal infants, and all this at a special friend-of-maharajas rate of fifteen bucks per diem.

There hadn't been a moment to lose – so Will began crowing right away, and kept it up under the eyes of Caius's many former landlords-and-ladies, as they struggled down the gangway. What a fucking cash-swaddled and corduroy-nappied idiot! No real empathy for the lower orders he treads beneath his Church's loafers, so he falls victim to them . . . *and rightly so!*

'Oh, who is it that has been ROLLING AWAY THE STO-O-ONE?'

The umpteenth question of this long and querulous day – one that began with his interrogator on the Delhi-bound train – howls round the YMCA hostel's courtyard. Will answers it with another: *Who indeed, Rohan? And what's underneath it* . . .

If only these earnest young Indian Christians could see the monstrous vermin currently infesting Room 421, flat out on his pus-ridden back . . . *I can feel your warm face, ev-er close to my lips* . . .

Will can see them too: querulous Rohan, sedulous Amit, serious Samreen, their eyes wide, as, sickened, they pick at sheets stained with blood and pus, before following the trail of foul footprints and discarded Band-Aids in search of *Our Failure and Junky . . . the Risen One* . . .

Caius moved into the second bedroom on the H. B. Ceylon, Rashid's womenfolk did his laundry, and for a few days he and Will attempted some tourism. They engaged a boat, and were sculled, shivering, about the lake, to visit the floating islands of shikaras, and the Mughal gardens on the far shore – grotty-Baroque terraces, overawed by the mountains, upon which newlyweds posed for photos, the men turbaned, the women veiled.

'And what,' Caius sneered, 'is the point of that?'

And what . . . Will howled inside . . . *is the fucking point of you?*

But then a guilty conscience makes the world an ugly place: to look upon his friend's pale and haunted face had very soon become a sort of exquisite torture for Will.

On Caius droned – about his dreadful parents, and the twisted branches of his family-fucking-tree. About his all-consuming misery – and the patent insufficiency of a world in which there weren't bottles of marc de Bourgogne and boxes of Montecristos stored alongside the dry biscuits and plastic clothes pegs, in the little boats, lit by hurricane lamps, that hawked their wares around the lake.

Most of all, about Will, who couldn't even keep off the smack for minutes – let alone days – and whose baleful influence had turned what was meant to be a redemptive pilgrimage into *a shoddy-fucking-binge!*

Caius took to dining on the far shore, at a four-star hotel. Will remained at the Ceylon – blaming him for the debacle, and, with Rashid, planning a Himalayan trek that would be both a redemption and a punishment.

Rashid claimed total competence: transport into these realms of ice and rock, guidance through them, catering and equipment: all would be handled by him, personally, for an extra fifty dollars, plus an increase in their daily rate to ten.

A handsome young man, Rashid, with a full lower lip and

a diffident manner. He wore a plain green shalwar kameez, and somehow managed – despite being very thin – to bustle. When it'd been just the two of them, they'd entered – Will felt – a comfortable enough bourgeois/proletarian symbiosis. But with Caius there came a large and vocal ruling class, which kept Rashid going with his picky requests: 'I say, Rashid, can't you do something about the draught in here? This isn't milk, Rashid, it's CONDENSED milk – do you understand? CONDENSED, which means it isn't milk AT ALL.'

When, Will wondered, would Rashid have the temerity to stand up to this fucking neocolonialist oppressor? When would he become part of the fucking change he wanted to see in the world – assuming, that is, he did.

Probably never.

He was as wreathed in false consciousness, Will thought, as his oppressors were . . . *in smack – two dollars a gramme! Two dollars a gramme!*

Caius was used to this saturation – a physical impact somehow synonymous with the fear of death – but this had been Will's biggest habit to date, and he felt himself *sinking in its quicksand* . . . as they sniffed up line after line: 'I say, Rashid, could you pass me that plate?'

With each village their Ambassador taxi drove through, it was as if the car were a zipper's pull: as they sped past the warped boardwalks, scores of shabby, underfed men had risen to their feet and chased after them. Such desperation – the entire disputed province must be populated by Ten Pence Toms. A real fucking downer, what? As, fortified with heroin, the young sahibs set out for the great proving ground of empire.

At least they'd provided their everything-wallah with a little amusement, when, at the head of the valley, they swapped the car for a couple of ponies and a donkey. Mounted on a little horse, with a striped blanket draped round his padded shoulders, and his pearl-grey fedora still clamped down on his shock of black hair, Caius looked at once pathetic – and absurd.

Will did too – anyone wearing this much denim looks idiotic on a horse . . . *unless he also has a Winchester rifle.* His legs stuck straight out to the sides, to relieve the pressure on what he'd begun to think of as . . . *my bed sores.* They'd rollicked around on their skinny mounts as they lurched along a rubbly track – that at first followed the course of a rushing river, then, after a couple of hours, began to mount the scree side of a steep valley.

That it was cold and pervasively damp went without saying so they'd kept shtum. The cloud cover sank down on top of them as they rose to meet it – the scenery consisted only in grey grass and greyer stone. His belly griping and his sores stinging, Will had ruminated gloomily: fuck the Marabar

Caves and the far-fucking-pavilions – really, they could be anywhere in north Britain, the Lake District or *the Black-bloody-Mountains* . . .

The cistern over the squat toilet gurgles – while Will, unwilling to take any risks, remains lurking in the bathroom of Room 421, crouching down then straightening up, hoping somehow to relieve these awful – and awfully familiar – sensations: the ill-fitting of his bones, the sandpapering of his skin, the liquefaction of his bowels.

The rest of the cast and crew must've assembled, because he can hear concerted murmuring in the courtyard outside, from which emerges: 'So, you will be saying this in a different sort of voice, yes?' And Will thinks that, yes, it would be great if his internal voice were suddenly to become someone else's – because this would mean he was *ceasing to be me* . . .

Rohan takes a different view: 'But I am Jesus,' he protests. 'See, I am wearing the Jesus robe – I have the Jesus face. I'm not going to be fooling these women, you know.'

'They are fooling themselves!' the director expostulates. 'That is why they don't recognise you sitting beside the tomb, yeah? Now, please just say the lines, Rohan – it's getting late and I'm wanting to head to my home for some rest and refreshment before evening rehearsal.'

At least Amit's right about that: it is getting late – and Will does want to go home. But he can't with a gramme-a-day habit, which is why his exit strategy includes this seventy-two-hour layover in New Delhi, where he'll puke and shit bile, until, wrung out and emaciated, he staggers on to the plane.

'Oh . . . okay, then . . . okay . . . "ahem" . . . Don't be alarmed if you are looking for Jesus the Nazarene, who was crucified. HE HAS RISEN!'

At around 13,000 feet, as they were struggling over a spur, the clouds parted to reveal the mighty peaks soaring thousands of feet higher, and their terrible flanks of snow, ice and rock. It was an awesome sight – the sublimity of which had been completely ruined by a single-storey green-painted weatherboard structure plunked down on the ridge above them.

As Rashid led their mounts away to a hut that would serve as their stable, the young sahibs goggled at this incongruity. It was the proof, Will felt, of the reality of their trek: no bold and manly progress into the wilds – but an ill-tempered and feeble retreat *into a cricket pavilion!* He'd half expected some Titmus or other to bound out on to the little veranda, bat brandished aloft to salute the empty, icy stands.

What transpired then was the worst ever bout of the stasis horrors, as the twelfth and thirteenth men were immobilised in this pavilion by a combination of altitude sickness and heroin addiction. There were two bunk beds, set at right-angles to each other in the corner of the main room – and these they took to, in their sleeping bags. Lying there, alternately shivering and gouching out, Will would regain consciousness to hear Caius reading aloud from his book on maharajas and their eccentricities – how this one had turned his entire principality into a working astronomical model, while that one maintained forty dwarfish concubines, and a third amused himself by building an extensive soup-and-curry-freighting rail network on his vast dining table.

Meanwhile, Rashid had fussed about them – producing, at periodic intervals, meals that tasted to Will *like a handful of dust* . . .

Rashid, with his thin and serious face, setting an aluminium saucepan of water on the primus stove and waiting — and waiting some more while the molecules of hydrogen and oxygen hauled themselves sullenly towards ebullition. They too had felt the effects of the altitude.

At some point during their sojourn – which lasted either three days or *a fucking eternity!* – depending on how you viewed it, Will stepped out on to the veranda and experienced a murky sort of epiphany, as the clouds lifted once more from the encircling peaks: surely these were the vaporous castles he'd laid siege to in earliest childhood – yet now they'd capitulated by this act alone, since such amazing grandeur should never bear witness to such pathetic squalor.

Back inside the pavilion, Rashid had been laying a newspaper tablecloth on a wonky card table, preparatory to serving their evening meal. Birthing from his sleeping bag, Caius flubbered towards them: a grub that had failed to metamorphose in its blue nylon pupa.

Will knew Caius was as angry and desperate as he – they were both entombed by the smack *finer than flour, alive, more poisonous than silica* . . . that *sifted, almost invisible, through the long afternoons of tedium* . . . but that hadn't excused his behaviour. And, as Rashid had pumped the primus, Will transposed its vaporous stench into a rotten certainty: *I'm never gonna get out of this fucking country alive* . . .

No . . . he'd end up wreathed in his dumb cotton scarves and lugging his silly tin suitcase, together with all the other dumb Westerners whose path to enlightenment had petered out into a dirty smack trail.

He'd seen them during their first few days in Delhi, on an excursion to the old town with Caius – clip-clopping past the Red Fort in a jingling gharry, the old hippy junkies eddied and whirled about them, begging with more desperate abandon than any Indian. *Fuck!* How moribund they'd looked – their pasty skins showing the dirt, their filthy flares and soiled cheesecloth shirts . . . *in tatters.*

'Rice, Rashid' – Caius had raised one of his spatulate fingers – 'and potatoes, Rashid' – he held up a second digit, with its weirdly recessed nail – 'and bread.' The third finger, at first simply adamant, then turned accusatory: 'That's three kinds of carbohydrate, Rashid, THREE KINDS OF FUCKING CARBOHYDRATE! HOW THE BLOODY HELL CAN I SURVIVE ON THAT? I'M ALREADY HIDEOUSLY FUCKING CONSTIPATED!'

His words hang before Will in the stinky little bathroom of Room 421 of the YMCA hostel in New Delhi – while beside them TIMMS' EXCELSIOR FOR SUPERIOR SMILLING manoeuvres for air space. And, despite his own precarious situation – lying once again athwart the shitty oubliette – Will laughs. Because, assuming he's made good on his own promise to kick before returning to London, whatever Caius is currently experiencing, it won't be constipation.

'Okay, okay, everyone – not so bad, really . . . Not so bad for a first full run-through . . .' Will feels he knows Amit now – and slightly admires his head-boy earnestness. Certainly, he recognises that the director is trying to be encouraging: 'But it is the practice that makes the perfection, so we'll be doing a second run-through now, but beginning with the Passover scene.'

A hiss of dissent whistles around the courtyard – Will wonders if it'll become an outright mutiny. But no – there's a click, a hiss, a squawk of feedback, and Rohan resumes his Messiah-impersonation.

'The one who has been dipping his hand into the bowl

with me will for sure betray me. The Son of Man will be going along just as it is written about him . . .' I'm going to die, Will thinks, in this ghastly shithole, 'but woe indeed to him who is betraying the very Son of Man!' Die listening to these po-faced fucking wowsers. 'It would be better for him IF HE HAD NOT BEEN BORN!'

5
August 1986

'How many times a day can you wank?'

'Hypothetically – or do you mean how many times in any given day do I, in fact, masturbate?'

'Yeah – that.'

'That what?'

'That – how many times a day d'you actually do it . . . an' that.'

Will ponders the phatic 'an' that'. Paul's the sort of kid who calls his grandmother 'Nan' – and was most probably brought up by her, another *potent class signifier* . . . He wears a parka, and stonewashed jeans that make his epicene legs appear *marbled with putrefaction* . . . Once sculpted into a Mohican, his massy-black hair has long since grown out into a sloppy pompadour that slumps on his spotty forehead.

Will says, 'I reckon I knock one out for getting on seventeen times a day.'

'Seventeen!' Paul's eyes widen with admiration. 'How the fuck d'you manage that?'

Will thinks for a moment. It's an exaggeration, certainly, but not that great a one.

He rises in the double dullness of a provincial suburban night to follow his bowshaft-taut cock as it dowses towards the bathroom, where, in a lilac-yellow stall, chilly zephyrs tickling his ankles, he rubs himself back into quiescence.

Most nights this doesn't work, so Will pads downstairs to the patients' lounge, where he sits and smokes a couple of fags with Alan, the nightwatchman, who confronts the world through eyeholes cut in a *massive port wine stain* . . . After which Will pads back up to the bathroom, knocks a second one out, then retires to the odd intimacy of darkness shared with strangers: the light arcing from the opened door to briefly stroke Paul's and Greg's heads, before wavering away over their prone bodies, humped beneath candlewick bedspreads.

Paul's in his third week at the Lodge, but anyway, as a self-confessed glue-huffing garbage head, he didn't really need much of a detox, just a couple of Librium to stop him bouncing off the walls. By contrast Greg required several handfuls – as he hasn't yet tired of telling Will – since, prior to his arrival in this place of safety, he was a highly conscientious alcoholic.

Greg's about to graduate from primary care, an event he regards as on a par with *receiving a fucking Nobel* . . . Another Northerner, like Paul, although of the Tory persuasion, his cheeks are rouged with burst blood vessels, while he has the lambent eyes and slightly vacant expression Will associates with those who've – in the Lodge's jargon – 'got the Programme'.

Greg carries a clipboard with him wherever he goes, as a nun might her rosary. Given any opportunity – not just the *Maoist criticism sessions* that constitute the essence of this 'treatment' – he'll detain his fellow alcoholics and addicts, in order to share his catechism of cupidity.

Both – so far as Will can tell – sleep soundly. Unlike him.

Upon his own arrival, a fortnight since, Will managed a cunning stunt, and actually increased his drug dependency while in treatment for it. Already stupefied by a half-gramme-a-day habit, he told the doctor who took his blood pressure and palped his lower abdomen he'd been taking twice that. Given eighty milligrammes of Physeptone daily, he'd spent his first four swimming through the *colourless green ideas' sleep, furiously* . . . from therapy group, to mealtime, to fag break.

Breasting the swirl of the fitted Axminster carpets, and the sheen of the polished parquet floors, Will would curl into one of the chairs in the circle, gouch out, then come to – gouch out, then come to again *annagain*, with the eyes of the group examining him from all angles, as he became reacquainted with the dismal cliché of his predicament:

A violent annexation of the island known as Will by the

main. And what a main! Floating in his caul of amniotic Physeptone, he'd tried to fathom the Lodge – and come up with The House of Sixty Fathers, a book he remembered reading, aged nine or ten, in the midst of his parents' hysterical break-up.

In the bloody flux of the Second World War's end game, as the Americans launch air raids on Japan from China, one of the millions of war orphans is adopted by a squadron of United States Army Airforce pilots. He sleeps in their huge dormitory, is dandled on their homesick knees – becoming their mascot, his starvation ending with the magical experience of curling tiny strips of sweetness on to his tongue . . . *and chewing*.

The Lodge also has communal eating and sleeping, combined with the charged atmosphere of shared and mortal endeavour – true, beyond the rhododendrons edging the property, Weston-super-Mare's environs bear scant resemblance to war-torn Jiangxi, while there are also plenty of potential mothers – as well as girls and boys – in residence. Nevertheless, since Will was sussed out, then precipitately tapered off the Physeptone, it's the fathers who've mostly *got on my case* . . .

Dodgy dads with fag burns in their V-neck pullovers, and, until very recently, Extra-Strong Trebor mints on their vodka breath. Greg and Dave and Ken and Brian – formerly solid chaps, eroded from within by their ravening thirst, who're only too keen to share their hollow wisdom and empty insight.

To describe Greg's cheeks as *rouged with burst blood vessels* is scarcely permissible poetry, rather, his face looks *like a fucking placenta*, it's so swollen-red and veiny. Yet, despite this mask of incompetence, Greg's quite convinced of his own wisdom and rectitude. 'Listen,' he says to Will at every opportunity, 'listen, if there's anything you need to share . . . anything that's troubling you, but that's too embarrassing to share in group, then I'd be honoured if you'd share it with me. Think of me as . . . as' – he struggled to avoid the paternity suit – 'your older brother.'

When Will thinks of his older brother, he remembers his instructions on how to mould pillows into a fuckable simulation of a body – or tossing himself off in an empty carriage on the Northern Line. Had his brother's abuse at the hands of his teachers been the cause of this preternatural sexualisation, or its effect? And should he share this with Greg, his group or his counsellor, the unctuous Bryn – who combines Low Church humility with the alcoholic's typically stratospheric arrogance?

One of the little zones of lucidity Will emerged into during his first four days at the Lodge had been occupied by Bryn's own 'chair', a more formal version of the confessional sharing everyone – staff and patients alike – is required to do, all day every day: a susurration of sins that accompanies them wherever they go.

The others had been sitting either primly upright in their plastic stacking chairs – or lolling promiscuously, when Will came to, and heard Bryn's triumphant fluting: 'Yes! Yes! I can admit it now – I was a piss-head, lit-er-all-y a piss-head. Why? Because sometimes I'd get so very drunk I would piss on my own head.'

It was an arresting image. Bryn's a pale, flabby man with reddish hair and geography teacher's sideburns, who wears white shirts over string vests, grey suit trousers and lace-up leather shoes. It took a fair amount of heavy imaginative lifting to crumple him up, and position his flaccid penis so it guttered on to his spluttering mouth.

Will wondered whether anyone else appreciated what was entailed by Bryn's literalism – wonders still why no one objected to such grandstanding. True, the head-pissing couldn't exactly be damned as *euphoric recall*, but hadn't Bryn been exhibiting a wayward *pride in his own disease*? *Pride* such as accompanies a *character defect* Will's very quickly come to identify in himself, namely . . . *grandiosity*.

'And petrol-sniffing,' Bryn had continued, 'that's meant to be some shock-ing new thing, isn't it?' No one saw fit to affirm or deny this, so: 'Well, I've known all about pet-rol sniff-ing for years now. Why? Because I'd get a great hooter-ful of the bloody stuff every time I grabbed the nozzle from the pump and stuck it in my bloody mouth!'

Will's mother, who'd studied journalism . . . *during the fucking Middle Ages*, still believes she holds the mystery when it comes to writing. Will remembers her stock response to almost any of his fuck-ups or misadventures: *that'll make good copy . . .* Which would be followed closely by: *Remember, any piece of writing must answer the following questions: Who? What? Where? Why? And when?* Sound advice – although, his ambition to write coaxed out of him by solicitous peers, Will's been bombarded with their histrionics: *You could write my story . . . This place would make a wicked book . . . Did I tell you about how I . . .*

However, there's such a thing as being spoilt for choice – Derek, the permanently employed cook, wields a cleaver with calm efficiency. As well he shouldn't, having – according to the Lodge gossip – killed his own wife during an alcoholic blackout. While Hervé, the suave, silver-haired counsellor who was formerly a pharmacist, sneers at his junky patients: 'You riff-raff don't know what drugs are – I've had access to more drugs than you've had hot dinners. I didn't have to do chemists – I was the chemist!'

Bryn's fantastical combination of the workaday and the Wagnerian is *well up there* . . . calling upon Will, as it did, to picture him dragging his desperate body across the oil-stained forecourt of some godforsaken Welsh filling station, hauling it semi-upright beside the pump, then unlimbering the nozzle so he might *suckle on the witch's tit* . . .

Fuck the house of sixty fathers – Will's trapped in a Catch-22 of monstrous proportions. To recover from the spiritual illness of chemical dependency – the principal deformations of which are an impoverishment of human relations and moral sense – the addict-alcoholic must shrive himself fulsomely, omitting no sordid detail, *leaving no stoned outrage unturned* . . . The form this takes is the writing down of examples of what they term 'powerlessness and damage': situations in which the addict-alcoholic's diseased will has caused harm to others – and, of course, himself.

The enthusiastic amassing of these 'examples' and their 'sharing', either with the group or 'one-to-one', makes of the Lodge a *mucky sort of murmuration* . . . as, when passing a window seat or colloquy of easy chairs, one's subject to hearing things like, *Then he grabbed my hair, so when he went out again I shat in the bath* . . . But, at the same time, Will must be ever-aware that the mere quantity of confession is besides the point – what's needed is high-quality sincerity: the full acceptance of sin, rather than its mere acknowledgement – for only then will the sinner truly be *on the Programme* . . .

It's bewildering – for how can you know whether your

urge to confess comes from you yourself, or from the very golem that's been summoned into existence by your addiction, and that resides in a secret chamber of your psyche? Yet more confusingly, while he was in the grip of his 'active addiction', Will personified it – while knowing that such magical thinking was, at best, unhelpful – and now, under the kindly eyes of these interrogators, he's required to resurrect this avid creature – if only to slay him.

At lectures and house meetings the foldaway tables are erected then covered with blue-jacketed pamphlets published by the legendary Hazelden Clinic in Minnesota, the font of all recovery wisdom – 'recovery' being a forever operative word, given that cure is an impossibility. Indeed, so far as Will can see, it's the progressive, incurable and fatal aetiology of what they stridently insist really is a bona fide 'disease' which excites the Programmers so much.

For, just as their drinking and drugging was a full-time job, so recovering from it will take forever, as they get half well, then halve the remaining illness, and halve that again – yet never get to a point where they don't *mouth-off a load of half-digested cod-psychological bullshit* . . . Much of it garnered from the pamphlets, which have titles such as The Triangle of Self-Obsession and The Circle of Deceit.

Will's particularly taken by Dr Harry Tiebout's geometric formulation of the not-so-subtle distinction between 'compliance' and 'surrender'. Surrender sounds good – alumni of the Lodge, who return for chairs that're at once popular and mandatory, speak of how it felt so very good to surrender – as if they were Taoists, stepping once into a stream that's nonetheless buoying them up *for-fucking-ever* . . .

Anyway, it's difficult to know how to frame your confessions, so as to find favour with these paternal O'Briens, who hold up three fingers while . . . *compelling you to say there're four.* Should he try to compete with Bryn, Derek and Hervé? Or, rather, should he emphasise the kitchen-sink nature of his travails as the Feminax Junky, knocking back period pills while cooking up that greyish, smokable morphine residue in the Baby Belling?

Or maybe it's his room-mate, Greg, Will should turn to – confining himself to matters which are, so to speak, *to hand* . . . Since the Physeptone – like some Sadducee – has been evicted from the temple of his body, Will's lust has become prodigious: a wank after breakfast – one both in advance and in the aftermath of morning group. A wank or four at lunchtime – followed not long after by some mid-afternoon *masturbatory delight* . . . as he reconfirms the tautological nature of his desire . . . *when it's right, it's right!*

For, while it's true that everything is painfully clear now in the light of drugless days, there remains an erotics of linoleum and wood-effect veneer, of his blurred hand and suppressed stertorous breath, as the fleshy-leaved garden shrubbery presses against the distorting panes of the down-stairs gents'.

In the evening there are edifying film screenings in the Lodge's main hall – such as Dr Harry Tiebout outlining the narcissistic nature of the addictive personality – a psychopathology to which he's given the catchy nickname 'King Baby'. Will has considerable sympathy with the good Doctor's views – for has he not been reborn? And is he not experiencing the polymorphous perversities of infantile sexuality anew?

Following afternoon group, before and after supper, precedent to one fag-break and subsequent to another, Will hies him to the stalls for wanks nine-through-thirteen – arraying before him in the antiseptic atmosphere these arousing images: Moira's bra clip, outlined by the stretched cotton of her polka-dotted top, the very slight – but, for all that, noticeable beneath her tight jeans – hem of Judy's knickers. And, most efficacious of all, the mere hint of a nipple, coddled by the half-cup of Edwina's Maidenform bra – an article of clothing that's become a votary object for Will, so obsessively does he dwell upon it.

Indeed, some fifty per cent of his wanks, daily, are predicated on these speculations: is it padded or patterned? Might there be some sort of lacy detailing? The bra is, Will thinks, a sort of veiled Christ or Hidden Imam, the substance of which can be seen, while its essence remains . . . *ineffable*.

And, although reluctant to mix allusions still further, he also feels himself becoming an Odysseus, lashed to the mast of his own erection, as he sets sail round Edwina – for she wears the tightest and the whitest of T-shirts, the most constricting and fanatically laundered jeans.

She thinks she shits chocolate ice cream . . . his mother's bitter cant rises up Will's gorge: it isn't fair of her to . . . *hang around so*, poised on one or other of his lower lids, peering out through his eyes, havering between . . . *claustro and aggro.* But yes, Mum, in this case you're at least half right: she probably does think she shits ice cream – but not chocolate flavour, vanilla. Edwina would never shit anything as shit-like as chocolate ice cream.

She's the on-off fiancée of a dreamily dissolute duke – and a precocious junky of nineteen, who, now she's starting to put on some weight, boasts a perfect figure. With her silky auburn hair and pert top lip, Edwina is the prettiest, most nubile female in the entire Lodge – everywhere she squeaks on the rubber soles of her immaculate white trainers, the eyes of male patients (and counsellors who've fallen, temporarily, off the Programme) track her, dwelling obsessively on every dip and mound.

And of course, *the scent of you invades cool evening air* . . . Or, at any rate, the closeness of the bedroom, such that Edwina reappears before him: *a whited sepulchre, indeed* . . . summoning him to his two final ejaculations of the day.

*

So: 'Yeah, seventeen – if, that is, you include the last two, though they're likely to be after midnight, and, frankly, pretty fucking negligible.'

Paul, who's only seventeen years old, so susceptible to Will's bitter antics and curdled comedy, takes flight at this point: levering himself up from the Melamine counter where they've been leaning and propelling himself out the dining-room doors.

Will hears his footfalls drumming along the corridor, then hammering up the stairs. A few moments pass, then down they come again. Paul reappears, his parka-clad arms flapping, and cries out, 'I'm a fruit bat! I'm a fruit bat!', circles one of the long refectory tables, before coming in to roost again beside Will – and a large fruit bowl, from which he takes a banana that he peels and begins to eat, such that his next words are *mushy*: 'I'm a fruit bat! I survive entirely on "nyum-nyum" fruit!'

It's Will's own shtick – an ironic celebration of his recovery. Given he's been using drugs for so long, sobriety is as peculiar to him as echolocation. And for the last week or so, as he's begun to feel he really is present, here, in this . . . *place of dead suburban roads*, so he's also felt compelled *to take flight* . . .

One of the sixty fathers, who's passing by the double-doors, pauses to tsk-tsk! Patrick's some sort of beadle or parish councillor, who's ridiculously self-important, always in jacket and tie, and who flaunts a bright enamel religious medal in his buttonhole. If Greg's at the touchy-feely end of the recovery scale, Patrick's part of the *militant-fucking-tendency* . . .

In his first week at the Lodge, banned from anything but the oxymoronic 'recovery literature', Will sneaked away whenever he could to read the novel he'd brought with him: Tolstoy's final feat of self-exculpatory tit-beating, Resurrection. Given the Programme is best absorbed by means of a sort of psychic osmosis its adherents term 'identification', this would seem the ideal primer, given Will certainly recognises a lot of Dimitri Ivanovich Nekhlyudov in himself.

After all, hasn't he always had at least the impulse to help those worse off than he – even if the follow-through left something to be desired. Moreover, if the opportunity arose for him to follow the woman he'd wronged into Siberian exile, Will's sure he'd seize it. Not least because anywhere's got to be better than the frozen wastes of Weston-super-Mare.

As for Patrick, and the other fathers of his ilk, they're on a much shorter path to enlightenment – their favourite reading being a work of cod-spirituality called *The Road-less-fucking-Travelled*. Bryn flutes that, 'Some of you with a re-li-gious background may object to the way the Programme deals with spi-ri-tu-a-lity . . .' while others 'might feel your drrrin-king and drrru-gging has, like, put you out in the cold, see, beyond God's sal-va-tion . . .'

But, far from believing God has forsaken him, Will suspects Patrick to be under the impression he is God – or, at any rate, Moses. For, having abandoned his pernicious dependency (to Crabbies Ginger Wine, Will snidely hypothesises), he's been supplied with the Tablets of the Law, in the form of the Twelve Steps and Twelve Traditions of Alcoholics Anonymous.

No doubt Patrick will raise the matter of Will's pernicious influence on the *highly vulnerable* Paul at the next house meeting. There are already, Will suspects, some black marks among the notes Bryn makes after their one-to-one sessions. Bryn's *confronted* Will with his *character defects* – the intellectualising, the grandiosity and, more worrying still, his liking for *euphoric recall . . .*

Will prevails upon Chloë to buy him boxes of twenty-five Sullivan's Export Virginia at Davidoff, which she then sends to the Lodge by recorded delivery. He sits in the patients' lounge puffing on these opulent smokes, oblivious to his prideful display, while his peers cluster around him, sucking on their humble roll-ups.

Everyone's seen this – but it was Patrick who grassed the addicts up to the counsellors when they – at Will's instigation – began taking snuff: little blue tins of Smith's No. 1 they bought from the newsagent at the bottom of Oldmixon

Road. Will put up a spirited defence, arguing it was simply another way of ingesting nicotine – and probably far less carcinogenic than smoking.

Bryn had counter-attacked: 'Oh-ho, yes, boyo! Soon enough you'll be making lines of the stuff, won't you – like it's co-caine, and where will you go from there?'

Where indeed, because Will's already chopped out a fair few of these snuff-rails, then ridden them straight to a head-banging and thoroughly nauseous terminus: propped in his favoured wank-booth, sinuses screaming, he's wondered if his *primary addiction* might not in fact be to toilet stalls.

Anyway, in this double-thinking cult, Will's choice of devotional literature is equally damning: 'If you've your head stuck in a book like that there Tolstoy, boyo,' says Bryn, 'then you can't have your mind on the Programme.'

'But I do!' Will protests. 'Really, I do!'

Which is the point in their sessions at which the coun-sellor usually *starts with the creepy mind-fuck*: 'Are you sure about that, Will – are you one hundred per cent cer-tain? Remember Step Two: "We came to believe that a Power greater than ourselves could restore us to sanity." Well, I'd say, if you want to be re-stored, you have to accept you've gone a little crazy – isn't that right?'

Will thinks his head may explode with the madness of Bryn's method – or, if not that, then with the horror . . . *the horror!* of his Jesus-at-the-beach poster, captioned with the

Serenity Prayer, and his Gonk collection: the hairy little bollock-beings diminishing across his desk blotter.

Will's utterly devoid of courage and a serenity-free-zone, so how the fuck's he going to change his awful situation, or accept this bullshit: 'A useful way of defining insanity, boyo, is to say it's making the same mistakes and expecting different results – yes . . . yes . . . I can see that gets home to you, doesn't it, you know what that feels like . . .'

Will does know what that feels like – although he thinks that, despite Bryn's low, Taffy cunning, he probably understands it better. No doubt, each time he dragged himself across the hardstanding and unlimbered the nozzle, he fully expected vintage Bollinger to gush out, rather than the *same old fucking two-star blend* . . .

'So, given you know what it's like, perhaps you're in a po-si-tion to know whether you're doing it again – doing it again here at the Lodge. Your mother's paying a lot of money, isn't that right? Paying it so you'll be treated for your chemical dependency – but are you truly surrendering to the treatment, Will, or are you just going along with it, see . . . Going along with it the way you went along with taking drugs and drinking, because it made you feel cool – made you the big I-am . . .'

All this had buzzed from Bryn's moist pink lips only yesterday afternoon – and this morning, after breakfast, Carol,

344

the Family Counsellor, told Will that Ted, the Head of Treatment, has asked to see him at two this afternoon.

'Cutting into valuable wanking time,' Will mutters – and Paul says, 'Wotcher onnabout?' as they join the others, who're being funnelled through the corridor into the large, parquet-floored room, where some twenty assorted chairs – plastic stacking, bentwood, cushioned and easy – are being arranged into a loose circle by those swivel-eyed zealots who've *got the Programme* . . .

Will explains about the summons in an undertone – and Paul klaxons: 'Ooh, I bet Ted'll be on your case proper, like – he'll say you've been complying wiv treatment.'

'Surely,' Will muses, 'that should be not complying –'

'No!' Paul cries – and then *with the air of some fucking Zen master*, pronounces: 'You, you're not on the Programme enough to get it – see, if you comply with treatment it means you're just going along with it . . . You do all the stuff they tell you to do – like writing down your examples of powerlessness and damage – but you don't believe in it, not really. You're just going through the motions . . .'

But isn't that life in a nutshell? Will thinks, as he takes his seat between Gary, a boss-eyed speed addict from Portishead, and Dale, a junky air steward from Louth. Isn't life all about going through the motions – the getting up and the lying down, the wanking and the shitting?

And yes . . . he further acknowledges . . . *quite likely* I am just complying, saying O'Bryn's holding up three fingers, when I know fine-fucking-well there're only two.

Carol, who's supervising this morning's bear pit, sits down and carefully arranges the folds of her beige, wraparound skirt. Everyone's aware of it – the sexual tension crackling through the Lodge. So-called 'special relationships' are among the many anathema – and, while the counsellors urge the patients to give each other hugs rather than drugs, these are scarcely even a maintenance dose of the human touch: being only the light clasping of shoulders in hands.

Will's a dreamer – he knows that. A dreamer who *strongly identifies* with what De Quincey said of his own opiate-addicted-nature: that it took up residence in some secret chamber of his brain, and from there engaged in a sickening commerce with his own heart. For what was Will's addict-self, if not the double of his actual one? Hasn't he proved himself to be, again *annagain*, the most spineless of individuals, completely lacking in any determination or fortitude?

Dale is reading the preamble to the group from a plastic-laminated card: 'This is a safe place to share, and what we say here will remain here . . .' No wonder everyone in the Lodge has what they call *trust issues* . . . and yesterday afternoon Carol had them performing what she calls 'trust exercises', such as falling backwards into each other's arms.

346

But is there really any comparison possible between those split-seconds of freefall and the long drop into cleanliness and sobriety — which Will sees stretching out ahead of him: an endless succession of rainy Tuesday afternoons in the dullest of suburban settings, a fate that makes the statis horrors that troubled him in active addiction seem like . . . *a walk in the fucking park.* He idly considers Cocteau's aperçu: that to talk of giving up to an opium addict is as futile as attempting conversation through an open window . . . *with a man who's just fallen off the roof.*

Dale sports blue tracksuit bottoms with red-and-white stripes running down the seams and a jolly smile. He's either deeply cool . . . *or a complete fucking idiot* – and quite possibly a psychopath. Because it's his turn to read his life story this morning, and after he's told the group all about what he's done, it'll be their turn to *do him* . . .

Some of the sixty fathers (and a few of the mothers) take genuine pride in what they call 'confronting' – they also favour 'giving strong feedback', but both activities just seem like bullying to Will. When he complains to Bryn about these orchestrated houndings – for the counsellors encourage the patients to go for each other's throats – he just shakes his formerly pissy head: 'It's all part of the re-cov-ery pro-cess, Will,' he claims. 'The dis-eased ego has to be broken down, see.'

Will's due to read his own life story next week – after

which he'll be adjudged to have *worked a Step Three* . . . Having subjected the Programme to a pitiless analysis, Will believes he sees it for what it is: a bogus syncretism of evangelical Christianity and sub-Freudian psychotherapy. This theoretic is yoked to a method not dissimilar to . . . *brainwashing.*

When Will accused him and the rest of the counsellors of being brainwashers, Bryn said, 'We have to wash your brain, see, because when you arrived here, Will, it was bloody dirty.'

But it isn't the dirtiness of Will's brain which really bothers Bryn – it's that Will uses it *to think for myself* . . . The counsellors' line is that the addict's very ego – and therefore their will as well – is diseased. Holding fast to the course plotted for them by the redoubtable Dr Tiebout – another nominatively determined man, since his aim is to *lash* everyone to his *mast* – they believe ego and superego to've leapfrogged each other in the addict noggin, such that he becomes his idea of what he's meant to be . . . *the cool dude, the big I-am* . . .

Only by smashing this false superego to pieces can the fledgling sober one be released, blinking, into the bright clean light of recovery. And in order to do this, it's necessary to *break the addict's diseased will!*

The group fidgets while Dale reads on, 'We made a decision to turn our will and our life over to the care of God as we

348

understood him . . .' The Twelve Steps – as befits the laws they truly are – are also inscribed on plastic-laminated tablets, to be read at the outset or the bloody culmination of therapy groups.

Bryn says, 'A-lot of peo-ple have trouble with the G-word . . .' But Will isn't fooled for a second by this seeming identification – Will isn't 'troubled' by the 'G-word': the very mention of God makes him want to puke.

Bryn claims, 'I simply call my Higher Power God because it's a short word.' Then makes this little moue to show he knows how funny he is, and that it's okay on this occasion to laugh.

Will doesn't oblige.

He knows *a sickening bunch of wowsers* . . . when he sees them – and sees also their second-hand hatchbacks parked on the tarmac apron outside the Lodge, all either with fish stickers in the back window or straw crosses on the dashboard. Will quotes William James to the Welsh-fucking-wizard: *The only known cure for dipsomania is religiomania* . . .

To which Bryn replies: 'You can be as clever as you like, boyo, but it won't help you – see, recovery isn't an in-te-llec-tu-al pro-cess at all, it's a spi-ri-tu-al one. It's about your feelings, see – your feelings, and the qua-li-ty of your rela-tionships with other people.'

Dale's finished reading, and tucks the card down beside his track-suited thigh. Carol clears her throat: 'Okay, thank

you, Dale – and the focus is going to stay on you this morning, as you read us your life story . . .'

Will's attention wanders away – he's no thought of giving
Dale anything but the most cursory feedback, and certainly
won't join in dog-fighting with the air steward – what is he,
one of the fucking few? He stares first at the bay window, then,
shutting his eyes, at its three bright *Rothko after-images* . . .

That fade expressionistically away, as he tiptoes along a darkening corridor. De Quincey writhed in withdrawal, terrorised
by the doubling and re-doubling of his addict-self – but
what resides in Will's secret chamber? There it is: a warped
and dented door of multi-density fibreboard, such as you
might see on any fucked-up council flat – grasping its rusty
knob, Will prepares to wrench it open.

What will he find inside? Some ghastly alter-ego, no
doubt, rendered albino by its dark reclusion, blubbery, and
with white feelers wriggling from its empty eye sockets.

Who is it, though? Who is it who crouches in the bony
cave of Will's skull, between the aching, snuff-filled cavities
of his sinuses? As Dale's voice – its accents as colourless and
flat as the landscape of South Notts – fades into the background, Will can hear this creature fulminating . . . *as it
foments rebellion.*

It or he? It's ambiguous, certainly, this great white spirit –
but shock-haired, and with pin-prick pupils piercing his doll's

blue eyes: he's the being who does indeed control Will, although not magically through the fifth dimension, only prosaically via the four ordinarily employed by the Royal Mail.

He drawls poison in Will's inner ear: *You're not going to just sit here, are you? Sit here listening to this pathetic drivel – the low life and high times of a man with writing on his fucking trousers! I thought you were an Übermensch, Will: a re-evaluator of all values, and a despiser of these people's slave-bloody-morality – yet here you are, lapping it up like a little kitten . . .*

. . . *Yes*: outwardly Will's nodding, and looking concerned as Dale drones up to the zenith of his narrative arc – nicking the morphine syrettes from the emergency first-aid kits on long-haul flights – but this is, indeed, *mere compliance . . .* for, inside his secret chamber, it's Caius who pulls on inky wires with spatulate fingers.

A letter arrived yesterday – violent words in violet ink on pale-blue paper: 'Where the fuck are you?' was Caius's salutation, followed without preamble by: 'Johnny's still attending these fucking na-na meetings, Ann's gone away on some bloody bourgeois villa holiday – and now you're in stupid-bloody-treatment. So, what's a man with a heart of oak to do? I'm sat here all alone, with only a quarter-ounce of smack and a half-ounce of coke for company. If I were you, I'd bust out of that hell-hole full of holy rollers and boss-eyed crystal-danglers, head back to London and help me finish it off . . .'

Yes! Finish it off, because – as every good mother's son knows – *waste not, want not* . . .

Last night, the nib of Caius's Mont Blanc pricking him, Will had lain awake and watched the silhouettes of shrubbery revolve across the wall as another car revved up the nominatively deterministic Totterdown Lane.

Listening to Greg's stuttered puffs, and Paul's dreamy mutters, Will imagined his great escape: the reef-knotted candlewick bedspread, the shin down the drainpipe, the cold shoulder of the slip road to the motorway – then the cab of the lorry hauling him towards London, smelling of stale fag smoke *and the rotting corpses of sausage rolls* . . .

And how would this – in the Lodge's idiom – feel? Fucking dreadful – no doubt about that. As he stared sightlessly at the headlights of the oncoming traffic, so he'd see in among the cars and lorries this ghost ship: his mother's Ford Fiesta, a fortnight ago, heading west, beside her the whey-faced and scrofulous passenger who was her very own *King Baby* . . .

Dale drones on – and Will burns with shame at this recollection: he'd begun by asking, then imploring – and finally begging. Begging his poor, neurotic, claustro-and-aggro mother: 'How much is it costing? Loads, right – thousands . . . You can just give me a fraction of that and I'll be gone, never darkening your doors again, and all that jazz . . .'

Had she wept – he rather thinks she had.

She looks utterly worn down nowadays – her hair rapidly greying, overweight. *Fat and old, fat and old, fat and old . . .* was no longer the mantra of her own neurosis, but a simple statement of the facts. And who was to blame for this? Why him, of course – her Benjamin, her baby, the *light of her fucking life . . .*

'You need to listen,' Carol said, during the first of their family sessions last Sunday, 'to what your mother has to say – she needs to be able to tell you how hurt and frightened she's been.'

And so his mother had obliged – and cried.

And Will saw her, sitting there, on the bottom stair, the phone's receiver cradled in her lap.

And she cried some more – until her face was quite wet with tears *like a seal – a fucking seal . . .*

She'd also brought all the penalty-charge notices with her to the Lodge, together with a summons for Will to appear at Lavender Hill Magistrates' Court in a month's time. Will found it hard to take it seriously as she pulled handfuls of the bright yellow-and-black plastic pouches out from her handbag – rather than being an impressive piece of Grand Guignol to rival Derek's uxoricide, amassing five hundred quid's worth of parking fines just looked like . . . *carelessness.*

The charge of driving with undue care and attention – although it carried a potential sentence of five years in

jail – seemed equally risible: there'd be no Götterdämmer-
ung, just a smack on the wrist for a naughty boy, followed by
an early bedtime. Of course, the group doesn't see it this way –
the group rounded on Will when Carol told them about his
poor mother, her careworn appearance and her unstinting
efforts simply to stop her son from killing himself.

Rounded on him still more when they learned – also via
quisling Carol – that Will's mother had funded his habit for
the three weeks before he came to the Lodge. How they
kicked off! Will was a sickening exploiter – according to
Jonathan, a prissy little drunk who chain-smokes menthol
cigarettes and irons a crease into his jeans – and his chosen
prey were women.

This hardly seemed just – after all, as Will's mother might
herself have observed, *nothing's worth having that isn't freely
given* . . . and so the heroin hadn't really . . . *hit the spot.* Anyway, there'd been too much pain for even a half-gramme a
day to eradicate: the pain of limping, carless, through early-
summer streets, face down to the ground . . . *down to the
ground!*

Will had done the same rounds he used to with Damian
when he first began using – from one ten-pound-bag mer-
chant to the next fucking chancer: from John down in
Stockwell to Terry in Kentish Town – until he switched his
business to Janey, over on the Mile End Road.

*

Genie had turned Will on to Janey, who, besides being the sister of some serious East End faces, also happened to be a nurse. When Will knocked for the first time on the door of her first-floor walk-up, he'd been surprised – first by the speed with which it swung open, then by the face that confronted his own: furry, sharp and toothy.

The door opened further – revealing a waif-like woman, while the Alsatian padded away to join its fellow in a large dog bed by the fridge. Janey had the shrivelled skin and drab hair of the career junky, incongruously combined with medical accessories: a steel watch pinned to the breast of her round-necked smock, and a taped-on and stoppered-off catheter in the crook of her skinny, track-marked arm. As she'd urged Will, cheerily, to *take a pew* . . . it became clear to him that the patient Janey was nursing . . . *was herself.*

She'd gone to the fridge, got out first a bag that looked to contain around an ounce of smack – then a five mil' syringe, the barrel of which was full of water with blood and heroin dissolved in it. She put these on the small kitchen table Will had sat down by and said, 'I was just 'aving me 'it when you rang – put the works in the fridge to stop the blood clotting.'

Without any ado, Janey unstoppered the catheter in her arm, attached the syringe – via a tiny rubber tube – and continued . . . *wiv 'er 'it*, altogether unfazed: as if, in fact, she really were undertaking a medical procedure with professional detachment.

'Now, love,' she'd asked, 'what can I do you for?'

A cue for Will to seriously consider *doing her* . . . as any properly macho career-junky might contemplate doing a chemist's. An ounce of gear – *an ounce of fucking gear!* He hadn't seen so much since the Sikh tuk-tuk driver tossed the bag into his lap: sod his mother's thirty-quid-per-day dole – here was the true motherlode. Enough to last him a couple of months — He could ride a moped all the way back to Oz, the way John in the Lands Department had.

The only serious impediments he could see to this excellent plan were the dogs – and his conscience: gangster brothers or not, Janey was a vulnerable woman. As for the dogs, they didn't look that vicious, spooning together in their bed – but if they weren't Janeys' protectors, who was?

Cursing Little Willy for *bottling it yet again* . . . he scored a half-gramme and left — On his next visit he'd remarked, casually, how surprised he was she was holding so much gear without any security.

'Security!' Janey cackled. 'There's nuffin' more secure than Sabre and Shadow, 'ere – so much as raise your 'and in my general direction, an' they'll rip yer fucking throat out . . .'

Oh, yes, indeed – it's a Hobbesian world out there, although you don't have to be in a walk-up off the Mile End Road to witness the violence of all-unto-each: Dale's finished reading his life story – a miserable coda saw him waiting in

356

Worksop for a bed to become vacant at the Lodge. At least the airline had paid for his health insurance – because his parents gave up on him altogether. Dale ended up sleeping in his aunt's garage, waiting, and undertaking his own miserable daily round – in his case, one of local chemist's, intent on codeine linctus to augment his methadone script . . . *and keep him straight.*

Dale had flown high, all right – flown high, while high – but here at the Lodge, although honesty is the only acceptable policy, it doesn't necessarily guarantee your safety. The group is, Will thinks, exactly the horrid duplication of dark natures that so tormented De Quincey when he looked inside – so saw, receding into his own psychic depths, mirrors reflecting mirrors . . . *a coruscating desperation.*

Predictably, it's Jonathan who's begun the torment known as 'feedback'.

'Didn't you think of your passengers, Da-ale?' he queries disingenuously, the repressed Scouse in him dragging two syllables out of his victim's dull little one.

Yes, the hunt is on! And the hydra-headed group begins to coil around the hapless air steward – who Will would quite like to protect: true, it was a little cavalier of Dale to've filched all those morphine syrettes, but, then again, *waste not, want not* . . . and what'd they been doing in those emergency packs if not *wasting away?*

But there's no way Will wants to raise his head above this

particular parapet – he's seen it happen time and again: the group uncoiling in an instant – then lunging, en masse, towards a new victim.

Nevertheless, given his awkward position – with only *one meagre buttock* on the Programme – Will better share Caius's letter with the group, and soon. If they and the counsellors discover he's concealed that quarter-ounce of smack and the half-one of coke, they'll rip him apart faster than any Alsatian.

Moreover, he must share the letter with pitiless clarity, so his peers see it floating before them, illuminated and eldritch, with Caius's face eerily emerging like a watermark from the pale-blue weave of his Smythson's of Bond Street notepaper. Because that's Caius – ever the class conformist, even unto the point of his own dissolution: *I floated . . .* or so he'd told Will *. . . floated up by the ceiling, in between the oak beams*, while his father, the erstwhile Member for Newbury South, undid Caius's snake-belt then got out *his own trouser-one . . .*

Caius had told Will about this abuse – his father's systematic raping of him, carried out over several years – during a long and frenzied night of shooting coke, a couple of days prior to his marriage to Ann.

Tipping pile-after-pile of white powder into the stained spoon, Will had thought: this is it, this is the white void of my childhood – the television studio with no limitation, the landscape with no horizon. But there's no gender-bender gyrating there, or Dougal doggily swishing about – only the dark and demonic Zebedee, telling little Caius – and Will's older brother too – that it's *time for bed* . . . *yes*, time for bed, although it's still light outside, and the pigeons roosting in the trees are happily *coo-burbling* . . .

Will thought this – but realised as well, as he'd looked upon his friend's face, blanched, haggard – and seen the black blood coursing down his white arm, how it was always Caius who got everything, whether they be material things, the beautiful, brainy Ann – and even these extreme experiences, which, self-annihilatory or not, would undoubtedly *make good copy* . . .

In the south of France, Will had stayed several times with Caius and others of his friends at his mother's villa, with its cool tiled floors, wood-beamed ceilings and silk-brocade drapes. There was a retainer with a jug-head who'd tended to Caius as a child, and who cooked for them in a large and ochreous kitchen. In the humming heat outside, over-ripe figs fell from outspread boughs to rot, empurpled, on the paving stones, while wasps dilly-dallied *combining business with pleasure*.

From the terrace they'd looked out across a valley to a recession of bluing hills, topped with walled villages – then they'd gone to the pool among the vineyards to swim, or driven down to the coast, where they'd lain on rental sun-beds, drinking vast cocktails in globular glasses.

And they'd paid visits to Caius's father . . . *the rapist* – who'd taken some sort of shine to Will, exempting him from the snide and snobbish put-downs he practised on his son's other friends.

They'd hit it off enough for him to invite Will, on more than one occasion, to drinks with him at his London club in Piccadilly, where they sipped dry martinis beneath a large and uglily irrealistic portrayal of the Light Brigade's spirited charge.

What had the old man spoken of? Will remembers tall-ish tales about how he'd ridden down this wild beast – or despatched, stuffed and had mounted that literary lion. For this had been his shtick: a combination of derring-do and intellectual braggadocio he'd passed on to his son *together with his semen* . . . and which with Caius had become a taste for shooting speedballs and delivering withering put-downs: *Why must you persistently misuse words!*

After finals, Caius had given up his Oxford flat – and when they returned from India, he moved out of the Kensington one and lent it to Will. He bought a Victorian terrace house off Holland Park Avenue – an unlovely thing, cold and recti-linear, that he filled with uptight furniture: haughty-looking escritoires and malevolent sideboards. The colour scheme had been devised by some Tilly or Tabitha, and executed with rag-rollers. In this fake marmoreal ambience, Caius staged dinner parties to which, for the most part, Will was not invited – lacking both the necessary suiting and the required attitude.

I knew my place . . . as a friend at once more intimate – and less creditable.

It had been in the Mitre, a pub adjacent to the new-old house, that Will had his final drink with the old man. He remembers the gloomy saloon bar, its engraved mirrors and purple-flock wallpaper, against which Caius's father's face appeared, a pink and mottled slab, in which were set the brilliant azure eyes they shared, together with his white moustache, ends upswept in the cavalryman's style.

His corner-table-talk had been, comme d'habitude, a melange of the louche, the snobbish and the liberal – the old man's time beneath the colours had mostly consisted in trawling the pubs of Kensington and Knightsbridge for his wayward troopers as it had in pig-sticking jaunts to the forests of Sikkim: 'The going rate for an old queer to get inside one of these young fellow's snowy-white pantaloons was only five bob! Which gives you a picture of how poorly the poor buggers were paid.'

Is it hindsight alone that affords Will this vision: the genial-old-duffer mask slipping from Caius's father's face to expose his leering paedophile features? If so, it's a hindsight he's now applying to much of his past, so as to scope out the darkest portions of that white void.

As for Caius's old man, that was it: he'd flown to Rome that evening and been found dead in his hotel room the following morning.

Will had been the last person he knew to see him alive.

In the back of Marvel comics there are adverts for Charles Atlas bodybuilding courses, concealed cameras, and X-Ray specs that would enable the spottiest of wankers to establish once and for all the true nature of Edwina's bra — And it's these Will longs for, as he becomes aware of a lull in the group. Have they finished attacking Dale? The lull extends into a genuine pause, during which Will sinks further into the sweaty cup of his stacking chair, attempting in emulation of his mentor to become . . . *El hombre invisible.*

But it's no use – there's a disturbance in the stale, air-freshened atmosphere, as the group re-focuses its attention on . . . *me!*

Fuck X-Ray specs! Will needs foresight if he's ever going to cope with this bear pit. It's Gary of all people who's rounded on him – Gary! Who admitted only yesterday that he became so psychotic once, when he was shooting up speed, that he got out his fishing rod, assembled it and began casting from the bedroom of his little council house in Portishead – flinging the hook way out into the Bristol Channel, where it caught in ferries and freighters he then reeled in, much to the consternation of his five children.

Five children! Ridiculous! And more ridiculous still is the idea of Gary confronting anyone, since with his wall-eye he can *scarcely look me in the face . . .*

'Ain't you got something to say, Will?' he demands – and Will wants to ask a supplementary question of his own, namely: *About what?* Because he's lost track of whether the group's still giving Dale feedback, or if they've moved on to *other business . . .*

'Well,' he blusters, 'I think Dale acted pretty irresponsibly – but then that's typical of addicts, isn't it.'

'Why do you say that?' Carol gently insinuates.

'Well . . .' he blusters on, 'it's a truth pretty universally acknowledged, isn't it – at least here . . .' And he's half tempted to continue, perhaps offering his peers . . . *who know fuck-all about Foucault,* some insights into the socio-culturally relative nature of 'addiction' itself, which, up until at least the nineteenth century, was *a wholly value-neutral term.*

Would continue, were it not that Gary now presses home his advantage: 'Maybe you're thinking of something you shouldn't've done,' he burrs in Bristolian accents, 'something you ain't shared with the group.'

And now it's *open-fucking-season,* as Edwina and Paul, Gary and Dale, Jonathan and Sally-the-dental-nurse-with-the-injecting-Valium-habit, all *push my buttons . . .* Not forgetting Felix-the-tramp – who took so much Hemi-nevrin one year it wasn't a year at all, and when he came out of the blackout discovered he'd been living in Shepton Mallet for quite a while, and, although not exactly its most solid citizen, *he'd been well liked* . . .

Either the group is an effective interrogator, or Will, true to type, is slavishly complying – either way, their manipulations call forth this: 'Well, I did get a letter yesterday from this friend of mine . . .'

'Using buddy, is he?' Gary, his wall-eye roving the ceiling mouldings, speaks for them all.

Will wonders quite how violently Caius would react to being called anyone's 'buddy' – wonders this, and also why it is he's been sucker-punched yet again: this awful feeling of exposure should surely be something the group's therapy seeks to heal, rather than its outcome.

'You can't really expect to work the Programme properly, Will,' Carol remonstrates gently, 'unless you're completely open and honest with the group . . .'

Yes . . . she says this gently – but Will hasn't been sitting here the past fortnight, listening to these *fucking wankers* . . . for nothing – he knows . . . *what's coming.*

In the queue for some mince muck Paul tries commiserating: 'They really care about you, Will – that's why they're so hard on you: it's tough love.'

Will grimaces, *tough love!* Out of all the Lodge's dumb slogans, this has to be the worst: *Tough love!* Meaning what? You have to be cruel to be kind? But Will wants sadomasochism done with – not some weird re-enactment of the pains and pleasures of so-called *active addiction* . . . Because that's what it'd felt like as the group's hydra-heads took it in turn to lunge and bite: there he was again *annagain*, wandering beneath the judgemental eyes of Nathaniel Woodard and Dennis Bovell, his heart hammering and the plastic leech sucking at the crook of his elbow.

Will spoons himself some mince muck, and two halves of boiled potato . . . *white as cocaine. Yes* . . . he really should bust out of this joint altogether – light out again for the Territory, or somewhere still more remote – but instead he adds some slimy-looking cabbage to his plate then takes his place beside Paul at the long refectory table.

The group may practise tough love – but inside Will there's just a capacity for *feeble self-hatred* . . . He doesn't even have Vassily's balls: the dopey son of some Greek shipping magnate, who arrived at the Lodge a few days ago, Vassily managed to conceal a wrap of gear from the nurses' search, then overdose in his bedroom. When the ambulance arrived, the patients were hustled into their lounge – but Will caught a glimpse of Vassily's blond ringlets . . . *a shower of gold*, cascading impotently from under an institutional blanket, as the ambulancemen carried him out on a stretcher.

365

Caught a glimpse – and suffered a pang of conscience: he too should be *busy dying*... (although Vassily had ignominiously survived), not shovelling down this awful pap, together with the Lodge's tasteless pabulum. After all, what love could be tougher or more brutal than Caius's, who sought to manipulate Will from a distance ... *to kill myself.*

Paul is truffling away beside Will – and all around the sixty fathers (and mothers) eat with grim determination, taking regular swigs of flat water from plastic tumblers. But there's no getting away from it – not with these posters bearing the *Twelve-tablets-of-the-fucking-law* hanging on the Artex walls: 'If you have diff-i-cul-ty with the G-word,' Bryn preaches, 'then we can think of it as an anagram, see: Good, Orderly, Direction – that's all.'

To which Will replies, ventriloquising Caius: 'You mean acronym, Bryn – it's an acronym.'

But Bryn won't have any truck with mere semantics: 'Clev-er-ness is what brought you here, Will – being too clever by-bloody-half. You thought it was a clev-er idea to stick a needle in your arm – that's what's in your head: no orderly direction at all, no path to the pa-lace of wis-dom, see, only a road straight to hell.'

Yes ... Will has to grant *O'Bryn* this much – a genius for twisting things round with his hoary rhetoric: 'If you can't surrender to God, Will, you can turn your will and your life over to the group – or the whole Lodge for that matter, because there's lots of us, boyo, but there's just the one of you. And if you think of the to-tal goodwill that we have for you, Will, you can see it's a lot stronger than your path-etic – and frank-ly arro-gant – self-ha-tred.'

Quite so . . . and Will has never felt greater self-hatred than when he sits in their one-to-one sessions, listening to Bryn come out with this *arrant-fucking-bullshit*. Because it'd only been a matter of time before the Welsh Wizard made a tedious pun on Will's name: *You're too self-willed, see, Will* . . . a matter of about *five-fucking-minutes* in point of fact. While it took him only a couple more to link this to yet another dumb little homily: 'If you want to re-cover, Will, you have to let go of your own dis-eased self-will. That's why I pray on my knees, because it reminds me every day that I'm not driving the car . . .'

When he came out with this, Will sneered inside: Yes, and it reminds you of your petrol-tippling days as well, because you were on your knees when you stuck the nozzle in your *fat-fucking-face!*

Eyes smarting with what he's learned to identify as *dangerous self-pity*, Will looks around at Patrick, his sancti-monious jaws working – and Greg, wagging his inflexible and nicotine-stained finger. Will tries yet again to see his future *clean-and-fucking serene*: the A-frame hugs in lieu of passionate lovemaking, the Sunday picnics in place of wild Saturday nights – all the caring-and-sharing stretching away, day after week after month after year after decade, until he too wears an enamelled religious medal, together with an expression of *the grossest insincerity* . . .

For there can be nothing, surely, without drugs? An inch of flat lager – or a huff of Evo-Stik, spinning round *annaround* until you collapse giggling on the floor: everybody must get stoned, right? When he was starting out, Will believed that for every possible experience there were a myriad drugged modulations – for it was intoxication which provided the vital principle of variation, thereby rendering the dullest Tuesday afternoon . . . *multicoloured.*

By the same logic, without these *synaesthetic sprinkles* . . . everything is now altogether too lucid, too full of itself: a plastic tumbler is just a plastic tumbler – a boiled potato only a boiled potato, nothing more – and nothing less. *Yes* . . . a future of the flattest realism, with no romance – and sex reduced to the mechanical insertion of cock into cunt, followed by its mechanical re-insertion again *annagain* . . .

Last weekend – the first Will was allowed a visit from Chloë – they'd attended the compulsory film show: a crowd-pleaser entitled The Truth About Chemical Dependency, then chatted for a short while to the other patients and their families, before making their excuses and heading out for a walk round the garden. The Lodge sits in a predictable half-acre of beds and bricky loggias, bordered by the dense rhododendron shrubberies that are the limits of Will's world – since he isn't allowed beyond them unless accompanied by two trusted peers.

Will had written to Chloë earlier in the week, asking if she'd 'wear a skirt – I want to feel you . . .' He had a frenzied and Lawrentian coupling in mind – the two of them rolling in muck as they *fucked and howled* . . . But it hadn't been like that at all: Chloë was transparently unhappy: Will squinted, and the beam of light *went right through her* . . .

They patrolled the lawn, waiting for a moment when, unobserved, they could creep into the dusty understorey of the rhododendrons. Then they'd crept further in – and she lifted her long, loose skirt, revealing silk net stockings, red panties and suspender belt. She'd trussed herself up to please him – Will knew this – but he thought only of . . . *a spatchcocked chicken*. Moreover, exposed in this way, she'd seemed thinner still – while Will was already aware that the counsellors had diagnosed them on sight: a co-dependent couple – the wanting swain and his wasting maid.

Anyway – what would it've been like to come inside Chloë then go back inside the Lodge and face the Formica faces of the counsellors *with their wipeable smiles?* They'd smell the sex on the two of them – then there'd be trouble. Because it was coming to an end – Will and Chloë both knew it: co-dependent or not, they'd reached the terminus of their shared journey, and were staring at the emotional buffers.

Carol says things like, *Maybe it was the best relationship you two could've had at this time in your lives* . . . But Will, slopping with guilt, just thinks of it as a colossal waste of that time — And what happens when you waste eight years of your life? Why, you want them back, of course – just as Chloë wants her two grand back: you want them back *with fucking interest* . . .

Before she'd left with Paul's nan, who was giving her a lift to the station, Chloë gave Will her accounts: well-worn file cards that reminded him of the fat figures his mother used to pencil on the walls of Number 43 – but, in this case, the sums related to piffling weights: grammes and fractions of grammes, rather than stones and pounds. Bryn caught him with these – and took them from him: just as he'd caught up with Will after this morning's group and demanded to see Caius's letter.

Will gets it: everything must be added into the calculus of his own *crapulent cupidity* . . .

And now what? It's all coming on top – while the idea of reading his life story to these *thick-fucking-pricks* brings more tears welling up into his eyes.

He stands abruptly, rasping his chair back – and, closely observed by the sixty fathers (and a few mothers), lunges for the dining-room door.

Will sits in the patients' lounge smoking concertedly — Except he's not here, really: he's already in Caius's house in

Kensington, his shoes and socks off, injecting coke into one foot while simultaneously injecting heroin into the other: he can taste the coke in the back of his throat . . . *if God made anything better, he kept it for himself.*

Carol enters the room and hustles over to where Will's sitting, in the middle one of a trio of armchairs tucked in the bay window. She's dark-skinned, Carol, with blue-black hair. She looks a little old-hippyish with her cotton-print skirt and scoop-necked T-shirt – a skirt she tucks round her knees as she sits, and, despite his distress, Will does, moment-arily, consider what might be up it.

'Ted will see you now,' she says, 'you know where his office is, don't you?'

Will grunts. Of course he knows – it's on the top attic floor of the Lodge, and for the most part the Head of Treat-ment remains up there, like some strange sort of household god, whose omniscience is only partially occluded by lino-leum, carpeting and William Morris wallpaper.

As he mounts the wide treads of the stairs, Will wonders how many newel posts there are in the Lodge – indeed, how many there are in Oldmixon and Weston-super-Mare more gener-ally: tapered newel posts, turned newel posts – ones carved in the shape of chess pieces or Saracens' helmets. He'd like, he thinks, to rip out all the newel posts in the Lodge and *shove them up the counsellors' arses . . . Christ! Enough!*

His calves ache as he gains the second floor – this is the greatest ascent he's made in weeks. Months, possibly.

A light tap on the door summons, 'Come!'

The Head of Treatment's office is a tetrahedron-shaped space with several dormer windows in its sloped roofs. A big bland desk sits in the middle of the room, and there are the expected filing cabinets, bookcases and – still more predictably – framed photos of happy, healthy un-neglected children, although, thankfully, there's none of the touchy-feely tat with which the counsellors clutter their cubbyholes.

There are a pair upholstered chairs angled in front of the desk, but Ted, who's standing with his back to Will, in the wedge of sunlight dumped down by one of the dormers, doesn't ask him to sit. There's a pause instead – one long enough for Will to see that Chloë's accounts, Caius's letter and the penalty-charge notices are stacked in the middle of the blotter.

With his back turned, Ted barks, 'D'you want to be here, Will?'

His accent is further east of mid-Atlantic than Will's mother's: *a bland twang* . . . that summons her apparition to sit in one of the upholstered chairs. She kneads a wad of tear-soaked tissues with her arthritic fingers – her glasses also lie in her lap. Her face is painfully naked without them – naked, and slick with her *sad secretions . . . she's like a seal . . .*

'D'you want to be here?' Ted reiterates – and, turning

round, he comes towards Will, radiating vigour in a way that's really *rather obscene*: it scintillates from his steely-grey hair, his bright white shirt and the steel frames of his fashionably blue-tinted glasses.

Will hates Ted's warm smile and his open, honest face *with a passion* . . . 'No,' he snaps back, 'of course I don't bloody-well want to be here.'

'In that case,' Ted says, 'I'm going to recommend you be discharged at the end of the week – which is when your mother's scheduled to pay the next instalment of your fees. There's no point in her chucking good money after bad, wouldn't you agree?'

The mother-apparition sobs softly, and keeps on with her painful kneading. He's killing her – Will knows that: he's been seeing this terrified expression for a long while now – and behind it, he knows, unspools her personal horror show: her baby, her Benjamin . . . *her little-fucking-Willy*, keeling over with a needle in his arm again *annagain* . . .

'Wh-What do you mean?' Will stands, his arms slack at his sides.

'I mean that, since you're really only complying with the treatment you're being offered here, Will, there's not a lot of point in wasting any more of your mother's money – wouldn't you agree?'

Is the Head of Treatment quoting Paul-the-garbage-head – or is it the reverse? What must their Higher Power be like if it pushes them to such weird parroting? Ammonia and synthesised lavender catch in Will's throat – is he going to puke on the rug, or throw himself through the other dormer? Anything now to escape this hall of polished and mirroring surfaces – he's tried saying what is not, in order to convince these torturers he believes in their fatuous credo, but they keep telling him he isn't convincing: and how ironic is that?

Ted goes behind his desk and sits down in his leather-covered swivel chair. He's every inch the sincere executive of a successful corporation. He puts his manicured hands either side of the pile of unpaid bills on the blotter and raises his neat eyebrows. It's these, Will feels, more than anything, that mark him down as a duplicitous smoothie – a man his age should have healthy untamed tussocks sprouting from a moorland forehead, not these well-groomed little parentheses . . . *ironising his face.*

'Well,' Ted says, 'what's it to be? Are you going to comply with the Programme, Will, or surrender to it? I know surrender sounds frightening, yeah? Like your ten-gallon hat's full of arrows and the Indians are overrunning the fort – but it can be a relief to just let go, and yeah, let God – or whoever else is willing and able – run the show. Listen' – he leans forward, blatantly smiling now, his cheeks *dimpled* with the impact of this *good-fucking-news* – 'you look all-in to mc, you look about ready to chuck in the towel, you look as if . . .'

Ted runs on, but Will isn't listening – he hasn't said, 'You've seen a ghost,' which is the truth of it, because it isn't only the apparition of his weeping mother Will's transfixed by: she's been joined by that of Hughie – or, rather, his ghost. The two barely met while Hugh was alive, yet here he is, making common cause with her *from beyond the fucking grave . . .*

The winter they squatted together in Brixton, Hugh's mental health had, once more, begun to decline. There'd been no more little-and-often – he didn't require any further stimulus: his own brain was crackling with electricity – and it'd been the Book of Revelation galvanising him. He carried a Bible with him at all times, and would thrust it beneath Will's dripping nose, urging him to read the same passage out – so much so, he knows it by heart: *And the heavens departed as a scroll when it is rolled together, and every mountain and island were moved out of their places . . .*

Late at night, if he awoke to take a piss, Will would hear Hughie in the room above, walking round *annaround – an island out of place . . .* and wonder if he were now part of that same fiendish mechanism to which Clive, Siobhan and Edmond had been attached. But sanity was just a social construct, right? One imposed by the secret psychiatric police on wayward, revolutionary souls such as Hugh. Will kept faith with his friend – following him up into his dizzy fugues, where everything made sense, at least for a while.

Then, one night when Will awoke, Hughie's shadow loomed over him, outlined by the uncurtained window. His friend – whom he knew to be the gentlest of men – spoke coldly: Will was a junky, while he himself was damned. He'd only been able to get hold of little amounts of Valium – but he'd saved them often, and he had enough.

'Enough for what?' Will asked.

Why, enough for them to kill themselves, of course – surely it was obvious this was the only way out of their impasse?

After that they'd drifted apart. Hugh went first to live with his girlfriend in the sticks, where her dad had a pub. But he had a freakout and was hospitalised – then sprung again by a couple of gay priests, whom he ended up living with at their vicarage, in a village outside Oxford.

Will and Chloë had gone to visit him there when Will returned from India – and stayed for the night at the house of a local wise woman. Young couples waited in her musty kitchen, piled high with old newspapers. Morbidly obese, she held consultations sitting fully clothed on a reinforced commode. Passing by the door, Will heard her tell them which herbs to gather, and how to prepare the potion.

The priests had been scarcely less weird – gaunt-faced men, stonily sympathetic, who besides being pastors also belonged to some mendicant order. They wore monks' habits and talked about Hugh in the third person when he was present. 'Hugh's a great help,' they said, and 'He's really no trouble.' But Hugh was right there – or at least some of him was – while the trouble was plain for all to see, in his lolling tongue and skewed eyes.

He'd always taken an interest in spiritual things – it was Hugh who'd passed on to Will Bashō's injunction that you should live your life *performing random acts of senseless generosity* . . . Although the compatibility of this with heroin addiction was at best . . . *tangential.* Anyway, a holy sort of fool he'd been, pottering in the vicarage garden, finding new snowdrops and an old roller equally a-maz-ing, while his friends sat inside talking gravely in their moist sitting room, with its mildewed walls.

At that time Will had wondered if there was any coming back from this: the dust blebs on the inside of the pre-war lampshades – for it was winter in rural England, so dark at noon.

Hugh returned to London – but Will hadn't seen him. Last heard of he'd been staying with his former girlfriend, who was squatting an old sweat-shop on the Commercial Road. The exact sequence of events had, the Coroner reported, been *difficult to establish* – which Will sincerely believes to be the truth of all human affairs.

There was an asthma attack, a heart one, and death.

It seems more than likely to Will that, given Hughie's

transcendent state of mind, his death was less the consequence of these than the beginning of some new and a-maz-ing adventure. Which begged the question: why did he put them all through the utter misery of his funeral?

A sodden affair, back in the sopping village with the flagstone-faced priests – the February day so very wet, the world turned copper-green, as the raindrops etched their way down to the bubbling ground.

Young peoples' funerals were, Will thought, a decadent sort of joke anyway – he and Chloë had already been to one for Danny, one of their London crowd, who'd died of leukaemia the previous year – but here they'd been again, the apprentice mourners in their grandparents' suits, handed down to them via charity shops. And silent – their tongues either knotted in grief or simply stuck to the roofs of their mouths by the priests' sweet sherry. So very silent that at one point during this interminable reception, Will realised the loudest thing in the room was *the sound of the rain falling outside.*

Will couldn't recall anything of the service Hugh's odd friends presided over in their chilly church – not even a word of the heartbroken eulogies: only that the speakers were indeed, heartbroken, while, cliché or not, there could be no denying it now: the best of them had died first — No. He was too far out in the waste of his own desperation, and when the mourners' umbrellas mushroomed by the graveside, he looked over the weeping wreaths and caught Genie's dry eye.

Within a couple of hours they'd been back in London, and scored.

Had he felt bad about this? Of course he had – about as bad as he had when sitting, gibbering Jane Austen to his grandmother, at her nursing home on Surrenden Road. It'd been a long drive to Grandmama's on that jittery occasion – while Little Willy had to pull off the road at frequent intervals, in order to inject himself with more cocaine – only managing to stop when, at Box Hill, he fixed up on a bench while not enjoying the celebrated view, then bent the needle and binned it.

Leaving Brighton, he'd driven straight back there, returned to the bench, rootled through the picnic detritus in the bin, retrieved the works, straightened the needle and shot up some more *nerve tonic . . . while Emma went down on Miss Bates, and Mr Knightley tossed himself off . . .*

. . . Yes: Will feels bad about this sort of carry-on – but far, far worse about Hugh, who may be dead, but whose moist brown eyes and gentle remonstrations live on, rendering him far more influential than any ineffectual parent or enfeebled conscience.

It's Hugh who ushers into Ted's office a representative selection of the many others – all the quacks who've tried to help Will over the past seven years with their own pet theories and patented nostrums. The aptly named Dr Salo, the psychoanalyst, is here – aptly, because it had indeed felt like *a hundred-and-twenty days of Sodom* when he'd cycled up Willesden Lane to go and lie down on the couch in the converted garage this chancer dubbed 'my consulting room'.

What kind of a man paints a dado on to a garage wall, hangs a colourful print on the wall, carpets the oil-stained floor, and imagines this will create the right sort of atmosphere in which to unbolt the rusted mechanisms of neurosis – only the sort who's prepared to trouser forty quid a session for sitting there saying fuck-all. But then whose fault had that been, really? Will's, and Will's alone – he gets that he's to this dreadful manner born: the legitimation of neurotic behaviours by their supposed palliation – the talking cure practised as *verbal diarrhoea* . . .

The maternal Jewish doctor who came on a call-out to Chloë's flat, where Will had been immobilised by withdrawals, and shot him up with Largactil *of all things* – she's taken one of the easy chairs in front of Ted's desk, while the shrink he'd seen at Queen Mary's takes the other. The one who didn't realise he could read upside down, so casually scrawled 'Borderline personality – schizophreniform?' across his notes, then prescribed him an antipsychotic so strong it laid Will out on the floor of the Kensington flat for almost a month. He'd been too tranquillised to go out and score – capable only of lifting the needle and returning it to the edge of the record, so he could venture once more into the slipstream, between the viaducts of her dreams – whoever she was . . . *or is*.

The toxicology report on Hughie had been ambiguous: in the twenty-four hours prior to death he'd taken a little Valium, a little amphetamine, a little marijuana and a little alcohol – not enough drugs, either singly or altogether, to do for him – but possibly implicated in the vomiting, which had led to the asthma attack, which in turn had stopped Hugh's clock.

Why had he died from this picayune dose of poison, while Will's still standing, arms akimbo, before the Head of Treatment? Hugh supplies the answer: unless Will fancies joining him in the cold morass of his grave, he really doesn't have anywhere else to go.

To go once to Casualty to be sectioned – only to have the duty doctor refuse to, on the grounds that you're too lucid – might be understandable, but to go twice, three times – four? No, this isn't even epic carelessness, it's far worse – it's the kind of insanity Bryn prates on about, the kind enshrined in their nauseating Second Step: it's the making of the same mistakes over and over, while expecting different results, again *annagain* . . .

*

So, at last, openly weeping, Will looks into Ted's Big-Brotherish eyes and says, 'No . . . no, I-I do want to work the Programme properly – I don't just want to comply.'

'In that case,' Ted says, tidying together Chloë's file cards, Caius's letter and the penalty-charge notices, 'this is what you're going to have to do.'

The waiter – who's got to be in his late sixties – pauses before pushing through the tired swing doors and into the kitchen clatteration: *He just couldn't wait* . . . Will wonders if he's been having one-to-one sessions with Bryn, because the waiter now enacts one of the counsellor's dictums by reaching back, firmly grasping the bunched-up cloth and yanking it from the cleft of his buttocks . . . *You can't save your face and your arse at the same time.*

Is he a child? Does he imagine that since he can no longer see the diners, they're no longer capable of observing him?

If so, *fair enough* . . . The waiter's gone – and Will's turned back to the desolate vista of the Grand Atlantic Hotel's dining room: a handful of elderly, overweight couples scattered among many empty tables, who're working their way through three courses, while sedating themselves with ethyl alcohol.

Will remembers the old Irish labourers he worked with, and their great skill when it came to husbanding energy, only expending it in a series of perfectly calibrated and regular increments. It's the same with these wrinklies noshing their way through the Carvery Sunday Lunch Special: they're eating slowly – but with tremendous steadiness. They've already despatched oxtail soup (or a prawn cocktail) with a crusty roll and butter – now they're engaged with the beef, the Yorkshire pudding and all the other clichéd trimmings. He suspects it would take nothing short of a direct Cruise missile strike, bang in the middle of the hotel's grandiose neo-Gothic façade – with its turret-topped towers and over-wrought balconies – for any of them to refuse the sweet trolley.

The dining room, with its faint reek of overcooked cabbage and greasy flock wallpaper, is yet more anachronistic than its clientele – it's high season, but surely anyone not confined to their bed, or a Zimmer frame, is doing all they can to escape the summery quagmire of Weston-super-Mare: its moribund accommodation, unfunny amusements and broad, polluted beach. Still, with its atmosphere of faded gentility and gentle gluttony, the Grand Hotel – and the somnolent town surrounding it – must also be a sort of sunny uplands for Will's old man, reminding him of his Hove childhood.

Looking across the table at his father, Will sees his ruddy face is, indeed, glowing, as he deftly spears sliver of beef, roundel of carrot and crust of Yorkshire pudding, then *pops* this sweetmeat in his hippo mouth, with its isolate, green-ish teeth.

The old man chews, his mild blue eyes unseeing – then picks up his tankard of bitter and takes a hefty gulp. Will knows what's coming next, a comic book exhalation, *Aaaaah!* as he sets the glass back down on the not-quite-white tablecloth, and it's partly to forestall this noise – which will bring with it, he knows, yet more revulsion from the flesh his own flesh is of – that Will *pops* his question:

'Dad,' he asks, 'you were an adult, effectively, in 1939 – you knew the world before the Second World War . . . Knew it in a sort of . . . quotidian way – its doorknobs and tablecloths, and light switches – and, I dunno, its beer glasses. What I want to know is . . . what was it like? What was that particular Gestalt of things and tools and words and mores like – what was its . . . quiddity. I'm not really interested in the whys and wherefores of events at all – it's the whatness of things that bothers me.'

It's a long question – more of a speech. Will can tell Polonius is impressed by a dose of his own prolixity. He sits back in his chair – his wool-knit tie is crusted with dried soup, but that's *par for the course* . . . The tan flannel flaps of his suspiciously off-the-peg suit jacket fall open, introducing the Professor Emeritus's belly to the conversation: 'Aaaaah!' He sets the tankard down and picks his napkin up from his lap to dab at his moist and full bottom lip.

'I know exactly what you mean by that . . .' he says – which immediately wrong-foots his son. Then he seems to feint in the other direction '. . . but I'm afraid I shall be unable to oblige you . . .' before delivering this knockout blow: 'You see, so far as I'm concerned, every time I've ever lived through . . . has been now.'

The ringing of the head – the pressure drop . . . *It is you-ou, oh, yes, it is you!* The sharp imprint of a bird's feet on fresh-fallen snow. There are such moments as these, Will believes, when transcendent states – artificially or otherwise induced – are stretched then pulled from here to there, and from then to now. Because he can see the justice in this eternal nowness – and accept it as explanation for his father's behaviour back at the Lodge, where 'I'm sure you'll be able to enjoy a bottle of wine or a few pints of beer again soon enough, old fellow' had been his sole response to a viewing of that box-office smash, An Introduction to the Disease Concept.

But then, unlike Will, the old soak isn't on Ted's 'special measures', which include yet more sharing of drunk and drugged derelictions, the foreswearing of several 'special relationships' Will hadn't even been aware of having – including one, hilariously, with Paul! – and further so-called 'small group work', in which, together with other hard cases, he gets to grips with the metastases of his primary tumour.

Yes . . . Will's growing accustomed to the Disease Concept — Not, he'd hasten to assure you, that he thinks it exonerates him for any of his past behaviour, rather, he's begun to grasp that the Programme can be viewed as a species of praxis, and that the therapy consists in progressively rewiring the addict brain, short-circuiting negative thought processes and their attendant behaviours, so allowing the recovering addict to reassume full responsibility for actions he can only, initially, be held accountable for – since, in common with Derek's blackout murder, they took place *when I wasn't in my right mind . . .*

It's putting his own philosophic gloss on the Programme that's enabled Will to read out his life story, then respond with the correct degree of histrionics to the group's aggressive feedback. Weeping, wailing, telling people they're *a bunch of fucking thicko arseholes . . .* is true grist to the therapeutic mill, as long as it's contained . . . *in a safe space.*

And Will craves a place of safety . . . *at least for now.*

The world outside the Lodge is a war zone when you've become so terrified of using again, you half expect loaded syringes to shower down from the heavens, impaling you – like some less than saintly Sebastian, who's relapsed, but, unlike Hugh, not had the temerity to actually die.

Which seems to be the attitude of the doctor Will's been seeing at the local hospital. Charged with testing him for hepatitises A-through-C, and HIV, he also gave Will a genital examination and found some warts he's now treating on a weekly basis.

On their second encounter, standing half naked in the consulting room, Will peered down on the doctor's dirty swirl of hair, while this thin, nervy specialist in sexually transmitted diseases painted his penis with an acidic substance, while applying a coat of his own caustic opinions as well:

'A simple solution to the epidemic would be,' he contended, 'to castrate all the known homosexuals and registered intravenous drug addicts in the country. Over. Finito.'

Then he told Will, quite innocently, to *pop your trousers back on* . . .

Who or what would Hughie have become in ten . . . twenty . . . thirty years from now? Will stands in the entrance to the Grand Atlantic, waiting for his father and watching donkeys plod along the beach with tubby children rolling about on their backs. Clouds are sailing in flotillas up the Bristol Channel: an attack of dreamy idealism on the rustily prosaic realities of Port Talbot. In years to come, Hughie will be deader – Will understands that: he won't fit into the world of the future, with his old suit jacket, its lapels spotty with badges, and his lopsided guileless grin.

Looked at another way, though, it's Hughie who'll stay forever more youthful – and, by extension, alive – than Will. It's Hughie, who, by cause of his premature death, resides outside of fluvial time: while Will's *condemned to surf the Severn Bore* . . .

A vertiginous progress, no doubt – but he's a proven sur-vivor, isn't he?

Because one minute he'd been standing in the Grays Inn Road, his petrol-soaked jeans a merry sort of conflagration, and the next a plumber's van had pulled over to the kerb, a bloke had leapt out and shouted: *Get on the fucking ground!* And when Will had, the bloke proceeded to pull them right off. Then, without waiting to be thanked for his life-saving, the bloke got back in the van and drove away. *It's always been now . . .*

Will hadn't been wearing underwear, and stood for a minute at least, dazed and half naked: a *fucked-up phoenix . . .*

It'd been the same after the car crash: the skid had taken the Veedub in a looping parabola, such that it slotted in perfectly between two oncoming cars. So, a three-car-shunt rather than a head-on collision – but Will's precious car had still been an undriveable wreck.

Shocked to the core, he did his best middle-class-act with the people in the other vehicles, and with the ambulancemen, who took one of them – who'd suffered whiplash – away. He'd fronted up to the cops as well, but they hadn't been too bothered, only saying he'd be hearing from them regarding possible charges.

Maybe twenty minutes after he'd lost control of the car, Will was alone in its cracked shell, waiting for the AA tow-truck. When it'd arrived, the burly operative took one look at the Veedub and said: *No point in towing that to a garage, you're best off letting me take it to my mate's place – he's got a breaker's yard off of Silverthorne Road . . .*

Will had ridden with him in the cab – and five minutes later the A A man waved goodbye, leaving him to negotiate with his mate, who'd been wearing oil-stained overalls, a leather waistcoat and a huge black beard. *I'll give you a tenner for it . . .* the man said *. . . it's only good for scrap.* And when Will bridled a little, muttering something about how it was a good car – and had cost him five hundred nicker, the man smacked the wrench he held in one hand into the palm of the other. *Take it . . .* he'd said *. . . or leave it, in which case shift that fucking wreck off my yard right away . . .*

Half an hour after that, Will had been back in the cool hallway, on the lower-ground floor of 1916, beseeching through John and Denise's letterbox: *I'm back . . .*

An eternal recurrence, indeed. But then that was Will's experience so far, whether summoned by bells or Genie's fists: he went under – then came to again *annagain . . . Yes*, a fucked-up phoenix *. . . in a fruit-bat suit.*

And if Hughie remains for Will *. . . forever young* – then what can be said of how the Will-of-the-future was for Hughie? He probably never so much as imagined this middle-aged being while he was alive – or, if at all, he'd've pictured a hazy creature, semi-existing at the intersection of bodily decline and failed ambition. Will-of-the-present understands this: he's thought about poor Hugh every day since he's died – and suspects he'll never stop thinking about him. But the Will-of-the-future's a ghost in full sunlight on a crowded street, and you *can see right through him* . . .

London, 4 March 2019